Len Bernhardt
1983

THE SURVIVAL BIBLE

THE SURVIVAL BIBLE

MAKE IT THROUGH ANY CATASTROPHE CALMLY, EFFECTIVELY, AND SAFELY

Bert Darga

A Stonesong Press Book

THE BOBBS-MERRILL COMPANY, INC.

Indianapolis/New York

Published by The Bobbs-Merrill Company, Inc.
Indianapolis / New York

A Stonesong Press Book
First Printing

Library of Congress Cataloging in Publication Data

Darga, Norbert
    The survival bible.

      Bibliography: p.
      Includes index.

      1. Survival skills. 2. Survival and emergency equipment.   I. Title.
GF86.D37   613.6′9   82-4261
ISBN 0-672-52707-3   AACR2

Manufactured in the United States of America

DESIGNED BY: BARBARA BERT/NORTH 7 ATELIER LTD.

for
Barbara Ann,
John Emil
and
Margaret Jeanne

CONTENTS

PART 2

THE BASICS OF LONG-TERM SURVIVAL
67

PART 3

FACING AND SURVIVING THE WORST
219

INTRODUCTION

To be called a survivor these days—as in, "Oh, he's a survivor, all right!"—has become the highest praise. The word stands for adjectives like *resourceful, self-sufficient, successful.* In fact, the whole idea of survival has taken on a new meaning for us in the decades since mid-century.

Thinking about survival—worrying about outliving a natural or man-made catastrophe—used to be the mark of the pessimist, the doom prophet. Spectacular advances in science and technology, as well as seemingly limitless expansion in our economy, gave Americans a sense of absolute safety in the years after World War II. We were immune to the devastations of war, economic collapse, earthquake, famine, epidemic. We were the Affluent Society, and the individual didn't need to be concerned about anything other than becoming affluent.

Change had come fast: automation, the computer, jet travel, television, the supermarket, fast food, millions of automobiles on thousands of miles of interstate highways. Agriculture became mechanized agribusiness, rural families swarmed into cities that sprawled into suburbs, and our population and economy boomed.

Our way of life changed faster and faster during those decades, but our future seemed forever secure.

But "forever" had begun to shrink long before the boom years had run their course, and we began the 1980s as certain that we needed to know how to survive—individually—as we were once sure we could put the question of survival out of our minds.

The shrinkage began in the 1960s. We saw the first signs that our technology was neither all-powerful nor without drawbacks. The wastes of our society were polluting our land, water, and air, and our natural resources were not limitless. Our military power did not prevail in Southeast Asia. In fact, war had become a more immediate and total threat because the intercontinental missile could now bring the thermonuclear bomb to our doorsteps, and all the nations of the world were clamoring for a weaponry that could depopulate the planet. We also learned that competition in the global marketplace was stiffening, other nations were gaining on us in our economic success, the American dollar might not always be almighty.

In the 1970s, the clearest sign that our future was not secure forever was one that said, "No Gas." The Arab oil embargo ended the era of cheap energy. Dollar-a-barrel crude oil had fueled our economic boom, but now the suppliers were setting and raising the price from a monopoly position and even withholding the supply. We had built an economic way of life that depended on oil, but most of the oil we needed belonged to the Arabs. At the same time, the Soviet Union had all the oil it needed, within its own boundaries. At the same time, our dream of nuclear power as a cheap energy source was not coming true. Doubts about its safety grew with every reactor breakdown, and Three Mile Island turned the dream into a nightmare.

We ended the decade of the 1970s struggling with an inflation that seemed beyond control, anxious about our dependence on foreign oil, at odds with ourselves about the international politics of thermonuclear confrontation, in grave doubt about nuclear power and other environmental concerns. At the beginning of the decade, some Americans had already proclaimed their loss of confidence in the new technological way of life: they moved to farms, joined communes, changed their diets to natural foods, marched in demonstrations against nuclear reactors. It took the ten years of the 1970s for this altered perception to sink in across the country and transform the way millions of Americans think about survival.

Our confidence in our technology has become deeply imprinted, however, and our sense of immunity to natural and manmade disaster yields to reality with great resistance. With a faith that is almost religious, we have come to trust in the reliability of the light switch. Turn it on, and there is light. Everything works for us and takes care of us. Dial the telephone, and a voice will answer. The television set glows with news and entertainment. The thermostat clicks, and there is heat from the furnace or relief from the air conditioner. Open the refrigerator door, and there's the supermarket, in miniature. And if you must leave this safe world, you simply go out to your car, turn the ignition key, and you're on your way. Or you can hail a cab, catch a bus, take a train, crowd into a subway. If you live in the city, your work as well as food, clothing, medical care, transportation, and entertainment are nearby. If you live in the suburbs, you'll only have to travel a little farther.

Most of us live in the cities and suburbs, where this regularity of daily life depends on a clockwork of private and public facilities. Most Americans now accept the fact that this clockwork can slow down, break down, even be obliterated. What do you do then? Can you manage? Can you survive? What if you are cut off from this sustaining system—out in the desert, or lost in the woods? Will you know how to survive?

Even in rural areas, where a farm family may live a more self-sufficient life, its crop is likely to be exclusively beef, or wheat, or whatever, making it as dependent upon the distant urban area for much of its food and all of its goods as is the rural village. The family might have an emergency generator, but if the truck from the refinery brings no gasoline, Farmer Brown is as blacked out as the millions in the cities.

No human was ever entirely self-sufficient, of course. But there was a time—not that long ago—when individual Americans were not as dependent as we are today on the organization and technology of the society around us. Some part of the nostalgia that became widespread during the 1970s surely has to do with a hankering for times when a family knew how to build its own house and raise its own food.

Looking backward—and yearning for what seem to have been simpler ways of life—has become a preoccupation in the books we read and the films we watch. A succession of best-selling novels has traced back through generations to find heroes and heroines of earlier decades who were able to control their circumstances and establish family dynasties. James Michener's *Centennial, Chesapeake,* and *The Covenant* are prominent examples. We watched *Roots* for hours on television and read the book: it is the story of survivors. For several years, television audiences have followed series like "Little House on the Prairie" for their tales of Americans who lived on the land. The Bicentennial of 1976 brought forth fiction and nonfiction in all forms celebrating times that are gone forever. Nowadays, most of our heroes and heroines seem to have lived in the past—back before the computer, back before technology seemed to have taken charge of our daily lives.

For a spell of recent years, we have also welcomed films and books that told disaster stories, and certainly that popularity has reflected a yearning to know what it takes to survive. Films like *Earthquake* showed city dwellers helpless against natural disaster. And a movie like *Towering Inferno* built its terror on our fear that a modern skyscraper's automated and computerized elevators, air conditioning, and electronic systems could actually transform an office building into a firetrap—a manmade disaster. In a film like *The Poseidon Adventure*—one of the many which come back again and again on television and in theaters, and even have their sequels—the marvels of our technology cannot save us when a cruel sea destroys a passenger ship. A jetliner crashes in the Andes, and we have the book *Alive,* recounting how some of the accident victims even turned to cannibalism to survive.

This fascinated fear of all that is menacing is as old as humankind, of course, but it seems especially acute in our times. We even seem to have a rediscovered fear of animal life. In *Jaws,* in *The Killer Bees,* and in many a similar horror story, wild creatures show us up as physically helpless, all our modern technology notwithstanding.

In reaction to this growing sense of insufficiency, Americans by the thousands have become campers, backpackers, hunters, fishermen, joggers, bicyclists, karate experts, do-it-yourself enthusiasts. We want that feeling of individual capacity that says, "I can provide for myself, I can find my way on my own two feet."

Our recreations began to change in the 1950s and 1960s, for instance. The family picnic at a nearby park was no longer enough for many Americans. The camping vacation developed, and a whole industry grew up to provide the clothing, equipment, and supplies necessary for spending days at a time roughing it in the woods. Many still need the conveniences of home at campgrounds with electric lights and hot showers. But other thousands of campers insist on living under canvas with pressure lamps and stoves, and they return to their homes smoky from their campfires and feeling like pioneers.

One of the symbols of this new kind of recreation and state of mind is the camper trailer parked in the suburban backyard, waiting for the summer-vacation season when it can become an instant tent. Another is the backpack. Loaded with sleeping bag, food, and basic gear, the backpacker says, "I've got everything I need, right here on my shoulders, and I can go anywhere, survive anywhere."

This growing need to feel individually self-sufficient reveals itself in many other ways. Joggers by the thousands, for instance, run their miles to keep heart and lungs and legs strong. But, deeper down, they run for the satisfaction of knowing that they *can* run and that good physical conditioning makes them better able to survive than those who don't.

Another example is the do-it-yourself enthusiasm that has produced thousands of books, manuals, guides since the 1950s. Economics are very much involved: If I can tune up my car engine myself, the money I save in payments to auto mechanics will add up to far more than the cost of my tools. But the satisfaction of knowing I am *able* to do it myself is as big a reward. Few of us become the jack-of-all-trades that we'd like to be, but that's our unadmitted goal—and increasing economic pressures make it more and more attractive.

We want to be survivors. In the years to come, hopefully that will mean nothing more menacing than one or two days of making do through a long power failure—using a kerosene lamp to read by instead of electricity, keeping the chops cold in a picnic cooler instead of the refrigerator freezer. But we also want to be able to feel that we could survive earthquake, economic depression, even the unthinkable devastation of thermonuclear war.

To be such a survivor requires a specific state of mind to begin with. Keeping your head while all about you are losing theirs is not a simple matter of remaining calm. In even the most elemental survival situation, you have to be able to size up the circumstances, understand the threat, recognize what you need to do and what you are equipped for and capable of doing—all of this is essential if you are to maintain the calm that allows you to decide and act.

There usually are several options in any survival situation—whether you are stranded in a blizzard in the North or along a desert highway in the Southwest, facing economic disaster in a depression or radiated death in a nuclear catastrophe. The critical factor is that, even lacking specific know-how, tools, and experience, the survivor will fall back on a sense of capability and improvise solutions. That capability grows out of continually adding to our resources for survival.

We read a newspaper report on the dangers of residential fires—and we buy an escape ladder and stow it in our bedroom. A television program tells us of the threat of skyrocketing costs for heating fuels—and we install solar heating in our home. Radioactive contamination escapes from a nuclear reactor in our region—and we purchase a dosimeter and store it away against the day of an accident. On the contrary, we may decide after all not to invest in any such equipment, but in the process we will have added information—and a kind of second-hand experience—to our resources for survival.

The survivor knows that self-sufficiency is a constantly receding goal. It is a direction you follow—toward information, skills, tools, goods, experience. It is also a process of finding out what you don't know and what you don't have. The three sections of this book are intended as a way to inventory what lies between you and survival.

Part one deals with short-term situations, temporary disruptions that can range from power failures to disastrous storms or being lost in the wilderness. Part two is concerned with long-term survival, permanent changes that affect our way of life like food and fuel shortages, rising energy costs, economic decline. Part three surveys such catastrophic possibilities as economic collapse, social turmoil, nuclear warfare—prospects for violent changes in our way of life that have produced the survivalism movement.

This book is for both the survivor and the survivalist, the one being a close kin of the other. Both have essentially the same needs. The difference between the two is largely a state of mind: The survivor wants to be ready when anything goes wrong, the survivalist believes that just about everything already has gone wrong and prepares for the coming of the worst.

Prices listed for the products and services presented in this book are subject to change: contact the company involved before mailing any payment for purchase. Inclusion of goods and services in this book is not intended as a warranty of quality or performance.

We are most grateful to the publishers, the manufacturers, and the hundreds of individuals who gave us information, photographs, time, and cooperation in putting this book together.

PART

1

SHORT-TERM EMERGENCIES AND DISASTERS

1
WAYS, MEANS, AND SKILLS

Just in Case
John Moir
1980/245 pp./$4.95
Chronicle Books
870 Market St.
San Francisco, CA 94102

This is the kind of book that every survivor needs to read, study, keep on hand. It covers all of the basics of emergency preparedness and action, for both natural and manmade disasters: blackouts, blizzards, fires, floods, hurricanes, earthquakes, nuclear accidents. It is handy-sized, concise, thorough. The book discusses the food, water, clothing, shelter, equipment you need in order to be prepared. Further, it outlines the practical know-how you must have in order to survive. There are chapters on first aid, as well as a guide to books on health and medical care. Also included is a state-by-state listing of emergency-planning offices, to which you can write for literature concerning your area. (If ordering from publisher, add $1 for postage and handling.)

Living Life's Emergencies: A Guide for Home Preparedness
Patrick Lavalla
1981/72 pp./$2.95
Survival Education Association
9035 Golden Givens Rd.
Tacoma, WA 98445

This booklet is a concise and useful summary of the basics of preparedness for power failure and the effects of severe storms of all kinds. Included are sections on survival and first-aid kits as well as on water and food supplies. Drawings and charts illustrate the booklet. (When ordering from publisher, add $1 for postage and handling.)

Flood Emergency and Residential Repair Handbook
Dept. of Housing and Urban Development and
    National Assn. of Home Builders
1979/60 pp./$4
(S/N 023–000–00552–2)
Superintendent of Documents
U.S. Government Printing Office
Washington, DC 20402

This manual deals with emergency measures to protect yourself and your home when a flood danger exists, steps to take in the aftermath of flooding, and long-range preventive action against flood damage. The directions for home-construction designs in a flood-prone area are particularly useful. The book is illustrated with both drawings and photos.

We are accustomed to a life of convenience that would seem unbelievable to someone who lived just a hundred years ago. And yet, the marvels of modern technology are often the first things to be swept away by a disaster. . . . *It is vital to realize that help may not be rapidly forthcoming.* No matter how well-organized the relief effort, it frequently takes from several hours to as much as a few days before help arrives and services are restored. Therefore, your ability to be self-sufficient is of critical importance. How well you fare depends largely on your plans, preparations and knowledge.

John Moir, *Just in Case* (San Francisco: Chronicle Books, 1980).

2

U.S. GOVERNMENT PRINTING OFFICE: INFORMATION FOR SELF-SUFFICIENCY AND SURVIVAL

The agencies of the federal government publish thousands of books, booklets, pamphlets, and other materials which are available to the public from the U.S. Government Printing Office. Many have to do with self-sufficiency and survival. Two special brochures—both free—will give you access to this information. The first brochure, *Consumers Guide to Federal Publications,* lists over two hundred subject bibliographies: You send for the free bibliographies you are interested in, and then order the publications you select. The second brochure, *Selected U.S. Government Publications,* is mailed to you eleven times a year: It catalogs current publications, with their prices. Write:

Superintendent of Documents
U.S. Government Printing Office
Washington, DC 20402

Survival/AFM 64–5
U.S. Dept. of the Air Force
1969/153 pp./$5
(S/N 008–070–00020–2)
Superintendent of Documents
U.S. Government Printing Office
Washington, DC 20402

Designed for the airman's survival kit for use after being downed in an isolated area on land, at sea, or on sea ice, this manual covers all climate and weather conditions. It is a thorough guide, with detailed information and directions, to food, water, shelter, communications, transportation. There is an extensive presentation on pathfinding and navigation using improvised methods. Basics are emphasized, and as such the book is a prime survival resource. Drawings illustrate the step-by-step instructions, and a section is included covering survival in areas contaminated by radiation.

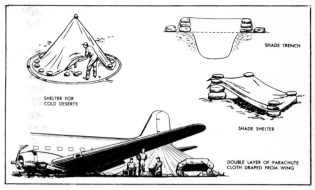

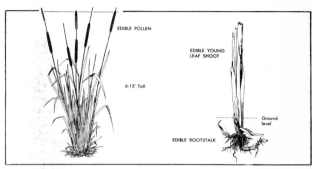

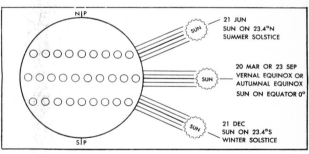

Drawings illustrate, from the top: desert shelters after a plane crash, the edible parts of the cattail, positions of the sun at equinox and solstice (from *Survival*).

Survival: Training Edition/AFM 64–3
U.S. Dept. of the Air Force
1969, 1978/408 pp./$9
(S/N 008–070–00019–9)
Superintendent of Documents
U.S. Government Printing Office
Washington, DC 20402

This large-format version of the Air Force survival manual will not fit easily in your backpack,

3

but it would be a valuable resource for study at home. The book covers the same basic subject matter as the survival-kit version, but in a more extensive and detailed way, with photos as well as drawings for illustration.

Survival, Evasion and Escape/FM 21–76

U.S. Dept. of the Army
1957, 1969/431 pp./$6.05
(S/N 008–020–00157–1)
Superintendent of Documents
U.S. Government Printing Office
Washington, DC 20402

This is a handbook and training manual for military personnel isolated in wilderness or cut off or captured by enemy forces. As a guide to wilderness survival skills and know-how, its usefulness is far-reaching. The book covers food, water, shelter, clothing, and pathfinding, with specifics for survival in cold-weather, tropical, and desert areas as well as at sea. Included are color illustrations of edible and poisonous plants, edible seafood, poisonous snakes. How-to instructions are illustrated by drawings.

Upper left, a log-fall trap for larger meat animals; upper right, a shelter made from willows and fabric; lower left, a system for condensing groundwater for drinking; lower right, improvised boots (from *Survival, Evasion and Escape*).

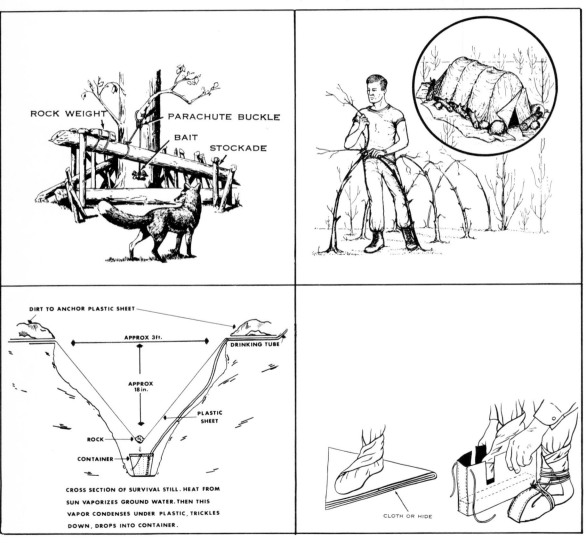

Outdoor Survival Skills
Larry Dean Olsen
1967, 1980/188 pp./$4.95
Brigham Young University Press
Marketing, 206 UPB
Provo, UT 84602

The author's premise is that to survive in the wilderness you need the Stone Age skills of the caveman: constructing shelters of all kinds; various methods and tools for making fire; identifying edible wild plants and collecting them; getting wild game (including insects and snakes) and fish for food; fashioning bone and stone tools and weapons; using rawhide for clothing and shelter. The drawings and photos are detailed and precise, with a special section of full-color photos for identifying wild-plant foods. This is an excellent resource, both for study and as a manual for your backpack.

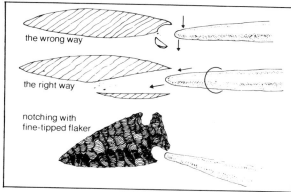

the wrong way

the right way

notching with fine-tipped flaker

Upper drawing details technique for pressure-flaking stone to shape arrowhead, lower diagrams food-storage pit in a cave floor (from *Outdoor Survival Skills*).

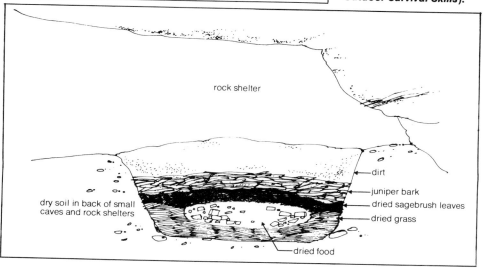

rock shelter

dirt

juniper bark

dried sagebrush leaves

dried grass

dry soil in back of small caves and rock shelters

dried food

Surviving the Unexpected: Curriculum Guide

Daniel E. Fear, Editor
1971, 1974/91 pp./$6
Survival Education Association
9035 Golden Givens Rd.
Tacoma, WA 98445

Designed as a teaching guide for survival-training classes, this book is devoted chiefly to the basics of wilderness survival, but it also deals with tornado, flood, earthquake, plane crash, civil disorder. (When ordering from publisher, add $1 for postage and handling.)

Surviving the Unexpected Wilderness Emergency

Gene Fear
1972, 1979/196 pp./$6
Survival Education Association
9035 Golden Givens Rd.
Tacoma, WA 98445

This how-to introduction to wilderness survival concentrates on the factors of physical and psychological stress. Its advice is basic, practical, and useful. Drawings and charts illustrate the book. (When ordering from publisher, add $1 for postage and handling.)

Emergency/Survival Handbook

Robert E. Brown
1979/45 pp./$2.50
The Mountaineers
719 Pike St.
Seattle, WA 98101

This small booklet is the ultimate in portable survival help: it measures four by five inches, is packaged in a waterproof clear-plastic envelope, and bound into it is a sheet of reflector material for signaling with sunlight. Prepared by the American Outdoor Safety League, the handbook concisely covers everything from first aid to finding food, water, shelter, with sections on being stranded with airplane, auto, boat, and with specifications for assembling your own emergency survival kits. Line drawings illustrate the booklet.

Upper drawing illustrates an improvised shelter with fallen tree trunk combined with windfall debris, lower drawing diagrams a snow cave (from *Emergency/Survival Handbook*).

And God said unto Noah, The end of all flesh is come before me; for the earth is filled with violence through them; and, behold, I will destroy them with the earth.

Make thee an ark of gopher wood; rooms shalt thou make in the ark, and shalt pitch it within and without with pitch.

And of every living thing of all flesh, two of every sort shalt thou bring into the ark, to keep them alive with thee; they shall be male and female.

And take thou unto thee of all food that is eaten, and thou shalt gather it to thee; and it shall be for food for thee, and for them.

And it came to pass after seven days, that the waters of the flood were upon the earth.

And the waters prevailed, and were increased greatly upon the earth; and the ark went upon the face of the waters.

Genesis 6:13–14, 6:19, 6:21, 7:10, 7:18 (King James Version, World Publishing Co.).

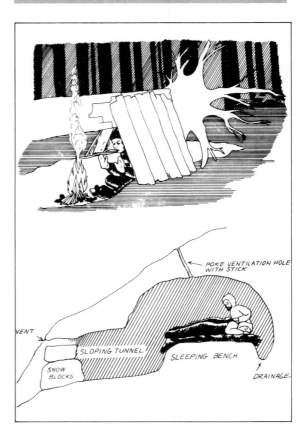

Keep a sketch map of your travels, showing landmarks, distances covered, and direction. It will help you keep on a direct course, show your progress, and enable you to retrace your trail.

Always pick the easiest and safest way, even if it is the longest. Save your strength by going around obstacles instead of fighting through or climbing over them. Don't spend an hour crashing through brush around which you can walk in 10 minutes. Don't go straight up a steep slope—climb at a slant, zig-zagging back and forth to save energy. Go around the edges of gullies and canyons; don't go down and climb up again out of them. Don't tackle a swamp or wet mud flat if you can walk around it.

Take it easy; keep up a steady pace. Travel a set amount of time and then rest. Periods of travel become shorter the longer you are out. You'll go farther and last longer with a steady, reasonable pace. When traveling in a party, adjust the pace to the slowest man. Don't crowd; stay 8 to 10 feet apart on the trail.

If traveling in a party, keep together. The easiest way to get lost is to get separated from your party.

If you get lost, stop. Keep calm and think back to where you went wrong. Return on the track by which you came until you recognize familiar ground. Then resume travel again.

A good way to follow a straight course is to choose two easily visible points (trees or other prominent objects) which are exactly on the line you want to follow and as far apart as possible; then walk, keeping the two points in line. Before reaching the first point, pick a third point in the same line ahead and repeat the method. Check your back course occasionally. Doing so will assure you that you are traveling in a straight line and will give a back view of landscape features which will help you recognize them if you have to backtrack. When resting, face the direction in which you are traveling, or make a pointer of stones, twigs, or scratches on the ground.

Streams and trails made by animals and human beings are the highways of the tropics and the arctic. Raft down streams. Walk the adjacent ridges—they are likely to have animal or human trails and may have numerous forks coming down to the streams. In hilly or mountainous country, ridges are also easier to follow, where the vegetation is less dense, footing is drier, and native trails are more likely.

Listen for the noise of rivers or surf. Look for trails and shelter cabins.

Keep your eyes open for plant and animal food to supplement your rations.

In case of storm or fog, make camp and wait for good visibility and better conditions before traveling. Any time you stop, mark your trail and direction of travel. You can get completely turned around even during a five-minute rest stop.

From: *Survival*/AFM 64–5, by the U.S. Department of the Air Force (Washington, D.C.: U.S. Government Printing Office, 1969).

A SHIRT-POCKET GUIDE TO WILDERNESS SURVIVAL

This guide is a set of three-by-five-inch plastic cards, with an eyelet at one corner to hold them together in a packet. The cards are filled with fine-print information about wilderness survival, highly condensed by Lee Nading from such sources as the U.S. Air Force and the American Red Cross. Finding water, improvising tools and shelter, getting vegetable and animal food, signaling, pathfinding, first aid are covered. Even in its condensed form, the information is clear and useful. A set of the cards in a pocket, backpack, or car glove compartment could save a life. Priced at $2.75 per set:

Survival Cards
Box 1805
Bloomington, IN 47402

NATIONAL OUTDOOR LEADERSHIP SCHOOL (NOLS)

NOLS is a private, nonprofit school specializing in teaching wilderness-living skills. Its courses are coeducational, with minimum age generally set at sixteen, and are accredited by over 150 colleges and universities. A sampling of courses: Yellowstone winter course, twenty-one days, $675; desert wilderness course, twenty-eight days, $900; mountaineering in Alaska, thirty-two days, $995. Write for catalog of courses:

National Outdoor Leadership School
Box AA
Lander, WY 82520

OUTWARD BOUND: WILDERNESS SCHOOLING FOR YOUNG AND OLD

This organization has seven wilderness-training schools across the country and has a reputation that goes back many years. Although known as a learning experience for teenagers, more than a third of the 75,000 people who have taken the courses have been adults, and nearly half have been women. The minimum age is usually sixteen and one-half, but there is no maximum age, though a physical exam is required for acceptance. The courses are a strenuous physical and psychological challenge, with emphasis on learning survival skills and know-how, and developing self-reliance, teamwork, and empathy for others. Some sample courses: twenty-three days of backpacking in the Colorado Rockies ($850), twenty-two days of canoeing and backpacking in the Adirondacks of New York ($875), winter camping and Nordic skiing in Minnesota (various courses, averaging a week, for individuals, couples, and families, at varying prices). Write for brochure and course schedule:

Outward Bound, Inc.
384 Field Point Rd.
Greenwich, CT 06830

For many years people have been strongly urged to store food and other necessities in their homes, against any one or a combination of the several possible emergencies—unemployment, sickness, strikes, famine, civil disorder, war and so on. To be unprepared despite the repeated warnings would certainly increase the nightmare quality of the experience.

Esther Dickey, *Passport to Survival* (Salt Lake City: Bookcraft, 1981).

Outward Bound: Schools of the Possible
Robert Godfrey
1980/273 pp./$8.95
Outward Bound, Inc.
384 Field Point Rd.
Greenwich, CT 06830
If you are intent on learning how to live and survive in the wilderness of mountains, desert, and ocean (even if you are never able to attend an Outward Bound school) this book will tell you what it is all about and will also give you some guidelines for any training program you may want to pursue on your own. The author, a former Outward Bound instructor, joined the students in the programs at each of the seven Outward Bound schools across the country. He recounts in vivid detail the experiences of the individual participants, taking the reader along for a sharing of the challenges, ordeals, and victories of the students. Illustrated with photographs.

WILDERNESS LANDS FOR TESTING YOUR SURVIVABILITY

The Forest Service of the U.S. Department of Agriculture manages 154 National Forests across the country. These are wilderness areas, with public access and facilities, for camping, hiking, climbing, fishing, hunting. Here you can test your survival skills and learn new ones. Write for the fifty-four-page booklet *National Forest Vacations:*

Forest Service
U.S. Dept. of Agriculture
Box 2417
Washington, DC 20013

Man in Nature
Carl O. Sauer
1939, 1975/286 pp./$9.95
Turtle Island Foundation
2845 Buena Vista Way
Berkeley, CA 94708
This book combines text and drawings to tell simply and clearly how the natives of North America lived here for the thousands of years before our European ancestors arrived. It is an education in the resources for survival that surround us. The book was prepared for children, but it is irresistible reading for young and old alike. (When ordering from publisher, add $.35 for postage and handling.)

DO-IT-YOURSELF KITS: SNOWSHOES, CLOTHING, BOATS, BANJOS

Country Ways specializes in kits of many kinds. You assemble the parts and finish the item, and not only save money but also have something that you made yourself. There are Ojibway snowshoes ($33 to $48), outdoor clothing, backpacks, sleeping bags, small boats, banjos, and other musical instruments. Write for catalog:

Country Ways, Inc.
15235 Minnetonka Blvd.
Minnetonka, MN 55343

TREE IDENTIFICATION—FOR PATHFINDING, FIREWOOD, LUMBER

If you are a stranger to trees but must survive among them and from them, here is a series of five shirt-pocket-size booklets to help you learn to identify them. The illustrated booklets average sixty pages and sell for $1.50 each. For the eastern portion of North America, see the *Master Tree Finder* and *Winter Tree Finder*. In the West, you would want the *Pacific Coast Tree Finder, Rocky Mountain Tree Finder,* and *Desert Tree Finder*. Write:

Nature Study Guild
Box 972
Berkeley, CA 94701

Now that I am my own power company, I have custom-designed the supply for my own real demand. I also avoid waste in a system that stores almost all of the electricity it produces. With proper planning and use of low-voltage technology, my independent power system generates and consumes just the power needed for use now or later, and not one bit more. An independently charged, battery-operated power system will serve you precisely because it is not too big. By combining new and old human technology with natural resources other than fossil fuels, you gain greater long-term security.

Jim Cullen and J.O. Bugental, *How to Be Your Own Power Company* (New York: Van Nostrand Reinhold, 1980).

Survival studies have shown that those who adapt successfully in a stress situation share some common attributes which set them apart from those who don't. A survivor possesses determination, a positive degree of stubbornness, well-defined values, self-direction, and a belief in the goodness of mankind. He is also cooperative. He does not feel that man's basic nature is to promote only self-interest; instead, he believes that most men are good and concerned about other people. Consequently, he is active in daily life and is usually a leader, though he may also belong to groups as a strong follower.

Larry Dean Olsen, *Outdoor Survival Skills* (Provo, Utah: Brigham Young University Press, 1980).

The American Boys Handy Book
D.C. Beard
1882, 1966/391 pp./$10
Charles E. Tuttle Co., Inc.
Box 410
Rutland, VT 05701
Originally published in 1882 and written for a Boy Scout audience, this book would give a young boy—or girl—a start on self-sufficiency in such things as making rafts, boats, games, fishing tackle. animal traps. But there are also do-it-yourself ideas for the adult as well. (If ordering from the publisher, add $1 for postage and handling.)

Winter Hiking and Camping
John Danielson
1972/192 pp./$4.50
Adirondack Mountain Club, Inc.
172 Ridge St.
Glens Falls, NY 12801
A manual on living in the wilderness in winter conditions, this book is a sound survival resource. The author explains how the human body responds to cold and relates our capacities to such factors as clothing, equipment and food. He covers travel on foot as well as on skis and snowshoes. The book is illustrated with diagrams and photos.

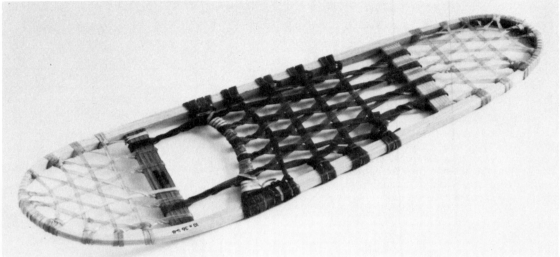

Two snowshoe models from Vermont Tubbs, from top: Alum-a-Shoe, $120, and Green Mountain Bear Paws, $77 ($69.50 with neoprene). The Trapper and Bear Paw models are available in do-it-yourself kits for $54.50 and $51.50.

SNOWSHOES: SURVIVAL TOOL FROM THE AMERICAN INDIAN

A pair of snowshoes—a life-or-death survival tool for thousands of years—can support your weight on the surface of the deepest snow. Vermont Tubbs Sales offers a line of wood-framed shoes as well as its Alum-a-Shoe, an aluminum model for $120 complete with bindings for the feet. The wooden shoes are made of New England ash, with rawhide or neoprene lacings: prices range from $68.75 to $86.75. Some shoes come with bindings; for those that don't, separate bindings start at $9.75 per pair. Write for catalog:

Vermont Tubbs Sales
Box 98
Ashford, CT 06278

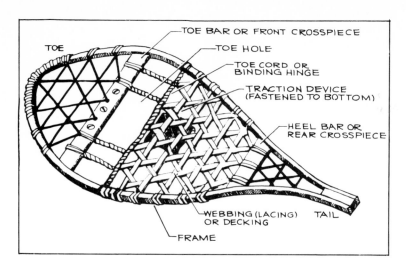

TOE BAR OR FRONT CROSSPIECE
TOE
TOE HOLE
TOE CORD OR BINDING HINGE
TRACTION DEVICE (FASTENED TO BOTTOM)
HEEL BAR OR REAR CROSSPIECE
WEBBING (LACING) OR DECKING
TAIL
FRAME

Snowshoeing
Gene Prater
1974, 1980/175 pp./$6.95
The Mountaineers
719 Pike St.
Seattle, WA 98101

Along with detailed coverage of the varieties of snowshoes and bindings, this book presents illustrated instructions in snowshoeing techniques, both for traveling cross-country and for climbing in high places. The book's drawings are clear and precise, with step-by-step directions.

Cold-Weather Camping
Ray Stebbins
1975/227 pp./$5.95
Dept. M
Contemporary Books, Inc.
180 N. Michigan Ave.
Chicago, IL 60601

The best way to prepare yourself for survival in the winter outdoors would be to camp in it, and learn how firsthand. If you can't do that—or don't want to—here is a book that can give you the experience, secondhand. The author covers everything from the equipment to the skills and know-how that it takes to live outdoors in the cold and snow. Particularly useful is a chapter that covers the troubles that can arise: avalanches, frostbite, hypothermia, whiteout, getting lost. The book is illustrated with photos and drawings. (When ordering from publisher, add $1.50 for postage and handling.)

Upper drawing indicates the various parts of a snowshoe, lower drawing illustrates technique for traversing a steep slope (from *Snowshoeing* by Gene Prater, The Mountaineers, publisher).

Drawings illustrate the use of a log base for cooking fire when there is deep snow (from *Cold-Weather Camping*).

Spit

Dingle stick

Movin' On

Harry Roberts
1977/135 pp./$7.95
Stone Wall Press, Inc.
c/o Stackpole Books
Box 1831
Harrisburg, PA 17105

This is a book of know-how for winter camping and backpacking, information and advice for keeping comfortable while tramping through the snowy woods for the sport of it—or for staying alive to survive the wilderness. The author carefully introduces you to the winter environment and how it affects the body, and then explains the clothing, shelter, sleeping bag, and food you need for cold-weather conditions. There are separate chapters on the use of snowshoes and skis as well as on pathfinding with map and compass. Line drawings illustrate the book.

The experiences of hundreds of servicemen isolated during World War II, Korean, and Vietnam combat prove that survival is largely a matter of mental outlook. The will to survive is the most important factor. Whether with a group or alone, emotional problems resulting from shock, fear, despair, loneliness and boredom will be experienced. In addition to these mental hazards, injury and pain, fatigue, hunger, or thirst tax the will to live. If you are not prepared mentally to overcome all obstacles and to expect the worst, the chances of coming out alive are greatly reduced.

U.S. Department of the Army, *Survival, Evasion and Escape*/FM 21-76 (Washington, D.C.: U.S. Government Printing Office, 1969).

But to expect is not enough; you must anticipate and prepare for the unexpected . . . Nature and the elements are neither your special friend nor your special enemy . . . they are actually disinterested . . . it is up to you, and the attitude you carry with you, whether you will survive or not.

U.S. Department of the Air Force, *Survival: Training Edition*/AFM 64-3 (Washington, D.C.: U.S. Government Printing Office, 1978).

Mountain Wilderness Survival

Craig E. Patterson
1979/192 pp./$4.95
And/Or Book Conspiracy
Box 2246
Berkeley, CA 94702

This useful handbook will fit in your jacket pocket, backpack pouch, or car glove compartment. The author, who has been both a survival instructor and Yosemite National Park ranger, covers his subject thoroughly and carefully: clothing, shelter, and food—both store-bought and improvised—coping with mountain storms, altitude sickness, lightning, the hazards of snakebite, bears, getting lost (with over thirty pages on pathfinding, with or without map and compass), survival kits. The book is illustrated with both photos and drawings.

Mountaineering
Peggy Ferber, Editor
1960, 1974/478 pp./$13.95
The Mountaineers
719 Pike St.
Seattle, WA 98101

The same skills, know-how, experience, and equipment that are basic to mountain climbing for fun and sport will help you to survive if you are there for other reasons. You might find yourself in the high country because of a plane crash, a sudden snowstorm, or a car failure during a highway trip, or because you want to live—or flee—there. In addition to covering all of the technical complexities of rock climbing, this book provides information on clothing, equipment, shelter, food, travel, safety, first aid, rescue, mountain geology, and weather. Drawings and photos illustrate the book throughout.

A PINK SHEET THAT COULD SAVE YOUR LIFE IN THE DESERT

Plans for a vacation trip usually don't include advance survival planning. But an agency in Arizona has prepared a concise fact sheet for people driving on the desert highways of the Southwest containing seventeen items of advice. For example: "If your vehicle breaks down, stay near it. A car has many items that may be useful in an emergency. Raise hood and trunk lid to denote help is needed. A vehicle can be seen for miles, but a person on foot is very difficult to discern. Leave a disabled vehicle only if you are positive of the route to get help. Leave a note for rescuers telling the time you left and the direction you have taken." Write for a free copy of *Desert Survival Safety*, enclosing a self-addressed stamped envelope:

**Department of Civil Defense
and Emergency Services**
Maricopa County
2035 N. 52nd St.
Phoenix, AZ 85008

Chart shows the effects of hypothermia, related to the loss of body temperature (from *Mountaineering*).

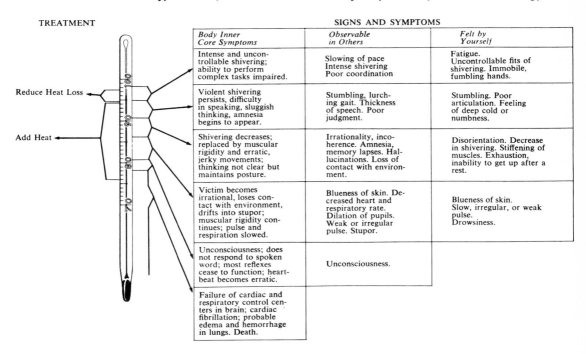

TREATMENT — Reduce Heat Loss — Add Heat

SIGNS AND SYMPTOMS

	Body Inner Core Symptoms	Observable in Others	Felt by Yourself
	Intense and uncontrollable shivering; ability to perform complex tasks impaired.	Slowing of pace Intense shivering Poor coordination	Fatigue. Uncontrollable fits of shivering. Immobile, fumbling hands.
	Violent shivering persists, difficulty in speaking, sluggish thinking, amnesia begins to appear.	Stumbling, lurching gait. Thickness of speech. Poor judgment.	Stumbling. Poor articulation. Feeling of deep cold or numbness.
	Shivering decreases; replaced by muscular rigidity and erratic, jerky movements; thinking not clear but maintains posture.	Irrationality, incoherence. Amnesia, memory lapses. Hallucinations. Loss of contact with environment.	Disorientation. Decrease in shivering. Stiffening of muscles. Exhaustion, inability to get up after a rest.
	Victim becomes irrational, loses contact with environment, drifts into stupor; muscular rigidity continues; pulse and respiration slowed.	Blueness of skin. Decreased heart and respiratory rate. Dilation of pupils. Weak or irregular pulse. Stupor.	Blueness of skin. Slow, irregular, or weak pulse. Drowsiness.
	Unconsciousness; does not respond to spoken word; most reflexes cease to function; heartbeat becomes erratic.	Unconsciousness.	
	Failure of cardiac and respiratory control centers in brain; cardiac fibrillation; probable edema and hemorrhage in lungs. Death.		

Survival at Sea
Bernard Robin
1977, 1981/239 pp./$15
International Marine Publishing Co.
21 Elm St.
Camden, ME 04843

The author, a French physician, divides his book into two parts. In the first part he reports on thirty-one historical accounts of shipwrecks and castaways, dating as far back as the 1400s. The second half of the book deals in detail with all of the practical considerations of survival at sea: equipment, emergency kits, life rafts, know-how for improvisation, and medical aspects. The text is illustrated with line drawings that include life rafts, devices for catching fish, and a gallery of species for identifying sharks. Survival advice throughout the book is based on the documented experiences of survivors.

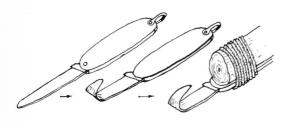

Drawing shows knife—with blade bent and handle lashed to an oar—used as a gaff to catch fish (from *Survival at Sea*).

Be Expert with Map and Compass
Bjorn Kjellstrom
1955, 1976/214 pp./$9.95
Charles Scribner's Sons
579 5th Ave.
New York, NY 10017

This is a handbook for "orienteering," which is a competitive sport with participants racing against the clock and each other to find their way with map and compass. But as such it is a complete and easy-to-follow learning tool for teaching yourself the skills of pathfinding. The book is extensively illustrated with how-to maps and drawings, and included with it are practice compass, protractor, and map.

MAPS: U.S. GEOLOGICAL SURVEY

The Geological Survey is a prime source for maps of all kinds, but particularly the topographic, or terrain, maps. Indexes showing maps for areas east of the Mississippi River, including Minnesota, Puerto Rico, and the Virgin Islands, are available free from:

Branch of Distribution
U.S. Geological Survey
1200 S. Eads St.
Arlington, VA 22202

Indexes showing maps for areas west of the Mississippi River, including Alaska, Hawaii, Louisiana, Guam, and American Samoa, are free from:

Branch of Distribution
U.S. Geological Survey
Box 25286, Federal Center
Denver, CO 80225

Residents of Alaska may request indexes directly from:

Distribution Section
U.S. Geological Survey
Federal Bldg., Box 12
101 12th Ave.
Fairbanks, AK 99701

These indexes list special maps, addresses of local map reference libraries, local map dealers, and federal map distribution centers. An order blank showing prices and giving detailed instructions for ordering maps is included with each index. The following brochures from the Geological Survey are useful for familiarizing yourself with the kinds of maps available:

- **Topographic Maps**
- **Topographic Maps: Tools for Planning**
- **Types of Maps Published by Government Agencies**
- **Topographic Maps: Silent Guides for Outdoorsmen**
- **Mini Catalog of Map Data**
- **National Cartographic Information Center**
- **Aerial Photographic Reproductions**
- **Looking for an Old Map**
- **How to Order Aerial Photographs**
- **How to Order Landsat Images**

Mapping
David Greenhood
1964/289 pp./$5.50
University of Chicago Press
5801 Ellis Ave.
Chicago, IL 60637

This informal introduction to the making and using of maps of all kinds is easy to read and full of know-how. The emphasis is on explaining the basic processes in making maps: by learning these elements, you are much better able to put maps to use. Drawings illustrate the text, which also shows you how to make useful maps of your own.

Coastal Navigation Step by Step
Warren Norville
1975/203 pp./$20

Celestial Navigation Step by Step
Warren Norville
1973/157 pp./$17.50

International Marine Publishing Co.
21 Elm St.
Camden, ME 04843

To assure your survivability at sea, you must have

the skills of marine navigation. These two books present instruction in all the basics, illustrated with drawings, photos, charts, and tables. You will need a sextant and reliable skill in using it, as well as some elementary math, though the author stresses that you need not be a mathematician.

> Had we lived, I should have had a tale to tell of the hardihood, endurance, and courage of my companions which would have stirred the heart of every Englishman. These rough notes and our dead bodies must tell the tale.
>
> **Journal of Robert Falcon Scott, who died with his antarctic expedition in 1912.**

Drawing illustrates method of steering between two dangerous shoal areas (from *Coastal Navigation Step by Step*).

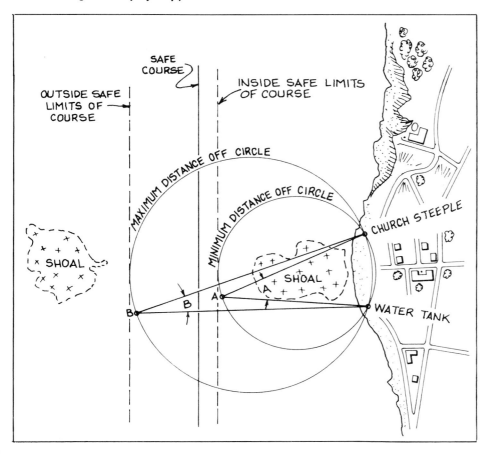

POCKET COMPASSES FROM BRUNTON

Brunton manufactures a line of compasses that ranges from a simple model 9020, for $9.95, to a variety of sighting compasses, some of which are designed as high-precision pocket transits for professional use by engineers, geologists, foresters and are priced accordingly. Model 8700 ($199.45) is a compass for general use designed with the features of the pocket transit. All of the models have liquid damping. Write for information:

Brunton Co.
620 E. Monroe Ave.
Riverton, WY 82501

Compasses from Brunton: from left, model 9020, $9.95, above model 8040, $27.95.

PRECISION COMPASSES FROM SWEDEN

Silva offers a variety of compasses, from a beginner's model for $5.25 to advanced models for such professional use as surveying and forestry for $42. All of the models feature a transparent housing and base plate so that you can read through the compass from a map. The housing is liquid filled to steady the needle. Other features are luminous points for taking readings in the dark and a sapphire-jeweled bearing for the needle. Advanced models are available with sighting mirrors for taking precise bearings. Also available are pedometer and altimeter/barometer units. The

firm conducts an education program for map and compass use (Orienteering Services, USA, Box 1604, Binghamton, NY 13902). For product and dealer information, write:

Silva Division
Johnson Camping, Inc.
Box 966
Binghamton, NY 13902

Silva Explorer III, Type 3, $11.25.

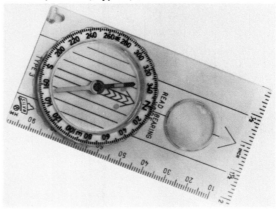

WHO FORGOT TO BRING THE COMPASS?

The husband and wife with their two children knew they were lost soon after they started down the ridge. It was already dark and they realized they should be seeing headlights from the highway down below.

In fact, the highway and their car were behind them—over and below the other side of the ridge.

They had climbed the ridge earlier that summer evening in the mountains. They were sometimes hikers, young people, the two children just eight and ten years old. Their vacation trip had taken them along the foothills of the mountain range. They wanted to be able to say they had climbed something, and so they hiked up the ridge and walked to its end so that they could watch the sunset on the high peaks in the distance.

It was an easy hike—no more than four hundred feet above the highway—and they angled up the ridge at a long diagonal to make it even easier for the kids. They made their own trail through the big timber.

They stayed until the very end of the sunset light and then started down the slope of the ridge in the darkness—in the wrong direction. They were just slightly off, but as they curved through the dark woods they swung around and down the opposite side of the ridge.

There was a sliver of moon, but it was not enough light for hiking at night with two young children, and the man and woman wisely decided to stay by a campfire until dawn. They did have matches and, in fact, owned the other tools they needed, but they didn't have them with them. There was a compass in the car glove compartment and in the trunk there was a rucksack containing a flashlight, camper's hatchet, and a light, waterproof tarp—all things they could have put to good use.

The family survived their misadventure, however, huddling in the shelter of the stump of a large fallen tree and keeping warm by their fire. A chill rain fell just before daybreak, but it didn't last long.

At sunrise, a state-police helicopter flew over and spotted them. After finding the car by the highway that night, the authorities had immediately prepared a search for dawn. They were taking no chances. Earlier that year, a sudden spring snowstorm had caught another group of hikers near the same highway. None of them had survived.

TAYLOR INSTRUMENT: FROM COMPASSES TO THERMOMETERS

This firm produces a variety of instruments ranging from compasses to barometers, rain gauges, and thermometers for weather forecasting. Check your local retailer or write for information:

Taylor Instrument
Sybron Corp.
Arden, NC 28704

Pocket compass from Taylor: model 2913, $5.95, liquid filled.

INSTRUMENTS FOR RANGE-FINDING AND NAVIGATION

Davis Instruments supplies mariners, but its rangefinder, a pocket-size unit for $39.95 that measures from six feet out, would serve well on land. The firm also sells a navigation kit, for $59.95, with several components, including sextant, parallel rules, dividers, and a booklet on how to use the sextant. Also available is a line of sextants at prices starting at $25. Write for information:

Davis Instruments Corp.
642 143rd Ave.
San Leandro, CA 94578

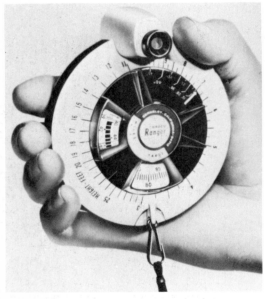

Davis rangefinder, $39.95.

Sager Weathercaster
Raymond M. Sager
1942, 1969/26 pp./$9.95
Weather Enterprises
Box 473
Pleasantville, NY 10570

The author brings weather-forecasting elements together in a simplified system: a booklet in which a set of four plastic dials is mounted. The booklet explains the system and gives directions, code tables, and charts for defining data. The four dials are then aligned in reference to wind direction, barometer reading, barometer change,

and current weather conditions. The booklet is sturdily made, with a spiral binding, and all you need is a barometer. (When ordering from the publisher, add $.50 for postage and handling.)

The Sager Weathercaster, with its plastic-dial instrument.

Instant Weather Forecasting
Alan Watts
1968/64 pp./$6.95
Dodd, Mead & Co.
79 Madison Ave.
New York, NY 10016

A method of weather forecasting based on a series of twenty-four color photographs of skies that are associated with bad weather, with no immediate change, with sudden change, with temporary deterioration, and with improvement. A scientific introduction shows how to "read" the photos, and specific forecasts are presented in tables facing the individual photos.

Weather

Paul E. Lehr, R. Will Burnett, and Herbert S. Zim
1957, 1975/160 pp./$2.95
Golden Press
Western Publishing Co., Inc.
1220 Mound Ave.
Racine, WI 53404

This small book—small enough to fit in a shirt pocket or purse—is an ideal way to start a study of weather and weather forecasting. It guides you from a simple and clear explanation of how weather works through the basic science of forecasting. The drawings and photos are in color, and they help make the whole subject easy reading.

Peace of Mind in Earthquake Country

Peter Yanev
1974/304 pp./$5.95
Chronicle Books
870 Market St.
San Francisco, CA 94102

Scientific study has mapped and identified the risk of earthquake around the country—but precise prediction of quakes is still in the future. If you live where there is risk—even slight or rare—you need to prepare for it. This book is largely devoted to building construction that will withstand earthquake. It uses text, photos, and drawings to show the destructive effects of a quake, how they function, and how they can then be counteracted by building materials and structural design. (If ordering from publisher, add $1 for postage and handling.)

EARTHQUAKES, VOLCANOS: U.S. GEOLOGICAL SURVEY

The Geological Survey publishes a variety of booklets on the earth sciences, such as *Earthquakes* and *Volcanoes of the United States*. Write for the agency's catalog, *Popular Publications of the U.S. Geological Survey:*

U.S. Geological Survey
101 National Center
Reston, VA 22092

WEATHER-WATCHING INSTRUMENTS

Dwyer Instruments manufactures two units for measuring wind velocity for data in weather forecasting, farming, and fishing. One unit, the Wind Meter, priced at $8.95, is hand-held and calibrated in mph, km/hour, and m/sec. The second unit, the Mark II Wind Speed Indicator, priced at $38.95, is more elaborate: it consists of a roof-mounted weather vane with pick-up tube from which pneumatic wind pressure is transmitted through a plastic tubing into a meter component in the house.

Dwyer Instruments, Inc.
Box 373
Michigan City, IN 46360

RECORDING BAROMETER: records barometric pressure on a seven-day chart, for altitudes of 0 to 10,000 feet, model 6450, $225. (Taylor Instrument, Sybron Corporation, Arden, NC 28704)

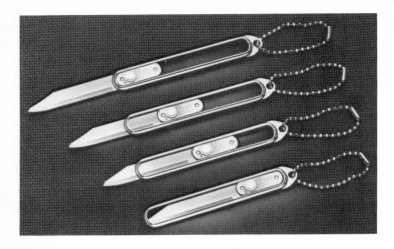

The Christy sliding-blade pocket knife, $5.

THE CHRISTY POCKET KNIFE

In times past, a pocket knife was in every man's possession. It was used to whittle kindling wood, dress game, cut a rope. Its survival value is still being proved in many an emergency. The Christy sliding-blade knife serves the same uses in some pockets—and purses—today. The knife is small, its stainless-steel blade locks into three different length positions, and it has a reputation for durability. Priced at $5. Check your retailer or write to:

The Christy Company
905 Dickinson St.
Fremont, OH 43420

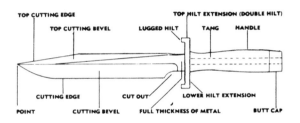

Drawing indicates the names of the parts of a knife: from the Randall catalog.

KNIVES: FOR SHEATH OR POCKET

Randall has a reputation for high-quality—though costly—knives. The Attack-Survival model is made of stainless steel, has a waterproof hollow handle, and is adaptable for use as a spear point: with 5½-inch blade, $140; and with 7½-inch blade, $145. Along with a variety of other knives, the firm also sells three Schrade pocket knives: the General Purpose, $17; the Stockman, $19; and the Folding Hunter, $32. Write for catalog ($1):

Randall Made Knives
Box 1988
Orlando, FL 32802

KNIVES FROM CASE

A well-known name in cutlery that goes back to the nineteenth century, Case offers a wide variety of pocket and hunting knives that range in price from as low as $12.75 to as high as $90. The company's line includes a selection of lock-open pocket knives. See your retailer, or write for catalog, and ask for the pamphlet, *How to Choose and Care for Pocket Knives and Hunting Knives:*

W. R. Case & Sons Cutlery Co.
20 Russell Blvd.
Bradford, PA 16701

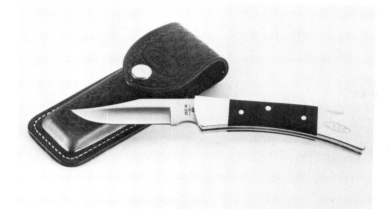

Case model 2159L
lock-open pocket knife,
$35.

SURVIVAL KNIFE: the Swiss Army knife, by Victorinox, with stainless-steel blades and tools, including scissors, bottle and can opener, three screwdriver sizes, reamer, wire stripper, tweezers, weighs three ounces, measures 3½ inches closed. Price $24. (Eddie Bauer, 15010 N.E. 36th St., Redmond, WA 98052)

SURVIVAL KNIFE: the Buck folding pocket knife, Ranger model, with three-inch blade, of high-carbon steel, that locks open and can be closed only with recessed safety switch, comes with leather belt scabbard. Price $33. (Eddie Bauer, 15010 N.E. 36th St., Redmond, WA 98052)

MAKE YOUR OWN KNIVES

Indian Ridge Traders specializes in finished blades and handle components for making your own knives—kitchen, hunting, and other types. The blades are American-made, at prices ranging from $2 to $18, as well as a line of English blades by Sheffield, from $6.25 to $19.75. The firm's catalog is a useful introduction to knife types, steels, care and sharpening; it also offers the book *How to Make Your Own Knives* by Jim Mayes ($7.95, illustrated). Write for catalog:

Indian Ridge Traders Co.
Box 869
Royal Oak, MI 48068

Step-By-Step Knifemaking
David Boye
1977/270 pp./$9.95
Rodale Press, Inc.
Organic Park
Emmaus, PA 18049
   Illustrated with both photos and drawings, this is a manual for beginners covering hand and power tools, techniques, materials, and designs. The how-to directions take the reader from raw steel to finished blade, and then through the process of making the handle and sheath.

A HANDY, HEAVY-DUTY JACK

The Handyman jack works on the same principle as the mechanical bumper jack you keep in your car trunk, but this unit has a 3½-ton capacity and is designed for such heavy-duty work as lifting a tractor, winching a car out of the mud, or stretching wire fencing. The jack comes in casting or all-steel models: forty-two, forty-eight, or sixty inches high with thirty-one, thirty-seven, or forty-seven inches of continuous lift. The forty-eight-inch size weighs thirty pounds. Prices range from $38.75 to $43.25. Write for information and prices:

Harrah Manufacturing Co.
Drawer 228
Bloomfield, IN 47424

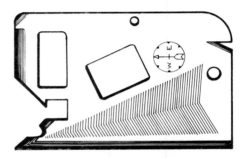

WALLET-SIZE SURVIVAL TOOL: measuring 2½ by 3½ inches and thin enough in its plastic case to fit in wallet or purse, the stainless-steel Walle Hawk is a multiuse tool as knife, wrench, punch, screwdriver, file, signal mirror, can and bottle opener, with built-in compass and a burning lens that can be used with sunlight to start a fire. Price $19.95. (Survival, Inc., Box 5509, Carson, CA 90749)

A selection of knife blades sold by Indian Ridge Traders.

MULTIPURPOSE HAND TOOL

The Red Viking is a hammer-size tool, eleven inches long and designed for eleven specific different uses: hammer, hatchet, pliers, nail puller, screwdriver, wire cutter, pipe wrench, tack pry, wire stretcher, bottle opener, and staple puller. Priced at $12.95, you might want more than one—for your home or farm, your cabin, your car trunk. Write for information:

Harrah Manufacturing Co.
Drawer 228
Bloomfield, IN 47424

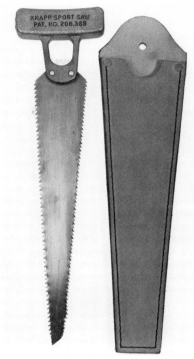

SURVIVAL SAW: eleven inches long, weighing nine ounces, saw fits in leather sheath to hang on belt, handle has waterproof compartment for emergency supply of matches. Price $14.95. (Eddie Bauer, 15010 N.E. 36th St., Redmond, WA 98052)

COLLAPSIBLE SAW: stowed in its aluminum handle, unit measures 24 × 1¾ inches, yet rigid buck-saw design makes it an efficient cutting tool. Price $12.95. (Eddie Bauer, 15010 N.E. 36th St., Redmond, WA 98052)

HOW TO EQUIP YOUR CAR FOR SURVIVAL

We spend a considerable part of our lives traveling in our cars, yet few of us think to carry emergency equipment with us.

Local climate and the kind of roads you travel may require some specialized items, but there are several basic things that make up a car survival kit.

A flashlight with spare batteries is essential when your car breaks down or you are lost or stranded along a highway. A small first-aid kit is also a must, as well as basic tools for car repair.

The lightweight bumper jack supplied with your car could be a dangerous tool if you had to change a blown-out tire off the edge of a country road. A heavy-duty jack is not only safer but also can be used to work your car out of a bad spot if you get stuck.

Signal flares could get you out of trouble if stranded.

Especially if you are traveling in desert country, a container of water could prove well worth the space it takes up in your car trunk. And a tarpaulin of canvas or plastic can provide emergency shelter.

For winter driving where heavy snowfall can be expected, stow a small shovel, a container of sand, and a set of tire chains in your trunk. The shovel will dig you out of a snowdrift, the sand and chains will keep you moving when the pavement ices up.

If you travel extensively by car, a CB radio is a sound investment: it could bring help when you need it most.

If you do not know how to change a flat tire, learn how to. Your spare tire is basic survival equipment: check it periodically to make certain it is properly inflated. (In a roadside emergency, your spare tire could also be burned to provide heat or to send up a distress signal.)

Getting lost has its hazards, particularly in an unfamiliar area, on backcountry roads, and in darkness or bad weather. Always travel with a road map. Combined with a car compass—or a pocket compass stowed in the glove compartment—a map will keep you out of difficulty.

Most of us do much of our driving in populated areas where help is usually not far away. But there are always exceptions, and unless you are prepared for them you leave your survival to chance.

SMOKE AND FLARE SIGNAL KITS

Penguin Industries offers a variety of signal kits, both smoke and flare. The Pengun flare model is pocket-size. Write for price and dealer information:

Penguin Industries, Inc.
Airport Industrial Mall
Coatesville, PA 19320

Equipment Lists
U.S. Coast Guard
1979/185 pp./free
Department of Transportation
U.S. Coast Guard
Washington, DC 20590

A boat could be your means of survival, or trouble with your boat could put you in a life-threatening situation. This manual lists various boat items "approved, certified or accepted" for use. Of particular interest are lifesaving equipment, distress signals, and survival kits. This manual could be useful as a guide to checking out equipment you already have or you intend to buy. Also available are such brochures as *Visual Distress Signals,* and *Everything You Ever Wanted to Know about Boating.*

PROFESSIONAL SURVIVAL EQUIPMENT

McElfish Parachute Service supplies the aviation industry and its *Survival Equipment Catalog* offers a variety of items designed for plane-crash situations. There are inflatable life rafts packed with survival kits, starting at $730. Individual survival kits include packs for both jungle and frigid-area conditions. There are also distress-signaling devices, including the Firefly, a battery-powered flashing strobe light. Write for catalog:

McElfish Parachute Service
2615 Love Field Drive
Dallas, TX 75235

Shown are specifications for an individual survival kit, model LSK-1, $84.95: from the McElfish Parachute Service catalog.

A meeting was called inside the Fairchild, and for the first time all twenty-seven survivors discussed the issue which faced them— whether or not they should eat the bodies of the dead to survive. Canessa, Zerbino, Fernández, and Fito Strauch repeated the arguments they had used before. If they did not they would die. It was their moral obligation to live, for their own sake and for the sake of their families. . . . [later] Canessa took it upon himself to prove his resolution. He prayed to God to help him do what he knew to be right and then took a piece of meat in his hand. He hesitated. Even with his mind so firmly made up, the horror of the act paralyzed him. His hand would neither rise to his mouth nor fall to his side while the revulsion which possessed him struggled with his stubborn will. The will prevailed. The hand rose and pushed the meat into his mouth. He swallowed it.

He felt triumphant. His conscience had overcome a primitive, irrational taboo. He was going to survive.

Piers Paul Read, *Alive: The Story of the Andes Survivors* (New York: Avon, 1975).

SURVIVAL KIT: compact unit weighs a few ounces, fits in the palm of hand, combines a stove that burns solid-fuel tablets with twenty-eight small but vital items including six-foot tube tent, windscreen, cooking pan, matches, magnesium match and flint, whistle, signal mirror, knife with two-inch blade, wire saw, snare wire, fishhooks, line, water-purification tablets, mosquito netting, aspirin tablets, bandages, soap, razor blades, broth packets, sugar cubes. Price $29.95. (Eddie Bauer, 15010 N.E. 36th St., Redmond, WA 98052)

LSK-1 INDIVIDUAL SURVIVAL KIT

A COMPACT, MULTI-USE GENERAL SURVIVAL KIT CONTAINING THE BASIC MINIMUMS IN FIRST AID, SIGNALING DEVICES, TOOLS AND FOOD.

CONTENTS: BURN COMPOUND, BANDAGES, AMMONIA, MERTHIOLATE, COMPRESSES, INSECT REPELLANT, WATER PURIFICATION, CHAPSTICK, COMPASS, DRIED SOUP, SIGNAL MIRROR, SUNBURN OINTMENT, U.S. AIR FORCE SURVIVAL MANUAL, FISHING KIT, SURVIVAL SAW, RAZOR KNIFE, MATCHES.

DIMENSIONS: 2x6x9 INCHES   WEIGHT: 2 POUNDS

Bushnell 20x Stalker spotting scope: 17¾ ounces, $149.

BINOCULARS

A pair of binoculars could save your life in a variety of situations, such as to find your way—with or without a map—by picking out distant objects, or to spot game when hunting for food. Bushnell offers a variety of sizes and features, and prices ranging from as low as $42 to as high as $525 for a Bausch & Lomb model. Their catalog provides tips on selecting size and features to suit your particular needs. Generally speaking, the 7×35 size is considered standard.

Bushnell Optical Co.
2828 E. Foothill Blvd.
Pasadena, CA 91107

TELESCOPES

Telescopes can take your eye beyond the power of the binocular, as high as 60 magnifications. Some models zoom from 20x to 60x with the turn of a ring. Such high-powered scopes are designed to be mounted on a tripod, but among Bushnell's offerings is a 10x telescope for $29.95 which can be used either hand-held or on a tripod. Prices range as high as $330. The company's catalog illustrates the various models.

Bushnell Optical Co.
2828 E. Foothill Blvd.
Pasadena, CA 91107

2 EMERGENCY LIGHTING

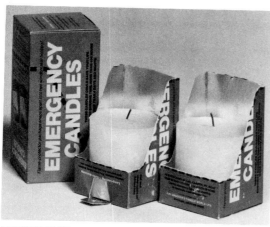

EMERGENCY CANDLES: these two three-inch candles come in a foil-lined box which you split apart to make two separate candle holders. Made of highly compressed paraffin, the two candles are rated for fifty-seven hours of burning life each. Price for pair, $5. (Stow-A-Way Industries, 166 Cushing Hwy., Cohasset, MA 02025)

LIGHT UNIT FOR POWER FAILURES

The Home Sentry security light, model 8350, plugs into any electrical outlet to draw on household current. Unit has three-position switch. While plugged into outlet, it can be used as a night-light, and its rechargeable battery can be kept at full capacity. Removed from outlet when there is a power failure, the unit serves as a flashlight. Price is $13.98. See your GE dealer, or write:

General Electric Co.
Housewares Div.
1285 Boston Ave.
Bridgeport, CT 06602

BATTERY-POWERED LANTERN: model 360 Sportsman lantern, complete with two fluorescent tubes and four six-volt batteries, $59.95. (Ray-O-Vac, 6414 Schroeder Rd., Madison, WI 53711)

SURVIVAL FLASHLIGHT: the Tekna-Lite measures only 5½ × 2½ inches, weighs only nine ounces, but produces 4,000-candlepower beam for 1½ hours on four AA nickle-cadmium batteries, watertight to 2,000-foot depth. Price $18. (Eddie Bauer, 15010 N.E. 36th St., Redmond, WA 98052)

DISTRESS-SIGNAL LIGHTS

ACR Electronics manufactures a line of distress-signaling equipment for marine use, with some units that would serve equally well on land. The ACR model L-10 ($14.95) is a powerful hand-held searchlight (with flashlight construction) that can reach out up to one-half mile and has a two-way switch for use as an S.O.S. signal. It is powered by six D batteries. The model L-10A ($39.95) is identical but flashes its S.O.S. signal automatically. The model SM-6 ($59.95) is another signal light in flashlight format, using two D batteries. It has two interchangeable top modules, one for a beam of light, the other for a high-intensity strobe-light signal. The firm's model 4F Firefly rescue light ($65) is the size of a cigarette package, with mercury battery, and gives a flashing strobe light visible for up to five miles. All units are waterproof. See a boat dealer, or write:

ACR Electronics Corp.
3901 N. 29th Ave.
Hollywood, FL 33020

From ACR Electronics: left, model L-10A automatic S.O.S. light, $39.95 (or $14.95 for L-10 model with nonautomatic signal switch); right, model 4F Firefly rescue light, $65.

From ACR
Electronics: model
SM-6, $59.95, signal
light in flashlight
format.

PRESSURE LANTERN: model
220K195, double-mantle,
designed to burn for eight
hours on two-pint filling of
Coleman naphtha fuel, about
$35. (Coleman Co., Inc., Box
1762, Wichita, KS 67201)

I tried to combat the fatality rate from
shipwreck by countering the four physical
shocks which kill the victim before his forces
are spent: drowning, which kills in minutes;
exposure, which kills in hours; thirst, which
kills in days; and hunger, which kills in weeks.
When I had done this, I found a fifth threat that
could also kill in hours, helped by exposure
and brought on by the terrible shock of
shipwreck—fear, panic, distress, the
crumbling of morale.

Alain Bombard, foreword to, Bernard Robin,
Survival at Sea (Camden, Maine: International
Marine, 1981).

3

HEAT AND POWER SOURCES

HEATING, COOKING WITH KEROSENE

Kero-Sun portable kerosene heaters offer a means of standby heating or can be used to conserve energy by reducing or shutting off the central heating and using the kerosene unit in an individual room. Eight models are available, rated from 8,200 to 19,500 Btu.'s per hour, weighing from fourteen to thirty-five pounds, and priced from $180 to $290. They are tested and listed by Underwriters Laboratories. The heaters are started by a D-battery-powered push-button device. Kero-Sun also sells a kerosene-burning stainless-steel cookstove, weighing thirteen pounds and priced at $110. Write for brochure and dealer information:

Kero-Sun
Box 549
Kent, CT 06757

The Kero-Sun kerosene-burning stainless-steel cookstove.

CAMP STOVE: model 425F499, two-burner, designed to burn (on high setting) for two hours on 2½-pint filling of Coleman naphtha fuel, about $40. (Coleman Co., Inc., Box 1762, Wichita, KS 67201)

MAKING YOUR STANDBY KEROSENE HEATER PAY FOR ITSELF WITH SAVINGS

Two or three kerosene space heaters, stowed away with a supply of fuel, can provide a practical hedge against the day when your home-heating system is disrupted. This kind of insurance can cost several hundred dollars, however, and with good fortune you might never collect on it.

A workable option is to cut your central-heating costs with kerosene space heating, and thus pay for your insurance.

The method is simple. In cold weather you turn your furnace thermostat down to an extra-low level and use the portable kerosene units to heat your house selectively. At night, only the bedrooms need to be warmed by the space heaters, while the rest of the house can be left cold. During the daytime, the same method can be employed, keeping the central-heating level low and warming only those rooms in regular use.

STANDBY KEROSENE HEAT AND LIGHT

Aladdin markets five models of kerosene space heaters and a wide selection of kerosene lamps. The heaters range in output from 7,800 to 15,200 Btu.'s per hour and in price from $183 to $274. They burn with a glass-fiber wick and have battery-powered ignition and automatic safety shutoff. The units are listed by Underwriters Laboratories. Said to be 99 percent fuel efficient, the heaters can be used for energy conservation as a supplement to or a substitute for the central heating system in a home. The Aladdin lamps are available in over twenty models, all of them in decorative designs and some of them with optional electric conversion. Prices vary; two models with porcelain bases sell for $49.95 each; other models come with metal bases. The lamps are designed to burn without smoke or odor and to produce an incandescent light equivalent to a sixty-watt light bulb. Write for literature and dealer information:

ALH, Inc.
Aladdin Industries, Inc.
Box 100255
Nashville, TN 37210

Two of Aladdin's kerosene space heaters. The Tropic radiant heater, on the left, has an output of 7,800 Btu.'s per hour, burns seventeen to twenty-two hours on .85 gallon, and is priced at $183. The Equator convection heater has an output of 15,200 Btu.'s, burn time of twelve to sixteen hours on 1.3 gallon, and costs $250.

CATALYTIC HEATER: model 512A708, 3,500-Btu. capacity, available in larger 5,000 and 8,000 Btu. models, weighs six pounds, burns Coleman naphtha fuel, about $45. (Coleman Co., Inc., Box 1762, Wichita, KS 67201)

The Winpower Powr-Pak 4000B ($1,100) portable generator has an output of 4,000 watts.

ALADDIN LAMPS AND HEATERS: MAIL ORDER AT DISCOUNT PRICES

Here is a catalog that offers discounts up to 20 percent on Aladdin kerosene lamps and heaters. The firm also sells a variety of grain mills, juicers, and food processors at discount prices, as well as spinning wheels and table looms.

The Underground
311½ S. 11th St.
Tacoma, WA 98402

PORTABLE GENERATORS: STANDBY ELECTRIC POWER

In a power failure, a standby generator could keep your lights lit and your freezer cold. This firm manufactures an extensive line of generators for home, farm, and construction that begin with small Powr-Pak portables, both gas and diesel powered, with output as low as 1,500 watts (model 1500B, $545) and ranging up to 5,000 watts in output. Write for literature and dealer information, particularly the brochure *Own Your Own Portable Electric Company:*

Winpower Corp.
1207 1st Ave. E.
Newton, IA 50208

COMPACT PROPANE STOVE: model 5418B700, 10,000 Btu. capacity, single-burner, uses disposable propane tank, stove unit weighs two pounds, about $20. (Coleman Co., Inc., Box 1762, Wichita, KS 67201)

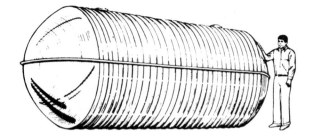

WHEN THE POWER FAILS

The lights go out. Or, if it's daytime, you notice that the electric clock has stopped. Either way, it's a sudden thing, and a shock. Your electrical power is gone. If it's nighttime, you go to a window—no, there are no lights on out there either.

You suddenly feel that everything has come to a standstill, and it has. The refrigerator is silent, the light does not come on when you open the door. Your radio and television set have died. Your air conditioner is a lifeless box, and you seem to sense the room temperature rising already, even though the unit has been shut down for only a few minutes. Or, if it's winter, you are almost immediately aware of a cold chill, knowing that the thermostatic-control system will be powerless to switch on your gas or oil furnace when the temperature does begin falling.

Power supply—and failure—is a completely unpredictable thing. You rely on your utility company to start the current flowing again. It could be just a few more minutes—or hours. Or it could be a matter of days. You can't really know—not until the blackout is over.

The simplest response you can make is to sit back and wait until the system returns to normal. But even during those first minutes you begin thinking about the possible consequences of the power outage and wondering what you would need to have and do in order to deal with it.

Here in your house or apartment you risk injury if you move around in the darkness. You need a flashlight, a candle, a gas or kerosene lamp. If you are in a public place (a stalled elevator, a windowless hallway) or out on a city street, you need a miniature flashlight in your pocket or purse to protect yourself from hazard.

With a battery-powered radio you could tune to news reports. Instead, several hours pass before a neighbor informs you and your family that a multistate power grid has been shut down. It will be at least twenty-four hours before the electricity returns.

It is late in the night now. The time for your evening meal has long passed—but you have an electric stove and it is useless. If you had a standby camp stove you could cook with it. You go to sleep in a cold house after a cold meal—it would be different if you had one of those gas or kerosene space heaters. You can't get heat out of your furnace—or you don't know how to. If it is wintertime in a northern state, you wonder how long it will be before your water pipes freeze and burst.

It is the next day. The food in your refrigerator and freezer compartment is still safe to eat because it is so cold in the house. But if it were summertime, the thawed meats and other perishables would already be spoiling. If you had kept one or two plastic gallon jugs water filled and frozen in the freezer, you could have preserved the meats a little longer. And if you had that ice in a camp cooler, the food would have lasted for two or three days.

If you had a standby generator, you could produce electric light in your home, run your refrigerator, even operate your electric stove. But you don't have a generator.

Now it is the third day of the power blackout. You can't drive your car to work because your gas tank is almost empty and the service stations aren't selling gasoline because their pumps run on electricity. And you don't have any spare gas stored at home.

Your supply of canned and dried foods is also running low. You drive to nearby stores—through traffic that is snarled because signal lights aren't working—and find the stores are closed or mostly sold out. If only you had kept a shelf or two of extra food on hand . . .

If you live in a high-rise apartment building on an upper floor, the water pressure is gone now because the tank on the roof is empty and there is no power to pump it full again. If only you had some jugs of water—for drinking and cooking, for washing, and to flush the toilet . . .

STANDBY GENERATORS

McCulloch sells a line of gasoline-powered generators that range in output from as low as 1,200 watts to as high as 5,000. Its model HP 1200, with 1,200-watt output, weighs 67 pounds and sells for $479.99. The HP 5000, weighing 141 pounds, is priced at $1,449.99. See your local dealer, or write for information:

McCulloch Corp.
Box 92180
Los Angeles, CA 90009

STANDBY ALTERNATORS

Poulan, a company well known for chain saws, sells a line of five models of alternators. The units are driven by Briggs & Stratton gas engines ranging from three to eleven horsepower, generating 1,250 to 5,000 watts. Write for literature and dealer information:

Beaird-Poulan Co.
5020 Flournoy-Lucas Rd.
Shreveport, LA 71109

Small AC Generator Service Manual
1981/290 pp./$7.95
Technical Publications Division
Intertec Publishing Corp.
Box 12901
Overland Park, KS 66212

This manual covers gas-engine-driven generators up to 8,000-watt capacity. It presents maintenance, service, and troubleshooting procedures, as well as wiring schematics for most current models on the market and for some models five to ten years old. Directions are step by step, with exploded-view drawings.

Familiarity with danger makes a brave man braver, but less daring. Thus with seamen: he who goes the oftenest round Cape Horn goes the most circumspectly.

Herman Melville, *White Jacket* (1850)

4

FOOD AND WATER

STOW-A-WAY INDUSTRIES: SURVIVAL STORAGE FOODS, FOOD APPLIANCES, SURVIVAL ACCESSORIES

Among the largest and oldest in the field, this firm has supplied provisions for the National Geographic Society and the Arctic Institute of North America. It sells a wide variety of storage foods, survival accessories, and goods and equipment for backpackers and mountaineers. Freeze-dried and dehydrated foods are available, as well as unprocessed bulk materials such as grains and beans packed in nitrogen-flushed containers. Prices vary widely, depending on type of food and quantity: a Stow-Lite twelve-month unit for one person is priced at $775, plus shipping costs. Among the food-processing appliances offered are grain mills, food dryers, dough mixers, ice-cream freezers, and home-canning equipment. The firm's survival accessories range from camp stoves and lamps to water purifiers, clothing, first-aid and survival kits, knives, heaters, and candles. Write for catalog:

Stow-A-Way Industries
166 Cushing Hwy.
Cohasset, MA 02025

STORAGE FOODS: OTHER SOURCES OF SUPPLY AND INFORMATION

Sources for survival storage foods have been increasing. Below is a sampling of manufacturers and retail outlets. Catalogs and brochures are free.

MARTENS: mail-order sales of dehydrated and freeze-dried foods, bulk grains, and legumes. Firm handles the Mountain House brand: Just In Case unit for one person for six months, $951; Mini version for thirty-five days, $310; Emergency 6 Pack for one person for eight days, $56. Also sells a selection of accessories, including an emergency dental kit ($19.95).

Martens Health and Survival Products, Inc.
Box 5969
Tahoe City, CA 95730

NELSON: mail-order sales of a wide variety of storable foods: whole and rolled grains, flour, beans, rice in bulk quantities (hard red winter wheat, forty-five pounds in plastic container,

Case 1: Protein	$35.40	**Case 7: Milk**	$71.40
4 Hamburger TVP		6 Milk, Regular Nonfat	
2 Chicken TVP		**Case 8: Milk**	$71.40
Case 2: Vegetables	$93.45	6 Milk, Regular Nonfat	
2 Carrots, Diced		**Case 9: Protein**	$33.10
1 Stew Blend		4 Ham Granules TVP	
1 Soup Blend		2 Unflavored TVP	
2 Peas, Green Garden		**Case 10: Vegetables**	$100.10
Case 3: Fruit	$86.20	2 Green Beans	
2 Apple Slices		1 Tomato Crystals	
1 Fruit Mix		1 Corn, Sweet	
1 Fruit Galaxy		1 Bell Pepper	
1 Dates, Diced		1 Cabbage, Diced	
1 Banana Flakes		**Case 11: Vegetables**	$47.00
Case 4: Grain	$29.90	2 Potato Dices	
1 Cornmeal		1 Potato Slices	
2 Rolled Oats, Instant		1 Soy Beans	
2 Rice, White		1 Lentils	
1 Wheat, Hard Red Winter		1 Onions, Chopped	
Case 5: Grain	$52.60	**Case 12: Adjuncts/Desserts**	$72.55
2 Elbo Macaroni		1 Pudding Mix, Vanilla	
3 Fruit Nut Cereal		1 Applesauce	
1 Cracked Wheat Cereal		1 Butter powder	
Case 6: Protein	$101.30	1 Salt	
3 Eggs, Scrambling		1 Drink Mix, Grape	
1 Peanut Butter Powder		1 Drink Mix, Orange	
1 Cheese Powder, Cheddar			
1 Baby Lima Beans			

From the Stow-A-Way catalog: chart shows contents of Stow-Lite twelve-month unit, designed to provide approximately two thousand calories a day for one person, stows in twelve cubic feet of space, priced at $755, plus shipping.

FOODS FOR SURVIVAL KITS: thèse Stow-Lite dehydrated and freeze-dried foods and fruit drinks—like any similar product you buy in your supermarket—are reconstituted by adding water. Pouches contain four servings, vary widely in price, depending on type of product: orange drink is $.85, while scrambled eggs with bacon-flavored bits are $1.85. (Stow-A-Way Industries, 166 Cushing Hwy., Cohasset, MA 02025)

BULK GRAINS AND BEANS: packed in nitrogen-flushed, five-gallon plastic cans, Stow-Lite bulk grains and beans are available in five selections—hard red winter wheat (37 pounds/$19.50), lentils (35/$38.50), long-grain white rice (37/$23.50), pinto beans (36/$29.75), soybeans (33/$25.75). (Stow-A-Way Industries, 166 Cushing Hwy., Cohasset, MA 02025)

DEHYDRATED AND FREEZE-DRIED FOODS: packed in no. 10 cans for long-term storage, these Stow-Lite foods vary widely in price, depending on type of food and weight of contents: two pounds eight ounces of fruit mix cost $15.95, while two pounds four ounces of carrots cost $11.50. (Stow-A-Way Industries, 166 Cushing Hwy., Cohasset, MA 02025)

$24.99). Also sells dried fruit, raw or roasted shelled nuts and in-shell nuts, as well as a selection of food-processing appliances.

Nelson & Sons, Inc.
Box 1296
Salt Lake City, UT 84110

SAMANDY: a manufacturer, markets dehydrated foods through retail outlets, packages complete units of basic foods for long-term storage as well as short-term emergency kits (a six-can case of no. 2½ cans, each can a one-day supply for one person, $49). When writing for literature, ask for booklet *Family Food Reserve Story:*

SamAndy Products, Inc.
1770 Chicago Ave.
Riverside, CA 92507

OREGON FREEZE DRY FOODS: produces the Mountain House brand of storage foods, sells through retail outlets. Write for brochures—to see not only the variety of unit combinations available, but also to see the appetizing full-color photographs of these foods cooked and served up.

Oregon Freeze Dry Foods, Inc.
Box 1048
Albany, OR 97321

RICHMORE: a pioneer in dehydrated foods—packaged for campers, backpackers, hunters, and fishermen—this firm sells through retail outlets. Offering a wide variety of food items of all kinds, this is a source for assembling your own storage-food program. Write for brochures and dealer information:

Richmore Corp.
Box 2728
Van Nuys, CA 91404

VITA GREEN: specializes in organically grown dried fruits, nuts, beans, edible seeds (pumpkin, sesame, sunflower), grains:

Vita Green Farms
Box 879
Vista, CA 92083

LOWERING THE COSTS OF KEEPING A STANDBY FOOD SUPPLY

The sources on these pages offer a variety of foods prepared and packaged specifically for long-term storage. Freeze-dried and dehydrated foods, as well as whole grains packed in nitrogen-filled cans, represent a large investment, however.

There are two main alternatives to consider.

One approach is to use the common canned foods you buy in the supermarket. These vegetables, fruits, and meats have a more limited shelf life, and so they must be kept in use on a rotating basis. After an initial investment to stock your shelves with a reserve supply, such canned foods simply become a part of your usual diet. You continuously add newer stocks as you routinely use the older supply. In this way, dollars are not tied up in foods that may never be eaten, and a reserve supply—ranging from several days to several weeks—can be maintained.

A second approach to long-term food storage is home canning. Vegetables, fruits, and meats—either home grown or purchased in season when prices are lowest—can be preserved and stored for routine and standby use in the same way as commercial canned foods. The dollar savings derived from home canning are substantial and make possible the storage of a long-term food supply.

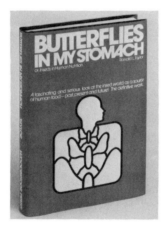

Butterflies in My Stomach
Ronald L. Taylor
1975/224 pp./$8.95
Woodbridge Press
Box 6189
Santa Barbara, CA 93111

The author, an entomologist and pathologist, makes a convincing case for the insect as a major nutritional resource. This is no textbook but a down-to-earth approach dealing with our prejudices about eating insects, their food potential, how to select and collect them, and how to prepare them for the table. There is background, historical and current, on the eating of insects, and a chapter on the role of insects in wilderness survival.

The New Healthy Trail Food Book
Dorcas S. Miller
1976, 1980/79 pp./$4.25
Ms. Dorcas S. Miller
Georgetown, ME 04548

Backpackers have refined their food-supply techniques to an art—one that can be applied to all kinds of survival situations. The author explains this art, dealing with nutrition, types of foods, trail cooking, recipes, sample meals.

The Well-Fed Backpacker
June Fleming
1976, 1981/112 pp./$3.95
Random House, Inc.
201 E. 50th St.
New York, NY 10022

A very practical how-to guide to the outdoor use of the various lightweight food products on the market. The author covers the dehydrated and freeze-dried products designed specifically for compactness, but she also shows how less expensive store-bought foods and home-prepared items can be adapted for the trail.

How to Prepare Common Wild Foods
Darcy Williamson
1978/108 pp./$6.95
Maverick Publications
Drawer 5007
Bend, OR 97701

If you are learning foraging you will also need to learn how to prepare the wild foods you find. You could cook up some milkweed shoots with mustard sauce, for instance—or scalloped wild onions and eggs, or some steamed serviceberry pudding. Over twenty wild plants and fruits are covered, with a guide to identifying them, and there are also recipes for preparing fish, wildfowl, and game meat.

Stalking the Wild Asparagus
Euell Gibbons
1962, 1970/303 pp./$5.95
David McKay Co., Inc.
Two Park Ave.
New York, NY 10016

Stalking the Wild Asparagus covers wild foods of all kinds: fruits, berries, leaves, roots, tubers, herbs, mushrooms. There are also chapters on wild honey and such other food sources as bluegill, carp, crayfish, frog's legs, and turtles and terrapins. The book is illustrated with line drawings for identification of edible plant species.

Roots
Douglas B. Elliott
1976/123 pp./$5.95
The Chatham Press
143 Sound Beach Ave.
Old Greenwich, CT 06870

Foraging includes what grows under the ground as well as on the surface and above it, and the author gives a thorough course on the wild roots, tubers, corms, and rhizomes of North America that can be used both for food and for their age-old medicinal purposes. The roots are illustrated with finely rendered drawings.

Courage is resistance to fear, mastery of fear—not absence of fear.

Mark Twain (Samuel Clemens), *Pudd'nhead Wilson* (1894)

Edible and Poisonous Plants of the Western States
Calvin P. Burt and Frank G. Heyl
1970, 1974/52 cards/$5.95

Edible and Poisonous Plants of the Eastern States
Calvin P. Burt and Frank G. Heyl
1973/52 cards/$5.95

Plant Deck, Inc., Publishers
2134 S.W. Wembley Park Rd.
Lake Oswego, OR 97034

You can study the edible and poisonous plants of your area from poker-deck-size reference cards, each of which has a full-color photo of the plant, with detailed text on the reverse side. (When ordering from publisher, add $.50 for postage and handling.)

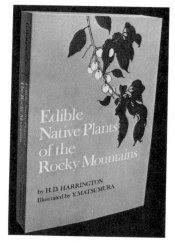

Edible Native Plants of the Rocky Mountains
H. D. Harrington and Y. Matsumura
1967, 1980/392 pp./$9.95

Western Edible Plants
H. D. Harrington and Y. Matsumura
1967, 1980/156 pp./$5.95

University of New Mexico Press
Albuquerque, NM 87131

Written for botanists and nonbotanists alike, these two books are first-rate manuals for food gathering. The larger book focuses on the Rockies, while the smaller covers the country from Kansas and Nebraska west to the Pacific. Both books are illustrated with line drawings.

The Mushroom Hunter's Field Guide
Alexander H. Smith and Nancy Smith Weber
1958, 1980/316 pp./$14.95
University of Michigan Press
Box 1104
Ann Arbor, MI 48106

A thorough and very readable guide to identifying mushrooms in the field. Combined with 290 vivid color photos, the text carefully shows how to distinguish the edible from the poisonous, with recommendations on the most desirable table species. The authors note that of more than three thousand species in North America not more than a couple of hundred are generally desirable as food. But those mushrooms that are "edible and choice" are well worth the search, and this book will lead you to them, particularly with its detailed information on season and locale for each type.

REFERENCE SOURCE ON MUSHROOMS

The following series of books on mushroom identification is the work of botanists and biologists. These are scientific books that grow progressively more complex and specialized as you read from Genus I to Genus V. (The Genus III book is really a laboratory study.) But the Genus I book, with its many clear and precise drawings, as well as the

Genus II book are sound resources for the mushroom hunter who wants to refine the practical skills of finding edible species. For the mushroom hunter with an extensive scientific background, these books would be a complete reference set.

How to Identify Mushrooms to Genus I: Macroscopic Features
David L. Largent
1973, 1977/86 pp./$4.85

How to Identify Mushrooms to Genus II: Field Identification of Genera
David L. Largent and Harry D. Thiers
1977/32 pp./$3.75

How to Identify Mushrooms to Genus III: Microscopic Features
David Largent, David Johnson, and Roy Watling
1977/148 pp./$8.50

How to Identify Mushrooms to Genus IV: Keys to Families and Genera
Daniel E. Stuntz
1977/94 pp./$5.75

How to Identify Mushrooms to Genus V: Cultural and Developmental Features
Roy Watling
1981/169 pp./$6.95

Mad River Press
Route 2, Box 151-B
Eureka, CA 95501

DRINKING WATER: YOU CANNOT SURVIVE WITHOUT IT

Unsafe drinking water can threaten your survival. One solution is the use of filtration devices like those made by American Water Purification. The company offers a range of products that use charcoal filters. Its pen-size Super Straw ($9.95) fits into a survival kit. The Portable Water Master ($24.95) comes with drinking cup, has a filtering capacity up to 1,000 gallons, and weighs twenty ounces. The firm also makes high-capacity filtration units that are hooked into the water pipes in the home: a Counter Top model for $49.95, and Under Counter models starting at $149.95. Write for catalog:

American Water Purification
115 Mason
Concord, CA 94520

PORTABLE WATER DISTILLER: the Clean Water Machine ($175), with a capacity of three gallons per day, is equipped with electric heating base, but with optional boiling pan ($29) it will operate on such other heat sources as stove top, camp stove. (Stow-A-Way Industries, 166 Cushing Hwy., Cohasset, MA 02025)

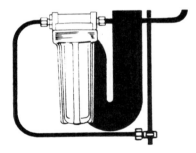

From American Water catalog: drawing illustrates hook-up of Under Counter water-filtration unit.

SOLAR STILL FOR DRINKING WATER

Vita Green Farms sells solar units for producing distilled drinking water. A smaller unit ($650) produces three to seven gallons of purified water weekly, depending on quantity of sunlight, and a larger model ($950) yields ten to twenty-five gallons weekly. Write for information:

Vita Green Farms
Box 879
Vista, CA 92083

PORTABLE SOLAR HOT WATER

Sun Shower is a plastic bag with an opaque side and a clear side. You fill the container with 2½ gallons of water at sixty degrees, place it on a flat surface with the clear side exposed to direct sunlight, and in three hours on a seventy-degree day the water will heat to above one hundred degrees. You rig the container overhead and turn on your shower. The unit weighs twelve ounces, costs $14.95.

Basic Designs
Box 479
Muir Beach, CA 94965

IMAGINE OPEC SAYING, "NO MORE OIL!"

The gasoline shortage of 1979 was nothing compared to this one, when even the big oil companies received a certain amount of public sympathy. First of all, there had been widespread strikes at the refineries during the summer, and reserves of gas and fuel oil fell. Then, just when the federal rationing program began to shorten the lines at the gas stations, OPEC went on strike. Member countries in the Middle East refused to sell crude oil to the United States, and it was almost six months before the political tensions eased and oil exports were resumed.

The crisis multiplied itself from day to day. Rationing allowed you just five gallons of gas a week—a little more if you were a physician or had some other priority rating. And then there were special "gasless" weeks, when the stations shut down for seven straight days. We learned to live with all that, though. Everyone belonged to two or three car pools—one for traveling to work, another for grocery shopping—and we all jammed onto public transportation whenever it was available.

But the real trouble was with food supplies and domestic heating oil. If you lived in an apartment building with oil heat, it was a very cold winter. Temperatures were kept just high enough so that the water pipes and the people wouldn't freeze, and there was never any hot tap water for bathing. If you had one of those small space heaters that burn kerosene, you could buy enough fuel to warm one room. In the suburbs, some neighbors moved in with each other: one family would shut its house down and take its fuel-oil allotment next door. A house with a good wood-heating system drew a lot of volunteer woodchoppers.

Food supplies went haywire all around the country. But it was especially bad in places like New England, where everything is shipped in by truck from long distances. Diesel fuel for trucks—and trains—was in short supply. The supermarkets weren't so super that winter. They limited the number of pounds or items you could buy at one time, and you could only stand in long lines for so long while your car pool was waiting for you. You could never count on what you would find at the stores. One day there would be piles of potatoes but no bread at all, and then for a week you wouldn't find a potato anywhere. And then, too, there were days at a time when the stores were closed entirely.

For people who had food stored away ahead of time, those months were not as grim. One woman in our neighborhood always kept a large supply of whole-grain wheat. She milled it herself and baked bread from it: that winter she bartered her bread for pork chops, and everybody was happy in the bargain.

If you had a storage tank of gas buried in your backyard—even as little as a hundred gallons—it gave you something to bargain with that was worth much more than money. Or if you had a motorcycle—or even a ten-speed bike—you could get around while others were stuck at home. In fact, you could get a ten-speed bike in exchange for a few gallons of gas.

5
SHELTER

Photo shows the Moss Optimum 200, with 192 square feet of space priced at $1,020.

TENTS, LARGE AND SMALL

Moss Tent Works supplies tents ranging from a twelve-foot Parawing, at $79, to the Optimum 1500, with 1,462 square feet of space at $6,800. The Parawing is actually an open-sided shelter, a fly with "wings" that slope down to increase protection: such a unit, kept in a car trunk, for instance, would be a useful emergency shelter from sun or rain. The Optimum series of tents—formed of arched alcoves around a vaulted central space and pole—vary in size from the 200 model, with 192 square feet at $1,020, to the very large 1500 model: such a tent could serve as a temporary family shelter or could be used as a stowable dwelling at a retreat site. Also available from this firm is a middle range of tents for backpacking and camping. Write for catalogs and prices:

Moss Tent Works, Inc.
Camden, ME 04843

43

TENTS FOR SURVIVAL STANDBY

Eureka tents—an old name in the field—offers a wide selection: wall tents in various sizes, as well as a range of tents with exterior frames, including compact small tents for mountaineering and backpacking. Some of the smallest tents—kept in a car trunk, for instance—have particular survival value. One example is the Sentinel: it is self-supporting with folding aluminum-rod frame, has double-wall construction, and weighs between five and ten pounds in its compact, two-person and four-person sizes. Write for catalog and prices:

Eureka Tent Division
Johnson Camping, Inc.
Box 966
Binghamton, NY 13902

The Eureka Sentinel model mountaineering tent.

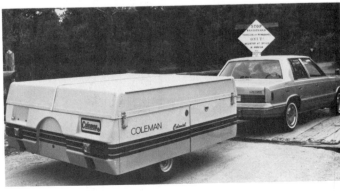

CAMPER TRAILER: the Colonial, one of several folding-trailer models, opens out (upper photo) to provide two double beds, includes galley equipped with two-burner range, sink, and built-in ten-gallon water tank. Folded for towing (lower photo), the 840-pound trailer has low profile for fuel efficiency. Suggested retail price, $3,345. (Coleman Co., Inc., Box 1762, Wichita, KS 67201)

THE YURT: A SHELTER DESIGN FROM CENTRAL ASIA

The yurt was developed over thousands of years by nomadic peoples. It consists of a collapsible, wooden-latticework, circular wall, with a conical roof, over which fabric or animal skins are stretched. The yurt has been transplanted and modernized, but the basic design remains unchanged. The yurts made by Pacific Yurts are canvas-covered, and come in fourteen-, sixteen-, twenty-, and twenty-four-foot diameters costing from $1,655 to $2,695. Do-it-yourself kits in the same sizes range from $1,090 to $1,985. A skylight at the peak replaces the smoke hole of the native yurt, and there are windows and doors in the sides. A fourteen-foot yurt has 155 square feet of floor space and over eight feet of headroom at the center. Two people can "pitch" a yurt in about two hours. The design—as any Mongolian would tell you—is very sturdy, and this firm's product is intended for durability. A yurt could be your emergency dwelling, or it could be your stowable shelter at a retreat site. Write for literature:

Pacific Yurts, Inc.
77456 Hwy. 99 S.
Cottage Grove, OR 97424

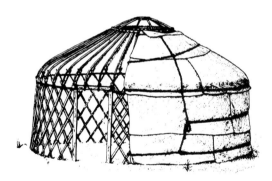

A Central Asian yurt (from Pacific Yurts catalog).

THE TIPI: SHELTER IN A ROUND SPACE

If the tipi seems a awkward shelter form to you, read Nomadics Tipi Makers' catalog. It explains how modern materials make the most out of what was a survival mainstay for the Plains Indians.

The company makes tipis from fourteen to twenty-six feet in diameter. A twenty-foot size ranges in price from $353 to $437, depending on the fabric of the cover. Tipi liners are available in matching diameters in either six-foot or nine-foot lengths; in the twenty-foot diameter, prices range from $124 to $219. The liner is a vital part of the tipi structure, serving both as insulation and as a source of the draft that carries smoke from the central fire up and out through the top flaps. The firm also sells kits for both covers and liners at reduced prices. Write for catalog ($1):

Nomadics Tipi Makers
17671 Snow Creek Rd.
Bend, OR 97701

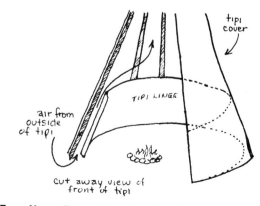

A Nomadics tipi set up for use.

From Nomadics catalog: drawing shows how the tipi liner creates draft to take smoke out of the shelter.

THE TIPI: A CANVAS SHELTER THAT TRAVELS WELL

The Plains Indians were travelers and wherever they went their tipis went with them. A tipi provides a great deal more living space than is immediately apparent. A tipi that is twenty-four feet in diameter at the ground is fifteen feet wide at the six-foot level. A tipi sheds the weather and stands fast in the wind. A modern version, like the Sioux design by Goodwin-Cole, could provide emergency shelter or a semipermanent shelter on a piece of woodland property. A twenty-four-foot tipi of flame-retardant canvas is priced at $485. Write for brochure:

Goodwin-Cole Co., Inc.
1315 Alhambra Blvd.
Sacramento, CA 95816

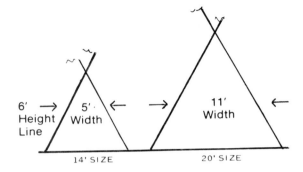

Tipi Size	14'	16'	18'	20'	22'	24'
Approx. Width at 6' high	5'	7'	9'	11'	13'	15'

From the Goodwin-Cole catalog, illustration shows the amount of living space that various tipi sizes yield.

BACKPACK TENT: two-person Twilight model made of Gore-Tex fabric, weighs three pounds nine ounces, packs into 5¼ × 17 inches, $250. (Marmot Mountain Works, Ltd., 331 S. 113th St., Grand Junction, CO 81501)

Shelters, Shacks and Shanties

D. C. Beard
1914, 1972/243 pp./$3.95
Charles Scribner's Sons
579 5th Ave.
New York, NY 10017

Written as a manual for the Boy Scouts, this book shows how to build shelters that range from primitive huts to log cabins. The how-to directions are illustrated with drawings, and the text is easy reading. It is a book for a young boy or girl, but there are useful shelter ideas for the adult as well.

Drawings show several shelters adapted from Indian designs (from *Shelters, Shacks and Shanties*).

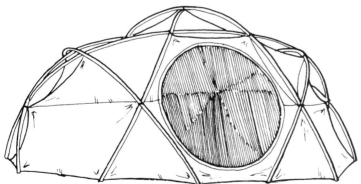

TWO-PERSON TENT: Oval Intention model pitches with two aluminum poles slipped into their sleeves, weighs five pounds eight ounces, sells for $232. (The North Face, 1234 5th Street, Berkeley, CA 94710)

6
HEALTH AND FIRST AID

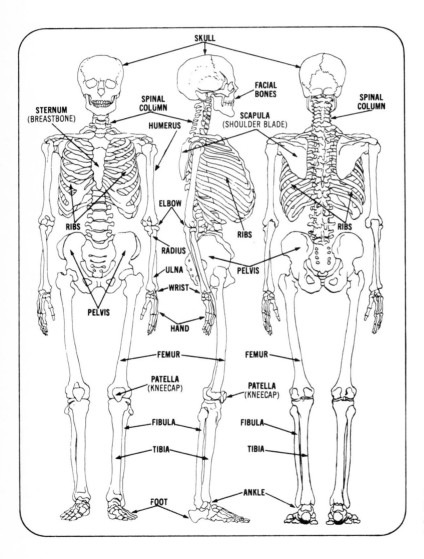

Illustration indicates names of bones of human skeleton: from *Advanced First Aid & Emergency Care.*

Standard First Aid & Personal Safety
1973/268 pp./$1.95

Advanced First Aid & Emergency Care
1973, 1979/318 pp./$2.50

American Red Cross
National Headquarters
Washington, DC 20006

Both of these detailed and illustrated manuals serve as textbooks for the Red Cross courses, and the organization emphasizes that training is essential to effective first aid. The Red Cross provides several such courses, which are administered through its local chapters. To take such a course or to order the manuals or other training materials, check your telephone directory for your local chapter. Ask for the brochure *Community Services Courses*. First-aid training—combined with experience in a local volunteer ambulance corps—could take you a long way toward self-sufficiency.

Emergency Medical Guide
John Henderson, M.D.
1963, 1978/681 pp./$5.95
McGraw-Hill Book Co.
1221 Avenue of the Americas
New York, NY 10020

A comprehensive manual for coping with simple and complex medical emergencies for those trained as well as untrained in first aid. All aspects of care, from removing a foreign object from the eye or splinting a bone fracture to resuscitation of a victim of heart or lung failure, are covered. A separate seventy-six-page section deals with such common medical emergencies and conditions as unattended childbirth. The book's line-drawing illustrations are exceptional, giving clear step-by-step directions.

Chart indicates treatment for certain kinds of poisoning: from *Standard First Aid & Personal Safety*.

TYPES OF POISONS FOR WHICH VOMITING SHOULD NOT BE INDUCED

Type of Poison	Diluting Fluids (One glass)	Neutralizing Fluid (Adult: 3-4 glasses) (Child: 1-2 glasses)	Demulcent (Several glasses but do not cause vomiting)
Strong acid (for example, toilet bowl cleaner)	Water or milk	Milk of magnesia or other weak alkali, mixed with water	Milk, olive oil, or egg white
Strong alkali (for example, drain cleaner)	Water or milk	Vinegar or lemon juice, mixed with water	Milk, olive oil, or egg white
Petroleum product (for example, kerosene, gasoline, furniture polish)	Water or milk	None	None

SAVING A LIFE WITH CPR

Training in cardiopulmonary resuscitation (CPR) has expanded continuously over the past decade and has become a part of high school teaching programs. The number of Americans who have learned this lifesaving system remains relatively small, however, even though its survival value has been proved by thousands of lives saved.

The main elements of CPR are mouth-to-mouth artificial respiration for inadequate or stopped breathing, techniques for clearing the airway of foreign obstruction, and the use of external chest compression to revive the stopped heart.

Learning the skills of CPR is not difficult but does require a training course given by a certified instructor. The course involves several hours of sessions and includes practice on an instrumented dummy which measures the student's proficiency.

To find out about CPR training available in your community, contact a local chapter of the American Heart Association or American Red Cross.

Drawing illustrates resuscitation procedures in CPR system (from "Standards and Guidelines for Cardiopulmonary Resuscitation and Emergency Cardiac Care," *Journal of the American Medical Association,* **August 1, 1980, American Medical Association, Chicago: reprinted by permission of the American Heart Association).**

SURVIVAL IN COLD WATER: MEASURES FOR DEALING WITH HYPOTHERMIA

Immersion in cold water leads to hypothermia, or subnormal body temperature, which can kill you. Even in fifty-degree water, however, a person may survive for three or more hours by using techniques that slow the loss of body heat. These techniques are explained in the Coast Guard brochures *Hypothermia and Cold Water Survival* and *A Pocket Guide to Cold Water Survival.*

Department of Transportation
U.S. Coast Guard
Washington, DC 20590

EMERGENCY MEDICAL INSTRUMENTS AND SUPPLIES

A mail-order source for your medical kit, Indiana Camp Supply serves backpackers and mountaineers who travel far out of reach of doctors. The catalog lists an extensive variety of instruments, appliances, supplies, and medications. A sampling: Hartman hemostat (to clamp off bleeding; $6.30), air splints ($9.50 to $14), suture-removal kit ($3.25), Percogesic tablets (for pain, fever; $2.10 for box of twenty-four), hydrocortisone cream (for poison ivy; $3.75 for one-ounce tube), Halazone water-purification tablets ($3.95 for 100 tablets). The firm also offers an Expedition Medical Kit ($25), Wilderness Medical Kit ($15), and Pocket First-Aid Kit ($7). Write for catalog ($1):

Indiana Camp Supply, Inc.
Box 344
Pittsboro, IN 46167

FIRST-AID KITS

Acme Cotton Products produces a wide variety of first-aid kits assembled for specific situations. An auto first-aid kit ($27.49) comes in a plastic case with reflector back for highway emergencies. A kit for outdoorsmen ($31.29) includes a snake-bite unit and is weatherproof, as is the packaging in a kit for marine use ($36.49) which includes a plastic mouth-to-mouth rescue breather. Write for brochures and dealer information:

Acme Cotton Products
Box 419
Dayville, CT 06241

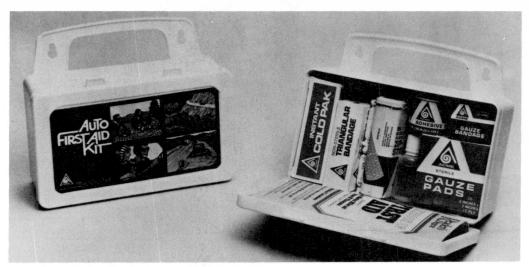

From Acme Cotton Products: auto first-aid kit, $27.49.

DENTAL FIRST-AID KIT: provides tools and materials for temporary relief of pain caused by toothaches, lost fillings, broken teeth. Called the ORx Dent-Aide, the kit includes a fifty-five-page instruction manual as well as elements for making temporary filings. Priced at $19.95. (Martens Health and Survival Products, Inc., Box 5969, Tahoe City, CA 95730)

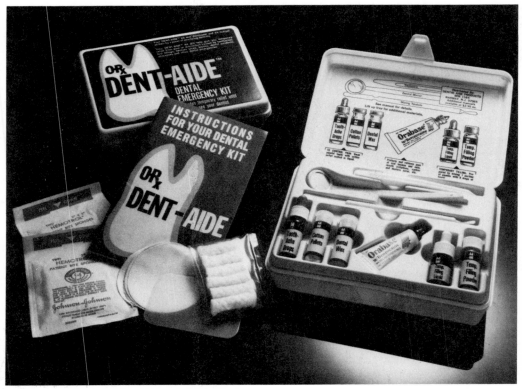

WALKING YOUR WAY TO PHYSICAL FITNESS

Your physical conditioning will probably be one of the largest factors in your chances for survival in any threatening situation. Whether you are stranded in a blizzard, fleeing an earthquake, or evacuating your family from the dangers of a nuclear-reactor accident, the physical demands for survival will be great.

A personal physical-fitness program can also make substantial demands, of course, particularly if you try to accomplish too much too quickly. One very practical approach is simply to start a regular routine of walking: daily walks that can be steadily increased to total several miles each week.

Walking exercise is a relatively painless way to begin a conditioning program. It can be a matter of a long, leisurely stroll in the neighborhood, or going on foot all or part of the way to and from your work. It can become a refreshing recreation, especially after a few weeks of walking have begun to tone up the muscles and given you an appreciation of your physical capacity.

Walking can be merely an easy first stage of a more substantial physical-fitness program. A next step would be to turn your stroll into long-range hiking in a park or woodland on weekends. A regular routine of walking can also prepare you for the more strenuous exercise of running.

Jogging has become a widely popular exercise because it so clearly pays off in good physical conditioning and health. Like walking, it costs you little more than time and determination.

There are other ways of developing physical fitness, of course. Exercises like isometrics or weightlifting, aerobic dancing, swimming, bicycle riding, tennis, and golf are all activities that, individually, or in combination, can promote fitness. But if you are not doing anything right now to condition your body for survival, a good way to get started is to take a long walk.

MEDICAL KIT FOR HOME, CAR, CAMP

Designed by a physician, this kit of nonprescription items includes topical antibiotic, disinfectant, and bandaging and surgical materials for wound care. Packed in a lightweight nylon belt pouch, the kit contains fifty items, including an instruction booklet: bandage scissors, forceps for removing splinters, butterfly closures, eye occlusor, various tapes and gauze, moleskin (for blister wounds), triple antibiotic ointment, Percogesic tablets (for pain). Called the Expedition medical kit, it is priced at $25. Write:

Indiana Camp Supply, Inc.
Box 344
Pittsboro, IN 46167

Mountaineering Medicine
Fred T. Darvill, M.D.
1966, 1980/55 pp. /$1.95
Darvill Outdoor Publications
1819 Hickox Rd.
Mt. Vernon, WA 98273
   Written for mountain climbers, hikers, and skiers, and published by the Skagit Mountain Rescue Unit, this pocket-size booklet presents the specifics of high-altitude first aid. Especially useful are sections on frostbite, exposure (hypothermia), altitude sickness, snow blindness, and sunburn. Included is a first-aid-kit listing of medications and prescription drugs—a helpful guide for anyone who might anticipate a survival emergency in the mountains. (When ordering by mail, add $.60 for postage and handling.)

Heimlich Maneuver
Henry J. Heimlich, M.D.
Clinical Symposia Reprint
1979/32 pp./$2
Ciba Pharmaceutical Co.
Medical Education Materials
Box R1340
Newark, NJ 07101
   Dr. Heimlich's procedure for dislodging an object caught in the throat. You can save a life with it, and—self-administered—you can save your own. Illustrated.

7
TRANSPORTATION

CHRYSLER OFF-ROAD VEHICLES

If you are partial to Chrysler products, its Dodge division offers two possibilities in four-wheel-drive vehicles. Its Ramcharger utility models include a four-wheel drive, priced at $10,095, and the Power Ram line of pickup trucks offers four-by-four models as well. See your local Dodge dealer for brochures and prices, or write:

Chrysler Corp.
Box 1919
Detroit, MI 48231

FOUR-WHEEL DRIVE FROM TOYOTA

Off-road survival mobility with four-wheel drive comes in more than one form. Toyota, for instance, sells its Land Cruiser—a jeeplike vehicle—a station wagon, and several pickup-truck models, all with four-wheel drive. See your local dealer for literature and prices, or write:

Toyota Motor Sales, U.S.A., Inc.
2055 W. 190th St.
Torrance, CA 90509

DRIVING AWAY FROM DANGER WITH FOUR- WHEEL DRIVE

We depend on the automobile for uses that are beyond its capacity in many cases. In a snowstorm, for instance, the family car is not a reliable means of transportation: it spins its wheels on icy pavements and bogs down in the drifts.

The exception is the car with four-wheel drive. When all four wheels are powered, a vehicle can go places and do things that may mean survival for driver and passengers.

In a blizzard, the four-wheel-drive vehicle will keep on moving down the highway while others are stranded at the sides of the road. In an evacuation situation, where a community's population must flee from natural or man-made disaster, a four-wheel-drive vehicle can bypass traffic jams and other obstacles by traveling off the paved roads in terrain that would stop the standard car.

Four-wheel drive is available as an option in cars and stationwagons that are otherwise standard, as well as in pickup trucks and in vehicles designed specifically for off-road use. Part of the cost of four-wheel drive can be "absorbed" by its routine use as a recreational vehicle or in work situations typical of a pickup truck.

The cost of four-wheel drive is not small, but it is an investment worth considering when weighed against its survival value.

FORD BRONCO FOUR-WHEEL-DRIVE

The Ford Bronco is a familiar name among off-road utility vehicles with four-wheel-drive. With a sticker price of $9,898, it is available with many options. Ford also offers a line of several pickup-truck models with four-wheel drive, ranging from $8,702 to $10,935. Your local dealer has literature and prices, or write:

Ford Motor Co.
Box 2053
Dearborn, MI 48121

The Ford Bronco.

UTILITY TRAILER: A WAY TO DOUBLE YOUR CAR CAPACITY

Think about the survival value of a small utility trailer to tow behind your car. This one weighs 265 pounds, costs $369.95, has a carrying capacity of 1,000 pounds with a volume of over twenty-one cubic feet. There is an optional fiberglass molded top for $164.95 and an optional oak side rail kit. It will haul your firewood out of the woods or you and your family out of an emergency. Write for catalog:

Cabela's, Inc.
812 13th St.
Sidney, NE 69162

Oak Side Rail Kit
(Optional)

Fiberglass Molded Top
(Optional)

Tilt Box Trailer

In the pith I saw some fat worms or maggots, and suddenly recollected that I had heard of them before as feeding on the sago (palm), and that in the West Indies they are eaten as a delicacy.

I felt inclined to try what they tasted like; so at once kindling a fire, and placing some half dozen, sprinkled with salt, on a little wooden spit, I set them to roast.

Very soon rich fat began to drop from them, and they smelt so temptingly good that all repugnance to the idea of eating worms vanished. Putting one like a pat of butter on baked potato, I boldly swallowed it and liked it so much that several others followed in the same way.

Johann Wyss, *The Swiss Family Robinson* (New York: Grosset & Dunlap, 1949).

Utility trailer from Cabela's is available with optional fiberglass molded top and optional oak side rail kit.

54

UTILITY TRAILER: Caboose model 5000-719, with hinged and removable top, weighs 175 pounds, about $450. (Coleman Co., Inc., Box 1762, Wichita, KS 67201)

Four Wheel Drive Handbook

James T. Crow and Cameron A. Warren
1970, 1976/96 pp./$3.95
CBS Consumer Publishing
PV4 Special Marketing
Box SG
Madison Hgts., MI 48071

This handbook is an introduction to the use of four-wheel-drive vehicles. There is a chapter on the various makes on the market. Driving techniques are covered, as is getting unstuck. There are also tips on repair and maintenance. (If ordering from publisher, add $1 for postage and handling.)

WINCHES FOR OFF-ROAD VEHICLES

A jeep-type four-wheel-drive vehicle can give you a mobility that could be a lifesaver. But for an added margin of mobility, you need a winch. Mounted on the front, it can pull your vehicle out of the rough, or it can do duty moving heavy objects. Superwinch makes several models, priced upwards from $100: they run on electric motors powered by the vehicle battery. Write for catalog ($1) and brochures:

Superwinch
Connecticut Rte. 52 at Exit 59
Putnam, CT 06260

Ox model CJ-7 from Superwinch, mounted on a jeep.

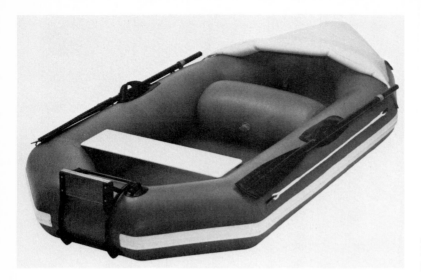

INFLATABLE BOATS

Seagull Marine imports the British Avon line of inflatable boats and life rafts. They range in size from small four-person models to large rescue boats. They are expensive: the smallest boat is priced at $1,095 and the smallest life raft is $2,415. But unlike many of the inflatables on the market that can be bought for less than $100— sometimes much less when made of plastic film—these boats have two or more air chambers and are constructed of a durable fabric that combines nylon with a synthetic rubber. These boats will keep you afloat when your life depends on it. Write for information:

Seagull Marine
1851 McGraw Ave.
Irving, CA 92714

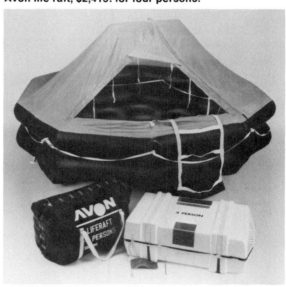

INFLATABLE RAFT

This raft is made of rubber-covered nylon and is available in a four-person model, weighing thirty pounds, for $99.50; and a six-person size, forty pounds, $129.50. Write for catalog ($1):

Airborne Sales Co., Inc.
Box 2727, Dept. C-81B
Culver City, CA 90230

Heroism, the Caucasian mountaineers say, is endurance for one moment more.

George Kennan, in a letter to Henry Munroe Rogers (1921)

8

COMMUNICATION

CB RADIO EQUIPMENT FROM PRESIDENT ELECTRONICS

This firm markets a full line of forty-channel citizens-band units that range from mobiles priced as low as $79.95 to a base-station model at $289.95. Included in the line are two hand-held walkie-talkie units (six-channel AX 55, $99.95; and three-channel AX 52, $79.95), as well as the forty-channel AX 43 marine model, $159.95. See your local retail outlet or write for brochures and dealer information:

President Electronics
6345 Castleway Ct.
Indianapolis, IN 46250

We immediately searched about for what would answer the purpose, and fortunately got hold of a number of empty flasks and tin canisters, which we connected two and two together so as to form floats sufficiently buoyant to support a person in the water, and my wife and young sons each willingly put one on. I then provided myself with matches, knives, cord, and other portable articles, trusting that, should the vessel go to pieces before daylight, we might gain the shore not wholly destitute.

Johann Wyss, *The Swiss Family Robinson* (New York: Grosset & Dunlap, 1949).

Hand-held CB unit from President Electronics: the six-channel AX55, $99.95.

A CB RADIO WOULD HAVE BEEN BETTER

You and your wife congratulated yourselves on the first day of the flooding. You had been very wise, when you moved to the area, to buy a house on high ground. There had been floods there in the past and now you and your neighbors were sitting pretty—on your own private island.

But the first day went by, and the river level did not go down. It went up. The rains continued and became heavier. The dam failed on the big reservoir up in the hills, making it all much worse.

The public water supply was cut off. The pumping stations were flooded, and the water had become contaminated anyway. But that wasn't going to be a problem because you had filled your five-gallon water cans before it all began.

The electrical power was out half of the time, but on enough so that food was safe in the refrigerator. The telephones were dead all of the time, and that became a problem. Someone should have had a CB radio.

Helicopters passed back and forth overhead, and on the second day one hovered long enough for a policeman with a bullhorn to call down and ask if anyone needed to be evacuated. Everyone shook their heads no. You knew from the radio broadcasts that things would keep getting worse until the floodwaters receded, and everything was all right on your little island.

That night the power was out again, and the gas and kerosene lamps were lit. One of the neighbors was also using candles. A child toppled a candle in a bedroom, and there was a fire.

No one was injured, but the house was a total loss—there was no water pressure to fight the fire.

Then, on the third day, food and drinking water did begin to become a problem. Everyone still had a supply left, but they could see it dwindling. That afternoon there were a lot of people waving at passing helicopters that were too far away to see the frantic signals.

In the evening, a man with a deep-V fishing skiff volunteered his boat for a try at getting across the valley to the main highway, which was passable now that the floodwaters had begun receding. An inflatable raft would have been better. The fishing skiff kept running aground in the shallows, and the expedition was postponed until morning.

The one really serious thing happened that night. A little girl slipped down a stairway in the darkness and broke her leg in two places. A woman who worked with the local ambulance corps splinted the leg, but the child couldn't lie still or sleep because of the pain. Finally, someone came up with a book on prescription drugs, and they calculated a safe dosage of sleeping pills to soothe the youngster for the night.

In the morning, everyone was ready for evacuation, but no helicopters flew in close enough to see the hand waving. A big fire made of car tires finally drew one in. A CB radio would have worked a lot better . . .

Part of me remained forever at Latitude 80° 08' South: what survived of my youth, my vanity, perhaps, and certainly my skepticism. On the other hand, I did take away something that I had not fully possessed before: appreciation of the sheer beauty and miracle of being alive, and a humble set of values.

Admiral Richard E. Byrd, *Alone* (New York: Putnam, 1938).

CB FROM RADIO SHACK

In addition to a wide variety of audio equipment, this retailer offers several CB units ranging in price from $69.95 for a mobile unit to $299.95 for a model which operates as either a base station or mobile unit. The Realistic model TRC-422A, $119.95, is a forty-channel unit with priority switch for instant access to channel 9 for emergency communication and channel 19 for highway information. See your local Radio Shack store or write for catalog:

Radio Shack
Tandy Center
Ft. Worth, TX 76102

CB RADIOS FROM COBRA

This well-known name in CB radios offers a variety of models, including the 29LTD. Priced at $129.95, this model is a forty-channel mobile unit, with switch for emergency use of channel 9. Write for brochure and dealer information:

Cobra Communications
6460 W. Cortland St.
Chicago, IL 60635

Into this fence, or fortress, with infinite labour, I carried all my riches, all my provisions, ammunition, and stores . . . and I made me a large tent, which, to preserve me from the rains, that in one part of the year are very violent there, I made double, namely, one smaller tent within, and one larger tent above it, and covered the uppermost with a large tarpaulin, which I had saved among the sails.

Daniel Defoe, *Robinson Crusoe* (New York: Macmillan, 1962).

Cobra model 29LTD CB radio. $129.95.

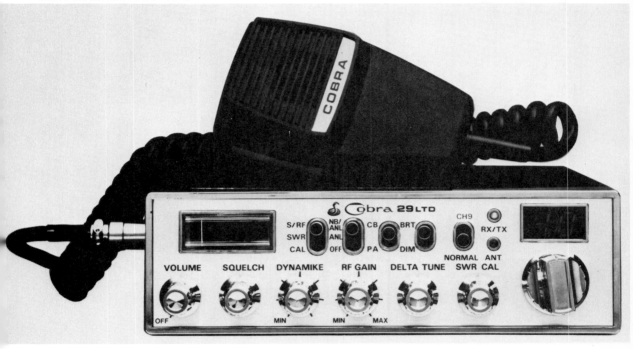

9
EQUIPMENT AND GEAR

CATALOGS FEATURING OUTDOOR GEAR

Outdoor gear—whether for use for recreation and conditioning now or as standby equipment for the future—is available in almost endless variety, from many sources, at varying prices. The list below is a sampling of manufacturers and re- tailers. Some manufacturers sell through mail order, some through retail outlets, some through both. Catalogs are free unless otherwise noted.

NORTH FACE: mail-order, high-performance down clothing and sleeping bags, tents, for backpacking and mountaineering:

The North Face
1234 5th St.
Berkeley, CA 94710

EDDIE BAUER: mail-order and retail outlets, widely known for goose-down clothing and sleep- ing bags, extensive selection of boots and various equipment and accessories for camping, back- packing—when writing for catalog, ask for brochure *How to Select a Sleeping Bag:*

Eddie Bauer
15010 N.E. 36th St.
Redmond, WA 98052

KELTY PACK: manufactures wide variety of backpacks, raingear, for camping, backpacking, and moutaineering sold through retail outlets only. Free catalog:

Kelty Pack, Inc.
Box 639
Sun Valley, CA 91352

STEPHENSON: manufactures and sells through mail order the Warmlite line of lightweight tents and goose-down insulated sleeping bags— high-performance products featuring Vapor Bar- rier design. The catalog costs $3, but is a how-to book in itself, explaining design functions and giving useful outdoor tips:

Stephenson
RFD 4, Box 145
Gilford, NH 03246

CLASS 5: manufactures and sells through retail outlets down- and wool-filled and wool-woven clothing, goose-down sleeping bags, backpacks:

Class 5
1480 66th St.
Emeryville, CA 94608

P&S SALES: sleeping bags, clothing, knives, and other camping accessories, including new, unused military field equipment sold by mail order at mid-range prices.

P&S Sales
Box 45095
Tulsa, OK 74145

DON GLEASON: a complete catalog for camping and backpacking featuring a wide variety of name-brand tents, sleeping bags, backpacks, raingear, clothing, and such accessories as canteens, lamps, stoves, coolers, cooking utensils, compasses, flashlights, and cutting tools. Catalog, $.75:

Don Gleason's Campers Supply, Inc.
Box 87
Northampton, MA 01061

JANSPORT: manufactures and sells packs and tents for backpacking and mountaineering through both mail order and retail outlets.

JanSport
Paine Field Industrial Park
Everett, WA 98204

INDIANA CAMP SUPPLY: complete selection for camping, backpacking, mountaineering, with tents, sleeping bags, raingear, and such accessories as camp and backpacking stoves, compasses, flashlights, cookware, cutting tools, trail foods, as well as medical instruments and supplies for kits. Catalog, $1:

Indiana Camp Supply, Inc.
Box 344
Pittsboro, IN 46167

> The civilized man has built a coach, but has lost the use of his feet. He is supported on crutches, but lacks so much support of muscle. He has a fine Geneva watch, but he fails of the skill to tell the hour by the sun. A Greenwich nautical almanac he has, and so being sure of the information when he wants it, the man in the street does not know a star in the sky. The solstice he does not observe; the equinox he knows as little; and the whole bright calendar of the year is without a dial in his mind.
>
> **Ralph Waldo Emerson,** *Self-Reliance* (Reading, Pa.: Spencer Press, 1936).

ARMY SURPLUS FOR SURVIVAL

Army field equipment, purchased from surplus retailers, can provide a variety of useful and inexpensive tools for a survival kit. The equipment is plain but durable: canteen, mess gear, pup tent, sleeping bag, entrenching tool . . .

One such piece of equipment—the G.I. can opener—is so small it can be carried on a key ring, yet it will do the same job that elaborate and much more expensive can openers can do. Veterans will remember this handy tool as an accessory in their combat rations.

The opener is available in army-surplus stores as well as from some of the companies listed in these pages. It costs about a quarter—and so you can buy several, spread them around, and never be caught without a can opener again.

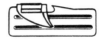

Drawing shows the G.I. can opener (from Stow-A-Way Industries, 166 Cushing Hwy., Cohasset, MA 02025).

MARMOT MOUNTAIN: manufactures tents and down-insulated clothing and sleeping bags sold through mail order as well as dealers. Equipment is lightweight, for camping, backpacking, mountaineering:

Marmot Mountain Works, Ltd.
331 S. 13th St.
Grand Junction, CO 81501

A COMPLETE SURVIVAL OUTFIT

Coleman is famous for its gas lanterns with integral pressure-pump system, but the company markets a complete line of outdoor products: naphtha-gas and propane lamps and stoves, ice-chest coolers, catalytic heaters, tents, sleeping bags, and camper and utility trailers, with a line of specialized lightweight gear for backpackers. See your local retail dealer, or write:

Coleman Co., Inc.
Box 1762
Wichita, KS 67201

Movin' Out

Harry Roberts
1975, 1979/151 pp./$7.95
Stone Wall Press, Inc.
c/o Stackpole Books
Box 1831
Harrisburg, PA 17105

This guide to backpacking equipment presents a useful introduction to all of the basic items: boots, clothing, backpacks, sleeping bags, tents, food, and cooking gear, with a separate chapter on compasses and how to use them. Throughout, the author uses text and drawings to explain how things are made and how they work, with advice on what to buy—or devise yourself—for your particular needs.

The New Complete Walker

Colin Fletcher
1974/512 pp./$12.95
Alfred A. Knopf, Inc.
201 E. 50th St.
New York, NY 10022

This book is a sound reference resource for campers, hikers, and backpackers. It is an illustrated guide for selecting the equipment of the outdoors, as well as a handbook for its uses.

Make Your Own Camping Equipment

Robert Sumner
1976/168 pp./$6.95
Sterling Publishing Co., Inc.
2 Park Ave.
New York, NY 10016

How to make your own survival equipment: tent, backpack, sleeping bag, down parka. With text and drawings, this book takes you through the process step by step. To get you started, there

CAMPING AND BACKPACKING: SURVIVAL TRAINING FOR THE FUN OF IT

Being able to make a campfire with a match and a few twigs does not guarantee that you will survive being stranded in a blizzard. But the tools and techniques of the camper and backpacker have many survival applications because these recreations are based on the idea of making do and doing without in outdoor places where there are few alternatives.

The specialized equipment and supplies of outdoor recreation can be turned to survival uses of many kinds. The backpacker's kit can be a model for the basic survival kit needed in home, car, or boat. And the know-how that is involved can be a guide to improvisation in emergency situations.

Such gear as stoves, lamps, and ice chests can do double duty as standby equipment in the home. Tents, sleeping bags, and improvised outdoor shelters can accommodate a family when hazard requires evacuation of a household. The knives, saws, hatchets, compasses of camping are all tools that have proven survival value.

Learning how to manage safely and comfortably in the outdoors is a sound preparation for surviving there. If you are a stranger to these ways, your introduction could be as simple as a Sunday hike through the woods in a good pair of walking shoes.

You may never want to sleep under canvas or climb to a mountaintop with a sleeping bag on your back, but you are free to borrow from the equipment and know-how of those that do.

are sections on materials (both fabric and insulation), as well as on design and sewing techniques. Make it yourself, and you not only cut cost drastically, but you are able to make it exactly the way you want it. (If ordering from publisher, add $1.25 for postage and handling.)

Drawing shows basic components of a middleweight hiking boot (from *Movin' Out*).

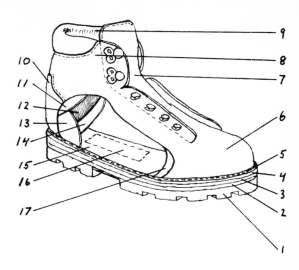

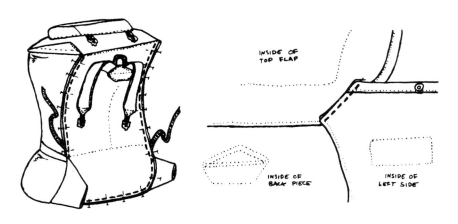

INSIDE OF
TOP FLAP

INSIDE OF
BACK PIECE

INSIDE OF
LEFT SIDE

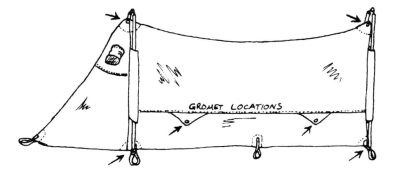

GROMET LOCATIONS

Upper drawing shows details from directions for making a rucksack, lower drawing illustrates a stage in process of making a mountain tent (from *Make Your Own Camping Equipment*).

BACKPACKER STOVE: model 400-599 Peak 1 stove, with integral pressure-pump system, no-priming design, rated to burn (on high setting) for one hour and fifteen minutes on 11.8-ounce filling of Coleman naphtha fuel, equipped with windshield, weighs 28 ounces, $40. (Coleman Co., Inc., Box 1762, Wichita, KS 67201)

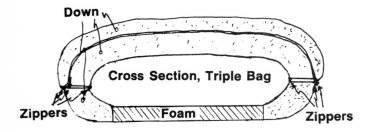

OUTDOOR GEAR: from the Stephenson catalog, cross-sectional diagram shows components of firm's triple-bag design in sleeping bags. (Stephenson, RFD 4, Box 145, Gilford, NH 03246)

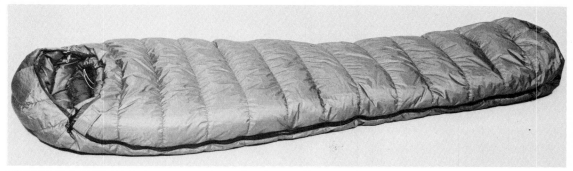

MUMMY SLEEPING BAG: for year-round use, insulated with goose down, weighs three pounds in five-foot ten-inch length ($382) and three pounds three ounces in six-foot four-inch length ($394). (Marmot Mountain Works, Ltd., 331 S. 13th St., Grand Junction, CO 81501)

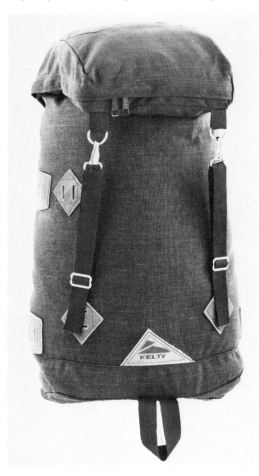

SOFT BACKPACK: Mockingbird model sells for $43, has padded back and shoulder pads, quick-release waist buckle. (Kelty Pack, Inc., Box 639, Sun Valley, CA 91352)

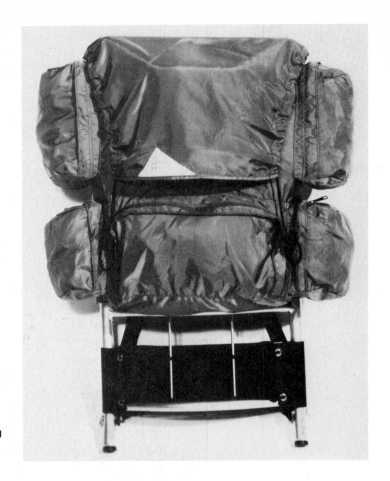

BACKPACK WITH FRAME:
Blueridge model sells for $89,
features heavy-duty zippers, has
space on lower frame for sleeping
bag. (Kelty Pack, Inc., Box 639,
Sun Valley, CA 91352)

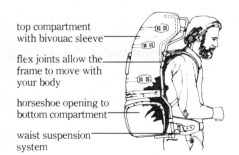

top compartment
with bivouac sleeve

flex joints allow the
frame to move with
your body

horseshoe opening to
bottom compartment

waist suspension
system

OUTDOOR GEAR: from the JanSport catalog,
drawing shows how components function together
in the firm's design for backpack with pack frame.
(JanSport, Paine Field Industrial Park, Everett, WA
98204)

WOOLEN CLOTHING FOR MEN AND WOMEN IN THE OUTDOORS

If wool is what you want for your wilderness kit, C. C. Filson specializes in it as well as in rugged work clothes. A pair of all-wool whipcord trail pants sells for $62.50, an extra-long mackinaw for $103. Write for catalog:

C. C. Filson Co.
205 Maritime Bldg.
Seattle, WA 98104

PART

THE BASICS OF
LONG-TERM
SURVIVAL

10
THE BASICS OF LIVING OFF THE LAND

Climates of the United States
John L. Baldwin
1973/113 pp./$2.50
(S/N 003-017-00211-0)
Superintendent of Documents
U.S. Government Printing Office
Washington, DC 20402

If you were to move your family to a farm near Des Moines, how many days of freezing temperatures a year could you expect? If you were to install solar heating, what kind of sunlight source would you have in your area? You will find answers to many such questions in the summarized data in this book, presented in charts and on maps in a format that is easy to read and understand. Local storms such as tornadoes and blizzards are covered, with data on effects and probabilities. This book was prepared by the Environmental Data Service of the National Oceanic and Atmospheric Administration, U.S. Department of Commerce.

Finding and Buying Your Place in the Country
Les Scher
1974/393 pp./$9.95
Macmillan Publishing Co.
866 Third Ave.
New York, NY 10022

This book covers in detail every aspect of buying land in the countryside. The author begins at the beginning—the search—with advice on dealing with real estate agents. There follows a series of chapters on how to evaluate the land—and dwelling—you are interested in, including water supply, soil, vegetation, and topography. All of the various legal aspects of buying property, as well as the process of negotiating and financing the purchase, are explained. Practical considerations are emphasized throughout the book, pitfalls and potential problems are identified, and solutions are offered. Included are listings of further sources of information.

TORNADO SAFETY RULES

Seek inside shelter, preferably in a tornado cellar, underground excavation, or a steel-framed or reinforced concrete building of substantial construction. Stay away from windows.

In Cities or Towns—in office buildings, stand in an interior hallway on a lower floor, preferably in the basement.

In Factories—on receiving a tornado warning, post a lookout. Workers should move quickly to the section of the plant offering the greatest protection in accordance with advance plans.

In Homes—the basement usually offers the greatest safety. Seek shelter under a sturdy workbench or heavy table if possible. In a home with no basement, take cover under heavy furniture in the center part of the house. Keep some windows open, but stay away from them. Mobile homes are particularly vulnerable to overturning during strong winds. Trailer parks should have a community shelter. Appoint a community leader responsible for constant radio monitoring during threatening weather or during watch periods.

In Schools—whenever possible, go to an interior hallway on the lowest floor. avoid auditoriums and gymnasiums or other structures with wide free-span roofs.

If a building is not of reinforced construction, go quickly to a nearby reinforced building or to a ravine or open ditch and lie flat.

In Open Country—move away from the tornado's path at a right angle. If there is no time to escape, lie flat in the nearest depression, such as a ditch or ravine.

Tornado Watch means tornadoes are expected to develop.

Tornado Warning means a tornado has actually been sighted.

Keep Listening—your radio and television stations will broadcast the latest tornado advisory information. Call the local National Weather Service Office only to report a tornado.

From: *Climates of the United States*, by John L. Baldwin (Washington, D.C.: U.S. Government Printing Office, 1973).

FINDING A PLACE IN THE COUNTRY WITH THE STROUT CATALOG

Strout is a nationwide real estate broker with local representatives across the country and an eighty-year reputation. The firm deals in rural properties—both farms and individual homes—as well as small-business opportunities. Write for the company's catalog, which is a sampling of its offerings, state by state: in it there is a listing of local representatives as well as a mailer you can use to request information about properties available in a specific area.

Strout Realty, Inc.
Plaza Towers
Springfield, MO 65804

Not since the Victory Gardens of World War II have so many people been raising and preserving so much of their own food as today. And people are not just raising tomatoes and green beans and strawberries, but a whole variety of vegetables and fruits, nuts, grains, and livestock as well. The number of organic gardeners and homesteaders has grown in recent years because people are discovering that just about the only way they can control the quality of the food they eat is to grow it themselves.

Carol Hupping Stoner, *Stocking Up* (Emmaus, Pa.: Rodale Press, 1977).

Back to Basics
Norman Mack, Editor
1981/456 pp./$15.99
Reader's Digest
Pleasantville, NY 10570

This book is a storehouse of self-sufficiency know-how, skills, and tools. Each of its hundreds of topics is covered thoroughly and concisely with how-to text, drawings, and photos. The book deals with buying land and building on it, using alternate energy sources, raising your own food, and processing and preserving it for the table. Skills and crafts are presented, including making and using natural dyes, spinning and weaving, tanning and leatherwork, woodworking and metalworking, soapmaking and candlemaking. Information sources are listed with each subject for further reading. (If ordering from publisher, add $1.32 for postage and handling.)

The Foxfire Book
Eliot Wigginton, Editor
1972/384 pp./$7.95
Doubleday & Co., Inc.
245 Park Ave.
New York, NY 10017

This book comes from the mountain people of the Appalachians in Georgia. It is a collection of material from *Foxfire* magazine, which is the work of high-school students using tape recorders and cameras to record the life experiences of their elders, some of them born in the late 1800s. The book—the first in a series—tells of times when the self-sufficient way of life was the only possible way. In these pages, you can learn how to make souse meat from the head of a hog, how to make tools out of wood, exactly how to build a log cabin the way cabins used to be built. There are sections on churning butter, slaughtering hogs, making soap, running a moonshine still. There are tales of folklore and folk methods—all from people who lived the folk life. The book is illustrated with detailed photos and drawings.

The Next Whole Earth Catalog
Stewart Brand, Editor
1980/608 pp./$16
Random House, Inc.
201 E. 50th St.
New York, NY 10022

The latest edition in a series that has found hundreds of thousands of readers, this catalog of products and books covers everything from life-styles to the nuts and bolts of fixing your own car. The broad variety of subjects, as well as the detailed and illustrated evaluations of products, make this a useful reference resource.

CoEvolution Quarterly
$14/4 issues per year
Box 428
Sausalito, CA 94966

This magazine grew out of *The Whole Earth Catalog* and its issues are a source of subsequent new editions of the catalog. *CoEvolution* covers self-sufficiency, appropriate technology, alternate energy resources, alternative life-styles.

The Mother Earth News
$15/6 issues per year
Box 70
Hendersonville, NC 28791

This magazine was one of the first voices of the alternative-life-styles movement, and it is devoted to self-sufficiency, appropriate technology, and alternate energy. Some typical articles: "How to Get a Patent"; "Make a Cider Mill/Press"; "The Art of Storytelling"; "Rate Your Windpower Site"; "A 'Less Than Half Price' Solar Home"; "Do Chemical Chimney Cleaners Work?"; "Quail, the Most Productive Poultry"; "Restore Barren Fruit Trees."

UNITED FARM AGENCY: A CATALOG FOR FINDING RURAL PROPERTY

United Farm Agency has been in business for fifty-five years as a nationwide real estate broker. Through its catalog and its local representatives you can follow up listings that include farms, homes, small businesses, and open land. The firm's catalog presents text and pictures of its listings, and it includes a mailer with which you can request listings that match your particular interests and the area you might want to buy in. The catalog listings are a convenient way to size up property possibilities around the country.

United Farm Agency, Inc.
612 W. 47th St.
Kansas City, MO 64112

Living the Good Life
Helen and Scott Nearing
1954, 1970/213 pp./$4.95

Schocken Books, Inc.
200 Madison Ave.
New York, NY 10016

If living in the city or suburbs has become a struggle for survival for you, and you are considering the alternative of going "back to the earth," then this book is one you should read. The Nearings left New York City during the Depression turmoil of 1932 and moved to a dilapidated and worn-out farm in Vermont. They learned the ways of farm life, grew their own vegetable food and stored it in root cellars for year-round use, built their stone house with their own hands, and found that making syrup from their sugar-maple trees gave them the cash they needed. Telling the details of nineteen years of their way of living "sanely and simply in a troubled world," their book has become a manual for the many others who have followed in their path.

Certainly we have made a mess of things in terms of the environment we are to live in. Just where we are going in this direction is a question we should all ask ourselves. Where, after all, has modern technology led us regarding the air we breathe, the food we eat, and the land we live on?

Robert Redford, foreword to, Larry Dean Olsen, *Outdoor Survival Skills* (Provo, Utah: Brigham Young University Press, 1980).

Continuing the Good Life

Helen and Scott Nearing
1979/194 pp./$4.95
Schocken Books, Inc.
200 Madison Ave.
New York, NY 10016

The Nearings continue their account of their homesteading life, describing how they left their first farm in Vermont and moved to Maine. There they established a new homestead, constructed new buildings, used composting to renew the soil and raise their own food—and found that blueberries would be their cash crop. The book has a personal style that is easy to read, and it is filled with how-to-do-it details.

Living on a Few Acres

U.S. Dept. of Agriculture
Jack Hayes, Editor
1978/432 pp./$7
(S/N 001–000–03809–5)
Superintendent of Documents
U.S. Government Printing Office
Washington, DC 20402

This book is a gold mine for anyone contemplating homesteading or small-scale farming. More than fifty individual contributors cover subjects including the style of life on a few acres; buying land or a farm; remodeling an old house; water and waste disposal; raising vegetables, fruits, and berries; beekeeping; woodlots; growing nuts; raising animals; marketing crops; dairying; horse-rental income; fish farming; raising earthworms; and running a vacation farm. The book is illustrated with photos and drawings

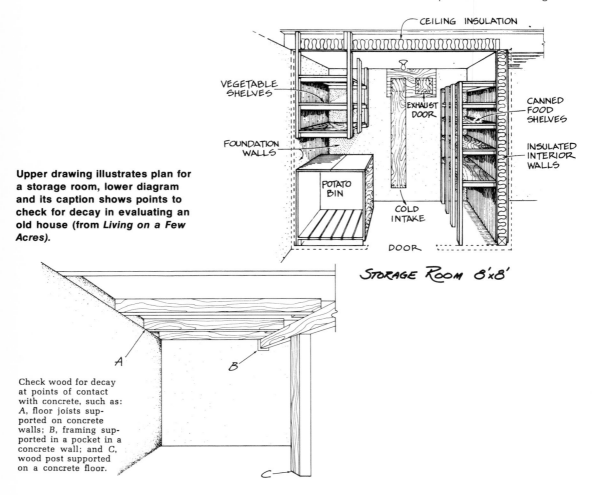

Upper drawing illustrates plan for a storage room, lower diagram and its caption shows points to check for decay in evaluating an old house (from *Living on a Few Acres*).

CEILING INSULATION

VEGETABLE SHELVES

EXHAUST DOOR

CANNED FOOD SHELVES

FOUNDATION WALLS

INSULATED INTERIOR WALLS

POTATO BIN

COLD INTAKE

DOOR

STORAGE ROOM 8'x8'

Check wood for decay at points of contact with concrete, such as: A, floor joists supported on concrete walls; B, framing supported in a pocket in a concrete wall; and C, wood post supported on a concrete floor.

A

B

C

Tools for Homesteaders, Gardeners, and Small-Scale Farmers

Diana S. Branch, Editor
1978/528 pp./$12.95
Rodale Press, Inc.
Organic Park
Emmaus, PA 18049

This big book catalogs tools and machines of all kinds for raising food. The equipment ranges from hoes and rakes to farm tractors and threshing machines, with listings of manufacturers and dealers.

Frontier Living

Edwin Tunis
1961/167 pp./$14.95

Colonial Craftsmen

Edwin Tunis
1965/160 pp./$12.95

Harper & Row
10 E. 53rd St.
New York, NY 10022

These two books are about how people lived in seventeenth- and eighteenth-century America. They will not tell you precisely how a log cabin or farm implement or blacksmith tools were made and used in those times, but the author will give you a clear idea of what was involved. His texts and hundreds of drawings are about a self-sufficient, preindustrial society, making these two books a valuable resource.

Downwind from Nobody

Joan Wells
1978/304 pp./$9.95
Garden Way Publishing
1538 Ferry Rd.
Charlotte, VT 05445

The author recounts her experience with self-sufficient living on a farm in Oregon. She tells of the lessons she learned personally and reports on the practical aspects of vegetable gardening, raising goats, and weathering the cold winters. (If ordering from publisher, add $1 for postage and handling.)

How to Build Your Home in the Woods

Bradford Angier
1952/310 pp./out of print
Hart Publishing Co., Inc.

Detailed directions for building a simple log cabin of the roll-roofing type including doors, windows, beds. You will have to find this book in a library, but it will be worth the search.

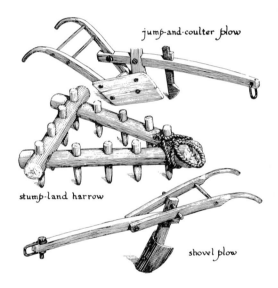

Upper drawing shows details of log-cabin roof construction, lower drawing shows farm implements (from Frontier Living)

It was as though the projectionist was suddenly running the movie version of twentieth-century American history in reverse.

People gave up on the cities in the late 1980s. There was a drift, and then a flow, to the suburbs and beyond. The already crowded suburbs expanded somewhat at first, absorbing the city population. But then Americans began giving up on the suburbs as well.

The original farm-to-city migration had to do with economics, just as the new reverse migration did.

It all began with the economic decline that made the cities unlivable. Tax revenues fell and government services shrank. Police, fire, health, and sanitation programs were reduced to minimum levels. People moved away, then corporations moved away to catch up with the people. As a result, tax revenues fell even further and government services became almost nonexistent.

Decay followed the migration to the crowded suburbs, and when the economic depression struck, the movement back to rural America was in full swing.

A revised way of life had already been growing up in the towns, villages, and farmlands of the country, and so the newest returnees found workable patterns to adapt to. There was employment, but on a different scale from that of the middle of the century. Conglomerates were beginning to undiversify themselves, and there were more and more small manufacturing companies turning up in the towns. There would always be paperwork, and jobs for those who knew how to do it. Various cottage industries were growing up: home computers provided incomes for many families. A man or woman who could overhaul a car or tractor engine, install a solar-heating system, or build a barn did not lack for work.

But for many years, almost everybody in the countryside earned at least some part of his living from the land. There were farmers large and small and no one lacked space for a vegetable garden. The family cow became as common as the family car.

Fears of social disintegration proved unfounded. State governments, which had abandoned the cities long before, took a firm hold during the population shift to exurbia and beyond. The federal government seemed farther away than ever during those years, preoccupied with international disarray and struggling to adjust to a national economy in which there was very little income to tax.

Cash was scarce and the banking system collapsed when the stock market did. People saved their old credit cards as souvenirs of the boom years. Barter became the common way of doing business, and sophisticated systems such as community bartering cooperatives in which you could accumulate trading credits developed.

Later, some observers would look back on those years as the era of a happy return to rural ways, but that proved to be a mistaken view. Life was harsh for many people, as it always is during times of drastic social change.

For the most part, the people who adjusted most successfully were the ones who had led the reverse migration back in the 1970s and early 1980s. Many of those homesteaders and small-farmers who went back to the land as outsiders were in the vanguard of the new establishment by the end of the twentieth century . . .

> And he gave it for his opinion, that whoever could make two ears of corn or two blades of grass to grow upon a spot of ground where only one grew before, would deserve better of mankind, and do more essential service to his country, than the whole race of politicians put together.
>
> **Jonathan Swift,** *Gulliver's Travels* (1726)

In 1973, the big news was the energy crisis as the Mid-East oil producers withheld their production from the U.S. and European markets. . . . Few persons heard about another significant event of 1973, though many were touched by it. For the first time since the Great Depression of the thirties, rising incomes did not keep pace with the increasing cost of goods and services. Real income in this country began to fall in 1973 and has been falling ever since. . . . We *are* on a treadmill running a rat race in which we move harder and harder, faster and faster simply to stay in place.

Sim van der Ryn, introduction to, Farallones Institute, *The Integral Urban House* (San Francisco: Sierra Club Books, 1979).

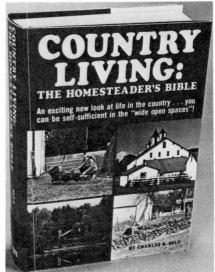

The Manual of Practical Homesteading
John Vivian
1975/340 pp./$9.95
Rodale Press, Inc.
Organic Park
Emmaus, PA 18049

The author presents all of the basics of living off the land: gardening and farming, maple sugaring and beekeeping, raising small and large livestock, raising orchard fruits and berry crops. Included are sections on preserving the harvest. The book is illustrated with drawings and photos.

Country Living: The Homesteader's Bible
Charles R. Self
1981/512 pp./$21.95
TAB Books, Inc.
Blue Ridge Summit, PA 17214

Beginning at the beginning, the author discusses the know-how needed for purchase of rural land, evaluating an existing home or building one, and the tools and equipment needed for a homestead. There are illustrated chapters on soil, and on raising vegetables, fruit trees, and livestock. Also covered is financing—particularly loans from the Farmers Home Administration of the U.S. Department of Agriculture.

The Forgotten Arts: Books 1–4
Richard M. Bacon et al.
1975, 1976, 1979/62 pp. each/$3.95 each
Yankee Books
Main St.
Dublin, NH 03444

These four books are collections of how-to articles from *Yankee* magazine. Illustrated with photos and drawings, the books are a valuable resource for self-sufficiency in the home and on the farm. The forty-one articles cover such topics as woodlot management, keeping a family cow, raising poultry, making bread, cider, soap, and paint, working a draft horse, repairing and rehandling hand tools, building bridges, chimney sweeping, making ice cream and maple syrup, herbal medicines, drying fruits and vegetables. The four books are also available in a boxed set for $13.95.

The Owner-Built Homestead

Barbara and Ken Kern
1974, 1977/394 pp./$7.95
Charles Scribner's Sons
579 5th Ave.
New York, NY 10017

A complete manual for homesteading from scratch: selecting and buying the property, developing it, constructing house and farm buildings, and then living off the land. The authors begin with the idea itself, helping you to think it out and try it on for size. From there they tell you about everything you need to know and do—and how to do it—in order to make a success of the venture. They cover water and soil development and management, tools and skills, crop and animal raising, fish farming, sanitation, food preservation. Drawings illustrate the text throughout.

Urban Homesteading

James W. Hughes and Kenneth D. Bleakly, Jr.
1975/276 pp./$15
Center for Urban Policy Research
Rutgers University
Building 4051, Kilmer Campus
New Brunswick, NJ 08903

A study by professional urban planners of the idea and practice of "homesteading" the abandoned housing of the blighted inner city. The term comes from city programs in which people are given title to housing upon fulfilling various requirements: basically, that they renovate, live in, and maintain the dwelling for a certain period of time. The idea behind the programs is to put the housing back on the tax rolls and restore the city as a whole. The authors examine four such programs (Baltimore, Wilmington, Philadelphia, and Newark): in general, they find that the actualities did not fulfill the idea, but they have sorted out the most successful elements from the programs for continued use. If you have wondered about your survival in the city—or thought about going back there to seek survival—this is a book to put on your reading list.

HOMESTEADING IN ALASKA: CLOSED

If you have ever dreamed of starting a new life on the wilderness frontier, you have probably thought about Alaska and homesteading there. The fact is that homesteading ended in Alaska in 1979. State land is available for purchase, however, but only by Alaskans, with one to three years of residency required, depending on the particular land-purchase program involved. For information write:

Alaska Department of Natural Resources
Division of Forest, Land and Water Management
323 E. 4th Ave.
Anchorage, AK 99501

Countryside

$11.95/12 issues per year
Countryside Publications, Ltd.
Highway 19 East
Waterloo, WI 53594

Here is a magazine to introduce you to homesteading and living on the land. It calls itself "the magazine for serious homesteaders," and its contents prove its claim. There are monthly articles on raising sheep, bees, rabbits, cows, hogs, goats, chickens. Special issues carry multipart features on a specific farm animal, as well as such other subjects as homestead marketing and cottage industry. Articles on gardening and cooking are regular features. The publisher also operates the Countryside General Store, with a mail-order catalog ($1) of things for the farm and home, as well as books related to homesteading.

An appreciation and tolerance of nature, of course, is essential. The quiet of the countryside, the smell of freshly mowed hay, the sight of livestock grazing in a lush green pasture, and the taste of vine-ripened tomatoes are there to be enjoyed. However, nature can also be harsh and unpredictable.

James Lewis, Ed Glade, and Greg Gustafson, article in, U.S. Department of Agriculture, *Living on a Few Acres* (Washington, D.C.: U.S. Government Printing Office, 1978).

LEARNING AND APPRENTICESHIP PROGRAMS FOR HOMESTEADERS

Becoming a homesteader is easier said than done. Here is a way to test your interest. Various groups across the country maintain centers devoted to self-sufficiency, farming, crafts, organic gardening, and appropriate technology. You can take part and learn: as a volunteer, a workshop participant, an apprentice. *Organic Gardening* magazine maintains a free listing of these groups and centers: address your letter, "Attn: Homesteader's List," and enclose a self-addressed stamped envelope:

Organic Gardening
Rodale Press
33 E. Minor
Emmaus, PA 18049

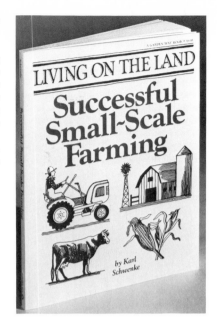

INFORMATION AND ASSISTANCE FOR FARMING OPERATIONS

Like the Federal Extension Service (with its local county agricultural agents), the Agricultural Stabilization and Conservation Service (ASCS), U.S. Department of Agriculture, is set up to provide specialized information and assistance for farmers. This agency deals with such aspects of farming as co-ops, commodity management, emergency conservation programs. Write for the brochure *ASCS Publications:*

**Agricultural Stabilization
and Conservation Service**
U.S. Dept. of Agriculture
Washington, DC 20250

Successful Small-Scale Farming
Karl Schwenke
1979/160 pp./$8.95
Garden Way Publishing
1538 Ferry Rd.
Charlotte, VT 05445
   The author writes from his own experience as a farmer, covering such subjects as soils and soil improvement, selecting farm crops, crop markets, and machinery for the small farm. He includes

illustrated how-to information on such subjects as repairing farm machinery, surveying, rough carpentry, and the various do-it-yourself skills needed on a farm. (If ordering from publisher, add $1 for postage and handling.)

Country Women: A Handbook for the New Farmer
Sherry Thomas and Jeanne Tetrault
1976/382 pp./$10.95
Doubleday & Co., Inc.
245 Park Ave.
New York, NY 10017
   A how-to book about women and their experience with self-sufficiency on the land. It is also a very personal account of the values found in a new way of life. The authors—as well as other contributors associated with *Country Women* magazine—explain how to find and buy land, build and repair house and farm buildings, provide water supply and tend the plumbing. There are sections that cover growing vegetables, keeping bees, raising small and large livestock, as well as preparing and preserving home-grown foods for the table. Illustrated with detailed drawings and photos, the book is a valuable resource for everyone.

GETTING FEDERAL "SEED" MONEY FOR YOUR FARM OR RURAL BUSINESS

The Farmers Home Administration, U.S. Department of Agriculture, conducts loan programs for the purchase and operation of family-size farms and ranches as well as for small businesses in rural communities. Eligibility for such loans includes requirements of skill and experience, but unless you are coming to the cornfields straight from the big-city pavements, the FmHA is a resource to investigate. Loan programs include money for single-family housing, soil-and-water development, income-producing recreational facilities, aquaculture enterprises. Write for the twenty-four page booklet *This Is FmHA*:

Farmers Home Administration
U.S. Dept. of Agriculture
Washington, DC 20250

Approved Practices in Soil Conservation

Albert B. Foster
1955, 1973/497 pp./$14
Interstate Printers and Publishers, Inc.
Box 594
Danville, IL 61832

This is a standard text aimed at farmers and landowners, with small as well as large acreage, including the homeowner with a minimum amount of land but with drainage and soil-erosion problems. All aspects of the subject are covered in detail, illustrated with photos and drawings. Included are chapters on managing woodland, encouraging wildlife, and commercial recreational uses of lands. If, for instance, you contemplate buying land for farming or as a survival retreat, here is a guide for protecting your investment as well as making it pay off in such by-products as timber and firewood, game meat, and rentals.

Drawing illustrates technique for planting tree stock (U.S. Soil Conservation Service: from *Approved Practices in Soil Conservation*).

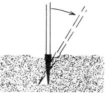

(A) DRIVE MATTOCK OR PLANTING BAR INTO SOIL WITH BLADE PERPENDICULAR. PUSH HANDLE FORWARD.

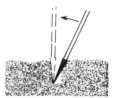

(B) RAISE BLADE AND DRIVE BACK INTO SOIL AT SAME ANGLE. TO GET NEW HOLD PULL BACK TO ENLARGE HOLE.

(C) SET AS DEEP AS TREES WERE IN THE NURSERY.

(D) CLOSE BOTTOM OF HOLE WITH PLANTING BAR OR MATTOCK.

(E) CLOSE TOP OF HOLE WITH HEEL.

The New Farm

$10/7 issues per year
Rodale Press, Inc.
Organic Park
Emmaus, PA 18049

The "new" in this magazine is the nonchemical, organic approach to raising vegetable, grain, fruit, and livestock crops. It is for farming from small to large scale, ranging from vegetable crops to dairy herds. The magazine covers equipment, seeds, and supplies of all kinds, and the advertising offers a variety of ideas for self-sufficiency seekers.

Small Farm Energy Primer

1980/57 pp./$3

Small Farm Energy Project Newsletter

$8/6 issues per year

Small Farm Energy Project
Box 736
Hartington, NE 68739

Both of these publications grew out of a three-year research and demonstration project conducted with forty-eight cooperating low-income farms in Cedar County, Nebraska. The primer is a collection of reports on energy alternatives and conservation techniques to help lower the costs of energy on small farms. The newsletter continues and follows up on these reports. The project involves the use of low-cost, home-built alternate-energy innovations—solar home heating, grain drying, water heating, barn heating—as well as the use of the solar greenhouse and the composting of manure as a field fertilizer. Both publications offer tested do-it-yourself ideas.

Practical Farm Buildings

James S. Boyd
1973, 1979/277 pp./$10.60
Interstate Printers and Publishers, Inc.
Box 594
Danville, IL 61832

A handbook of basic engineering for the construction of farm buildings of all kinds covering such aspects as selection of lumber, computing loads on structures, framing systems, designing joists, beams, and columns. Included is a section on the use of wind power for mechanical applications as well as generating electricity. This is a valuable reference resource for a farm of any size.

Barns, Sheds and Outbuildings

Byron D. Halsted, Editor
1881, 1977/240 pp./$7.95
Stephen Greene Press
Box 1000
Brattleboro, VT 05301

This facsimile edition of a book from 1881 is full of ideas for useful buildings for the farm—large scale or small. Over 250 drawings illustrate the various structures: barns, stables, sheds, cornhouses, pigpens, poultry houses, icehouses, smokehouses, doghouses. (When ordering from publisher, add $1 for postage and handling.)

JOHN DEERE TRACTORS FOR GARDENING AND FARMING

With a name equivalent to Ford in the automobile field, this is one of the manufacturers you turn to for mechanical horsepower when your gardening gets too big for hand tools, or your small-scale farming becomes larger. Deere markets a line of diesel-powered tractors that range from 14½ to 50 h.p. Prices range from $5,680 to $15,400. The firm also sells the implements that go with the tractors: rotary tillers, mowers, plows, discs, front-loaders, scrapers. See your local John Deere dealer or write for brochures:

Deere & Co.
John Deere Rd.
Moline, IL 61265

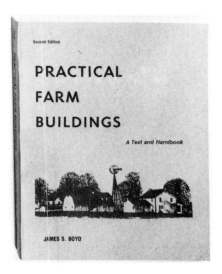

From John Deere: model 1050 diesel tractor ($10,015), disking farm field, below, and, above, drilling fencepost hole with augur operated by power takeoff from tractor.

CASE TRACTORS FOR GARDENING AND SMALL-SCALE FARMING

This manufacturer's name is long established in large farm tractors. It markets a line of medium-size tractors in its 400 series, which range in power upwards from the 444 and 446 to the 18 h.p. model 448. With a hydraulic system for power-take-off, the units work with such implements as tiller, mower, and earth-grading blade. See your local dealer, or write:

Case Co.
119 S. 1st St.
Winneconne, WI 54986

TRACTORS: BOOKS FROM AAVIM

Specifications for Tune-Up and Service of Farm Tractors
1979/85 pp./$5.95

Tractor Maintenance: Principles and Procedures
1975/152 pp./$7.95

The Tractor Electrical System
1966/64 pp./$3.25

American Association for Vocational Instructional Materials
120 Engineering Center
Athens, GA 30602
(When ordering from publisher, add $1 for postage and handling; catalog available.)

SHOP MANUALS FOR TRACTOR MAINTENANCE AND REPAIR

If a farm tractor comes into your self-sufficient life, particularly an older model, you will need to keep it running. For that you will need a shop manual. Intertec publishes an extensive series of manuals for the major tractor makes: John Deere, Ford, Case, International Harvester. Prices vary, write for catalog:

Technical Publications Division
Intertec Publishing Corp.
Box 12901
Overland Park, KS 66212

IRRIGATION EQUIPMENT FOR THE FARM

The Domestic Growers Supply catalog is of primary interest to the farmer who must irrigate: it shows water-storage tanks, water pumps, drip-irrigation emitters, hose of various kinds, as well as other farm items. An item of interest: a collapsible reinforced nylon water "tank" which is designed to be placed in a truck, then filled with water for transport: capacity in gallons ranges from 73 to 1,340, and the 73-gallon size ($244.95) in the back of a pickup truck could be a lifesaver in a water crisis. Write for catalog ($1):

Domestic Growers Supply, Inc.
Box 809, Dept. BD
Cave Junction, OR 97523

SEARS: TOOLS, EQUIPMENT AND SUPPLIES FOR GARDENING, FARMING

With over sixty pages, the Sears *Farm & Ranch* catalog offers a variety of tools, equipment, and supplies for raising everything from vegetables to fruit trees and livestock to honeybees. The catalog is a short course in the things that go with farming. Write for catalog:

Sears, Roebuck and Co.
Sears Tower
Chicago, IL 60684

THE SCYTHE—AN ANCIENT CUTTING TOOL WITH A HUMAN ENGINE

Hand & Foot specializes in tools dependent on human energy. The company's scythe blade is imported from Austria and sells for $29: the snath—or handle—is available in metal ($18) or wood ($33). A cradle attachment for reaping grain is priced at $24. Also available are hayforks and hayrakes, blade-sharpening accessories, sowing and planting equipment. Write for brochure and prices:

By Hand & Foot, Ltd.
Box 611
Brattleboro, VT 05301

The Scythe Book
David Tresemer
1981/120 pp./$6.95
By Hand & Foot, Ltd.
Box 611
Brattleboro, VT 05301

The scythe is a tool that goes back thousands of years, but in some parts of the world it is still the mainstay for harvesting grains, mowing hay, cutting weeds and brush. The author describes the tool thoroughly—its history, design, parts, variations, and different uses. There are detailed directions, with drawings, for employing the scythe on various crops.

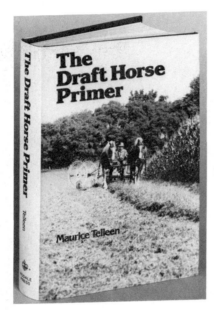

HARNESSING THE POWER OF A DRAFT HORSE FOR YOUR FARM

The use of draft horses takes farming another step closer to self-sufficiency. The Big Sky Leatherworks is one source of the harness equipment required. Its catalog will show you such items as bridles, bits, belly bands, collars, and traces. Write for catalog ($2):

Big Sky Leatherworks
Rte. 3
Billings, MT 59101

SOME ADVICE ABOUT DRAFT HORSES, FROM A MAN WHO FARMS WITH THEM

If you decide to go out and get yourself a good broke team, try to take an experienced horseman with you, pick up pieces of usable horse machinery you can find at local farm sales, prepare to work a little harder physically than your mechanized neighbor, and go at it kind of easy, not all in one jump. Work a pair for a while on the spreader, corn planter, and seeder before you put four on the disk. You may just discover that horse farming is what fits you, your concept of what farming should be, and your place on this earth.

And if you do like the company of good horses, you will be richly rewarded by working with them. There is a sense of partnership between a teamster and his horses that is worth a great deal. To take them in and care for them after hitting a good lick in the field is a fulfillment. If it isn't—if it is a burden—then you best not have them.

A working team, at its best, is a part of the family and the very embodiment of the life on the farm. For me, and for many others, the quietness of working with well broke horses is a pleasure and satisfaction that covering more acres simply wouldn't yield. I'm often asked questions such as "How many acres did you plow or cultivate or disk, or whatever, today?" Once in awhile, it is a loaded question, and my answer in those cases, I'm sure, generally serves to convince the questioner that I am, after all, a bit feeble-minded. But I remain quite unconvinced that "faster" and "more" is always better.

From: *The Draft Horse Primer*, by Maurice Telleen (Waverly, Iowa: Draft Horse Journal, 1977).

Draft Horse Journal
$10/4 issues per year
Box 670
Waverly, IA 50677

This magazine is about workhorses for the farm—the Clydesdales, Belgians, Percherons. It covers the care and breeding of draft horses as well as the plowing, cultivating, and mowing machinery that goes with them. History and lore is included, and the ads offer both horses and equipment.

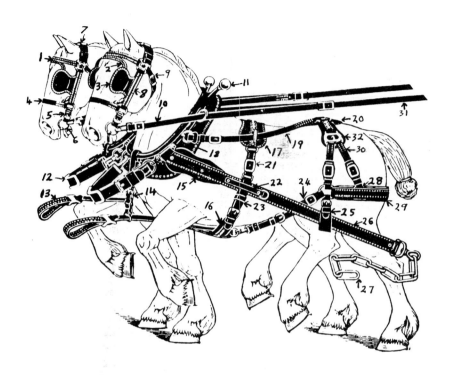

The Draft Horse Primer
Maurice Telleen
1977/386 pp./$12.95
Draft Horse Journal
Box 670
Waverly, IA 50677

Covering both workhorses and mules, this book takes you through all of the basics. There are chapters on the breeds of draft horses, buying them, farm machinery. Other chapters cover care, feeding, shoeing, and housing, as well as harness and hitching. The book's opening chapter discusses the return of the draft horse to more common use. Photos and drawings illustrate the book.

The Modern Mule
Paul and Betsy Hutchins
1978/148 pp./$6.60
Hee Haw Book Service
Box 65
Denton, TX 76201

You might want to consider using a mule on your small farm—it is an animal that sets a good example for hard work. This book will tell you what you need to know about the mule as a farm and pack animal. Also available from the publisher is *The Mule* by Harvey Riley, a reprint ($4.60) of a book from 1867, as well as *The Brayer*, a quarterly magazine ($10) published by the American Donkey and Mule Society.

SUPPLIES FOR ANIMAL CARE

If isolation or economics, or both, require you to care for your own animals—dogs, cats, horses—here is a mail-order source to consider. The firm's catalog carries several pages of vaccines, antibiotics, and veterinary instruments.

PETCO Animal Supplies
Box 1076
La Mesa, CA 92041

Horseshoeing
Anton Lungwitz and John W. Adams
1884, 1913, 1966/216 pp./$12
Oregon State University Press
101 Waldo Hall
Corvallis, OR 97331

This is the standard book on horseshoeing and it has a long history. The original book by Lungwitz was first published in Germany in 1884; this edition is a 1966 facsimile of the 1913 translation by Adams. Its history speaks for its soundness. This book covers the horse itself—its anatomy, down to the hoof—the shoes, the farrier's tools, the techniques for putting the shoes on. Numerous drawings illustrate the text.

Horses, Hitches and Rocky Trails
Joe Back
1959/117 pp./$8
Johnson Publishing Co.
Box 990
Boulder, CO 80301

The author has made his living hauling goods on packhorses. Here he presents his many years of accumulated know-how: techniques, equipment, and special tips, both about the packs and the horses. He uses his own drawings and personal experiences for illustration. If you are going to use a horse to carry things, here is where to learn how to do it.

Whether you attempt to become totally self-sufficient and live entirely off your few acres, or decide to just raise the family's fruits and vegetables in a backyard garden, be prepared for certain facts of rural life: water freezes in winter—crops fail—fences fall—and livestock get sick. Realizing that sickness, injury and disappointing harvests can occur, and being able to cope with these events are all part of the rural experience.

James Lewis, Ed Glade, and Greg Gustafson, article in, U.S. Department of Agriculture, *Living on a Few Acres* (Washington, D.C.: U.S. Government Printing Office, 1978).

Raising Small Meat Animals
Victor M. Giammattei
1976/433 pp./$12.35
Interstate Printers and Publishers, Inc.
Box 594
Danville, IL 61832

If you have decided to raise your own meat for the table, here is a sound place to start. This book covers five meat animals in thorough detail: Cornish game hens, chicken broilers, turkey roasters, fryer rabbits, and squabs. It combines text with photos and drawings and deals with all of the basics of meat production, including breeding and the health care of the animals.

From the left, drawings show acute-angled, normal-angled, and upright hooves (from *Horseshoeing*).

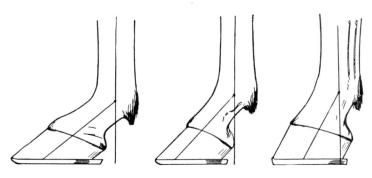

THIS IS THE GEAR

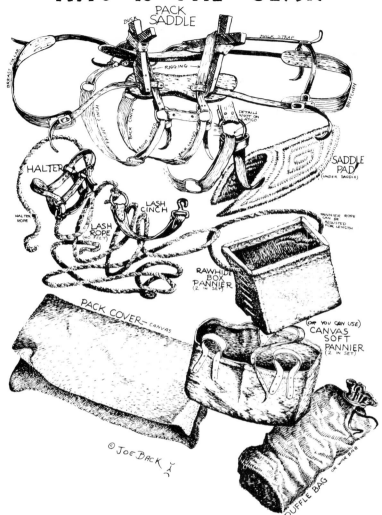

Basic equipment for use with a packhorse (from *Horses, Hitches and Rocky Trails*).

Minnie Rose Lovgreen's Recipe for Raising Chickens
Nancy Rekow and Claire Frost, Editors
1975/31 pp./$2
Pacific Search Press
222 Dexter Ave. N.
Seattle, WA 98109

This small book is based on the author's sixty years of experience raising chickens. It is a personalized how-to book that covers all of the basics, with emphasis on successful egg and chick production. (When ordering from publisher, add $1 for postage and handling.)

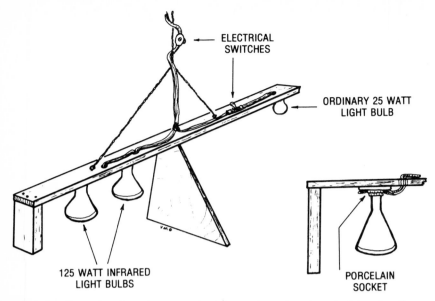

Drawing details a plan for a home-made infrared brooder (from *Raising Small Meat Animals*).

CHICKS, HATCHING EGGS, DUCKLINGS, GOSLINGS

If you want to raise poultry—for your own table or for profit, or both—Stromberg's is a place to start. They will ship you the day-old chicks you need to begin your flock. The company sells hatching eggs for duck, turkey, pheasant, quail, and other bird species, and it also offers equipment for poultry raisers and books on how it is done. Write for catalogs ($1) and prices:

Stromberg's Chicks and Pets
Pine River, MN 56474

CHICKS FOR YOUR CHICKEN FARM

The Murray McMurray Hatchery has been in business for over sixty years and sells over sixty varieties of chicks of all rare and popular breeds.

The firm's catalog is an education in the many varieties, described in words and pictures. Write for catalog and price list.

Murray McMurray Hatchery
Webster City, IA 50595

Raising a Calf for Beef
Phyllis Hobson
1976/120 pp./$4.95
Garden Way Publishing
1538 Ferry Rd.
Charlotte, VT 05445
The author promises superior beef for less than half the supermarket cost: six hundred to seven hundred pounds of beef in fifteen to eighteen months, with just one-half hour of care per day. She gives complete information for care, feeding, housing—and step-by-step photos for home butchering. (If ordering from publisher, add $1 for postage and handling.)

OTHER BOOKS FROM GARDEN WAY ON RAISING ANIMALS FOR FOOD

The "Have-More" Plan
Ed and Carolyn Robinson
1973/70 pp./$3.95

Keeping Livestock Healthy
N. Bruce Haynes, D.V.M.
1978/324 pp./$10.95

Raising Rabbits the Modern Way
Bob Bennett
1975/160 pp./$4.95

Raising Poultry the Modern Way
Leonardo Mercia
1975/240 pp./$5.95

Raising Your Own Turkeys
Leonardo S. Mercia
1981/160 pp./$5.95

Raising the Home Duck Flock
Dave Holderread
1980/192 pp./$5.95

Garden Way Publishing
1538 Ferry Rd.
Charlotte, VT 05445
(If ordering from publisher, add $1 for postage and handling.)

Goat Husbandry
David Mackenzie
1957, 1980/375 pp./$23
Faber and Faber, Ltd.
Merrimack Book Service
99 Main St.
Salem, NH 03079

This book comes from England, where raising dairy goats has long been a part of the way of life in the countryside. It has gone through many reprintings and is a standard manual on goat raising. The book presents a brief history of goat husbandry and then goes on to cover housing, feeding, breeding, health care, milking practices, dairy products, kid meat. A separate chapter discusses goat-farming systems, from the small-household scale to large flocks. The book is illustrated with both photos and drawings.

Raising Milk Goats the Modern Way
Jerry Belanger
1975, 1980/160 pp./$4.95
Garden Way Publishing
1538 Ferry Rd.
Charlotte, VT 05445

This how-to book has chapters on selection, housing, fencing, breeding, kidding, goat-milk products. There are diagrams and photos to help get a new goat raiser started. (If ordering from publisher, add $1 for postage and handling.)

Domestic Rabbit Production
George S. Templeton
1955, 1968/213 pp./$10
Interstate Printers and Publishers, Inc.
Box 594
Danville, IL 61832

A thorough introduction to raising rabbits for food explaining the various breeds and giving advice for purchasing starting stock. There are chapters on shelter, feeding and feeding equipment, breeding, meat production, marketing of meat and skins. Also covered is the marketing of wool from the Angora rabbit, as well as preparation of rabbit meat for the table. The book is illustrated with photos and drawings.

Small-Scale Pig Raising
Dirk van Loon
1978/272 pp./$6.95
Garden Way Publishing
1538 Ferry Rd.
Charlotte, VT 05445

Why not start with pigs? On a homestead, that would mean low-cost, high-quality pork chops and bacon. The author tells how a growing season between spring and Thanksgiving can produce top results for your investment. Among the many areas covered are butchering and smoking. (If ordering from publisher, add $1 for postage and handling.)

Raising Sheep the Modern Way
Paula Simmons
1976/240 pp./$6.95
Garden Way Publishing
1538 Ferry Rd.
Charlotte, VT 05445

The author tells you everything you need to know from starting a flock of sheep to making mutton sausage. With over 100 illustrations, the book covers feeding, breeding, care, shearing. (If ordering from publisher, add $1 for postage and handling.)

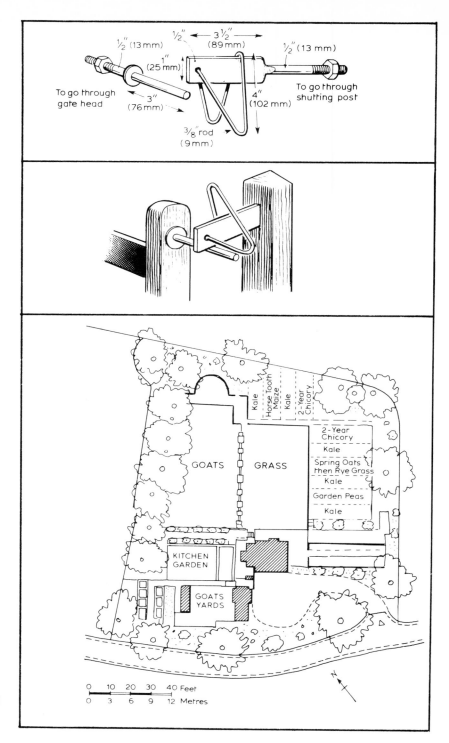

Upper diagram shows a design for a goatproof gate latch, lower drawing is a plan for a layout of goat yards and fodder crops (from *Goat Husbandry*).

Live weight pounds	Number days required to produce 1 pound live weight	Pounds feed required for 1 pound increase live weight
6 to 6.9............	12	5.5
7 to 7.9............	15	8.0
8 to 8.9............	21	11 5
9 to 10............	26	14.0

Chart indicates number of days and amount of feed required to increase rabbit live weight by one pound (from *Domestic Rabbit Production*).

RAISING RABBITS—OR HOW TO GET A MEATY RETURN ON A SMALL INVESTMENT

Of all of the small livestock, rabbits generally require the smallest investment of time, money, and space for the amount of protein they can provide for your table.

Compared to chickens, goats, sheep, pigs, or cows, the domesticated rabbit is easy to raise. Rabbits are silent creatures, feeding contentedly in their small hutches behind the garage or barn. Even in the limited space available in the city, room can be found to raise them.

Feed costs are relatively low. Rabbits thrive on everything from carrots to greens and apples, as well as on commercial pelletized feeds. If you can locate a source—supermarket produce departments, for instance—you can feed your animals on scrap vegetables and fruit. Shelter for rabbits is a minimal investment: simple cages of wood and wire mesh that you can build yourself.

Rabbits reproduce rapidly. If you start out with a male and two or three females, you can turn your modest investment into a regular supply of tasty high-protein food in a matter of months.

Spinning and Weaving with Wool
Paula Simmons
1977/222 pp./$12.95
Pacific Search Press
222 Dexter Ave. N.
Seattle, WA 98109
This how-to book covers selection of wools, carding fleeces, choosing a spinning wheel, or making your own equipment. There are photos and details about over forty available spinning wheels, as well as a listing of sources of supplies and equipment. (When ordering from publisher, add $1 for postage and handling.)

VETERINARY SUPPLIES

Kansas City Vaccine is a mail-order firm offering medicines and surgical instruments for use with livestock, poultry, and pets. The catalog is chiefly devoted to products for livestock, but the section on dogs and cats is a useful source for providing medical care for dogs and cats at home. Write for catalog:

Kansas City Vaccine Co.
Stock Yards
Kansas City, MO 64102

From Kansas City Vaccine catalog: illustration shows injection points for cattle.

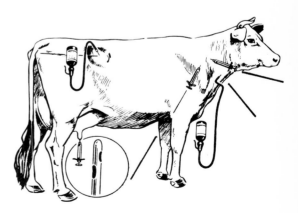

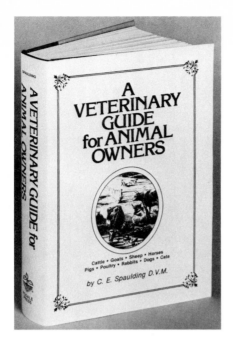

A Veterinary Guide for Animal Owners

C. E. Spaulding, D.V.M.
1976/420 pp./$14.95
Rodale Press, Inc.
Organic Park
Emmaus, PA 18049

This is a book for the layperson—a kind of "Dr. Spock" for caring for cattle, goats, sheep, horses, pigs, poultry, rabbits, dogs, and cats. The author's aim is to enable you to prevent, identify, and control health and medical problems and know what to do in an emergency. Drawings illustrate the text throughout.

First Lessons in Beekeeping

C. P. Dadant, M. G. Dadant, J. C. Dadant,
 G. H. Cale, and Howard Veatch
1917, 1976/127 pp./$1.40
Dadant & Sons, Inc.
51 S. 2nd St.
Hamilton, IL 62341

This small book tells the hows and whys of beekeeping, including chapters on equipment and supplies as well as on the uses and marketing of honey and beeswax. This introduction to beekeeping is presented in simple terms, with drawings and numerous photos.

The ABC and XYZ of Bee Culture

A. I. Root, E. R. Root, J. A. Root, and L. R. Goltz
1878, 1978/723 pp./$12.95
A. I. Root Co.
Box 706
Medina, OH 44258

A standard work on beekeeping, this book was originally published in 1878 and has gone through thirty-four editions. The bees will provide you with honey, wax, and pollination in your garden and orchard—once you learn how to keep them busy and happy at their work. This book can tell you how to do it, including how to process the honey and wax and how to market it. It is an encyclopedia, and its topics range from the anatomy of a bee to the presence of zinc in honey. The book is illustrated with both photos and drawings.

The Hive and the Honey Bee

Charles Dadant, Roy A. Grout, et al.
1946, 1975/740 pp./$12.95
Dadant & Sons, Inc.
51 S. 2nd St.
Hamilton, IL 62341

This book is the work of many hands, going back to its original source in the writings in the mid-1800s of L. L. Langstroth, who is credited with being the founder of modern beekeeping. Written by specialists, the book combines the practical with the technical. For instance, while there is an eighty-five-page chapter devoted solely to the "activities and behavior of honey bees," there is an equally clear and detailed twenty-five-page chapter for the beginner in beekeeping. Everything is covered, illustrated with drawings and photos.

EQUIPMENT, SUPPLIES, AND BOOKS FOR BEEKEEPING

Betterbee is a mail-order firm offering everything from hive components, pollen traps, foundations, and package bees to tools, protective clothing, containers, and how-to books. Write for catalog:

Betterbee, Inc.
Box 37
Greenwich, NY 12834

A. I. Root sells through both dealers and mail order. Their catalog offers a large selection of hive components and honey-processing equipment, as well as protective clothing, containers, tools, how-to books. Write:

A. I. Root Co.
Box 706
Medina, OH 44258

Make Your Own Honey Extractor
1977/8 pp./$3.95
Garden Way Publishing
1538 Ferry Rd.
Charlotte, VT 05445

If you take up beekeeping, you will need a honey extractor. A new extractor costs about $200, but if you build it yourself, you can save over half the cost. Here is a set of detailed plans that will show you exactly how to do the job. (If ordering from publisher, add $1 for postage and handling.)

American Honey Plants
Frank C. Pellett
1947, 1976/467 pp./$9.10
Dadant & Sons, Inc.
51 S. 2nd St.
Hamilton, IL 62341

This book is a reference resource about the hundreds of flowering species from which the honeybee collects nectar and pollen. Usually, however, a beekeeper depends on a few abun-dant local species. In a year when these crops fail, a keeper can often move the hives a few miles to a flowering crop and save the honey harvest. All depends on the keeper knowing the species, which this book describes with text and illustrates with photos.

Fish Farming in Your Solar Greenhouse
William Head and Jon Splane
1979/43 pp./$5
Amity Foundation
Box 11048
Eugene, OR 97440

Part of the premise of this book is that since water stored in a solar greenhouse is an efficient medium for storing heat, why not grow fish in the water, along with the vegetable crop. The authors explain how to proceed, with photos and drawings, as well as plans for building greenhouses efficient for aquaculture. They include a listing of books related to the subject.

Elementary Fishing
Joseph D. Bates, Jr.
1967/192 pp./$.75
Wright & McGill Co.
Box 16011
Denver, CO 80216

A bargain book that has all of the basics you need to start out in fishing, from a company that

An assembly of Root Company hive components.

has been selling tackle and promoting fishing for many years. With drawings for illustration, the author gives step-by-step directions for the beginner. Included are instructions for making improvised rods, reels, and lures.

Whole Fishing Catalog

Editors of *Consumer Guide*
1978/320 pp./$7.95
Simon and Schuster
1230 Avenue of the Americas
New York, NY 10020

This comprehensive guide combines a catalog of fishing equipment with instructions for its use. Both freshwater and saltwater species are covered in large-format presentation that illustrates both products and methods with drawings and photos.

Complete Guide to Game Fish

Byron Dalrymple
1968, 1981/506 pp./$14.95
Outdoor Life Books
Fulfillment Office
Box 2033
Latham, NY 12111

Written by an authority, this book combines identification data with how-to tips on catching all of the major species of freshwater and saltwater game fish. The species are illustrated and range from the panfish, bass, and trout of freshwater to the bluefish, bass, and sharks of saltwater.

WRIGHT & McGILL FISHING TACKLE

This firm is best known for the Eagle Claw brand name on its fishing tackle. Fishhooks are its specialty, but its line of products includes rods and reels. For your survival kit, the firm's Trailmaster rods come in four-piece and six-piece units which pack in a screw-top aluminum cyclinder. The firm sells through dealers only, but its catalog is available free:

Wright & McGill Co.
Box 16011
Denver, CO 80216

FISHING TACKLE, HUNTING EQUIPMENT

Cabela's mail-order catalog is a useful resource for fishing, hunting, and outdoor equipment. Included are knives, binoculars, clothing, and camping equipment. Ask for the spring catalog to get the best selection of fishing tackle:

Cabela's, Inc.
812 13th St.
Sidney, NE 69162

TURNING A STREAM INTO STORAGE FOOD AND WATER

If you have bought—or you are shopping for—land to fall back on, a dammable stream is a resource with considerable survival value.

Stocked with fish, even a small man-made pond can yield a reliable food supply. And if drought dries up your well or spring or the stream itself, the pond will provide a standby reserve of water.

The earthen dam, constructed with a bulldozer, is the most common means of creating a pond. Construction costs can range up to several thousand dollars, depending on soil and water-flow conditions on the site, but the investment's dividends can even include cash.

One way to make a pond produce income and pay for itself is to offer sport fishing for a fee. Another method is to raise a fish crop for market. Either approach requires a substantial pond and government regulations vary from state to state, but such ponds have become a well-established means of earning income for their owners.

Aside from any dollar payoff, however, a pond on your land can put food on your table year round. And in an emergency it could be your standby food and water supply.

The Farmer and Wildlife
Durward L. Allen
1949, 1977/63 pp./$1
Wildlife Management Institute
Wire Bldg.
Washington, DC 20005

If you live on rural or wild land—or you are going in that direction—you need to know about wildlife resources and how to encourage them. This booklet will give you a basic introduction, covering ways to use land to benefit wildlife and showing how wildlife benefit the land.

MONTHLY MAGAZINES:

Sports Afield
$11.97/12 issues per year
250 W. 55th St.
New York, NY 10019

Field & Stream
$11.94/12 issues per year
1515 Broadway
New York, NY 10036

Outdoor Life
$13.94/12 issues per year
380 Madison Ave.
New York, NY 10017

If you are entirely new to hunting or fishing, the three large monthly magazines in this field are especially useful for your introduction to the skills and equipment you will need. These magazines cover such related topics as guns, boating, hunting dogs, and camping. How-to basics are emphasized, and the advertising gives you an opportunity to shop for the equipment, clothing, and supplies that you will need. By buying single issues at the newsstand you can sample all three of the publications.

REMINGTON: GUNS FOR TARGET SHOOTING AND HUNTING

This firm is one of the best-known names in the field of sporting arms and ammunition. Its line of rifles and shotguns include both inexpensive models and higher-priced high-performance firearms. The company makes a full line of rifle and handgun cartridges and shotshells. See your local gun dealer or write for catalog:

Remington Arms Co., Inc.
939 Barnum Ave.
Bridgeport, CT 06602

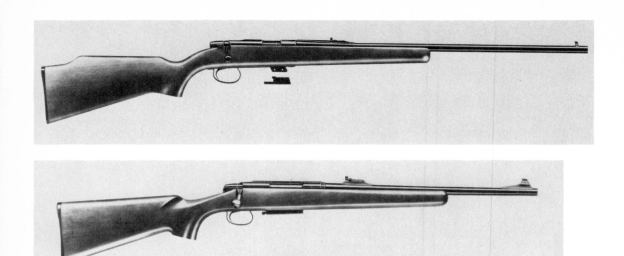

From Remington Arms: from top, model 581 bolt-action .22-caliber rifle, $141.95; and model 788 bolt-action rifle, available in .243, .308, or 7mm caliber, $269.95.

AIRGUNS: SAFE, ECONOMICAL PRACTICE FOR SKILL WITH FIREARMS

It is simple enough to arm yourself with rifle, shotgun, or handgun, but to become skilled with firearms requires time, opportunity, and money. A practical approach is to use an airgun. Because its range, lethal effect, noise, and ammunition cost are very limited, an air rifle or pistol can be fired in target practice in a minimal space indoors or out, and hundreds of times at a session. Even top-grade pellets will cost only $4 to $6 per 500, compared with prices many times that amount for

cartridge ammunition for a firearm. In its ninety-page catalog ($1.50) Beeman's offers a wide variety of air rifles and pistols, specializing in precision European imports, at a range of prices. Write:

Beeman's Precision Airguns, Inc.
47 Paul Drive
San Rafael, CA 94903

AIR RIFLE: German-made, high-performance model SI 145 generates velocity of 800 feet per second with one cocking motion, designed for precision target shooting. Price $297.50 (Survival, Inc., Box 5509, Carson, CA 90749).

TELESCOPIC SIGHTS FOR RIFLES

If you have access to wild animals as a source of food, you will need a large-caliber rifle for the bigger mammals or a .22-caliber rifle if your targets are such smaller species as rabbit or groundhog. In either case, a telescopic sight will make your shooting more consistent. Bushnell sells a variety of models in a wide range of magnifications, either fixed or variable. Prices range as high as $224.95, to as low as $34.95 for a 4x

scope designed for use on a .22-caliber rifle. Their catalog includes explanations of such scope features as built-in rangefinders and bullet-drop compensators, both devices for long-range shooting.

Bushnell Optical Co.
2828 E. Foothill Blvd.
Pasadena, CA 91107

Five Bushnell Banner scopes, from 2.5x magnification to 10x, from $92.95 to $146.95.

Bushnell
BANNER® RIFLESCOPES with Multi-X® (MX) Reticle
FIXED POWERS

	MODEL #	Magnification
	71-1143	10x 40mm
	71-1603	6x 32mm
	71-2103	4x 40mm
	71-1403	4x 32mm
	71-1203	2.5x 20mm

The survival values of the skills of fishing and hunting are many. Both sports are a means of food supply and provide an opportunity to learn the ways of the outdoors and the wilderness. In addition, hunting requires a proficiency with firearms that can double as self-defense weapons, and fishing usually demands experience with boats that can add to an individual's survivability.

However, a newcomer to either of these sports may find access to them difficult, particularly in urban areas where opportunities for fishing and hunting are limited or nonexistent.

Both sports require the kind of learning process that goes most smoothly when you have an experienced teacher. If you can apprentice yourself to a friend who is an accomplished fisherman or hunter, you can become as proficient in the skills of these sports as your time, money, aptitude, and interest will take you. If you don't have such a friend, you will have to improvise your own training.

Fishing is probably the easier sport to learn on your own. A beginner's spinning reel and rod will cost you only a few dollars and lures or bait will be even less expensive. Whoever sells you your tackle can give you tips on its use and where to fish locally. The fishing and hunting column in your daily newspaper, as well as the monthly outdoor magazines, will be useful resources.

If you live near the seacoast or a large body of inland freshwater, seek out the party boats or fishing guides and get your beginner's instruction and experience for a fee. Once you get started, you will probably find that your opportunities are greater than they first seemed.

Without a friend as tutor, the beginner in hunting faces more of a challenge. The newspaper columnist and the monthly magazines can give you some ideas, but you must start out by learning how to use a shotgun or rifle, and a firearm will cost you much more than a beginner's fishing tackle. One practical approach would be to join a local shooting and hunting club. In many parts of the country, you can find commercial target ranges, and these can be a resource for the beginner. A week spent with a licensed hunting guide in your region would be a substantial investment but well worth your time and money.

Once you have made your start on your own in either of these sports, you are likely to find teachers—and friends—as you go along. Fishermen and hunters are at least as willing to welcome newcomers as other sportsmen—and often a bit more so.

Fur-Fish-Game
$7/12 issues per year
A. R. Harding Publishing Co.
2878 E. Main St.
Columbus, OH 43209

This magazine is a standby for those who still earn dollars by trapping furbearing animals, and it is a popular publication among hunters and fishermen as well. If you contemplate trapping, this is a useful resource with its advertising of equipment and supplies.

TOMAHAWK LIVE TRAPS

In many parts of the country there is money to be earned by trapping furbearing animals. As an alternative to traditional foot-and-leg traps, live traps do not injure the animal or damage the pelt. Live traps are wire cages with doors that close in on the animal after it has entered the unit seeking the bait. Tomahawk sells traps for a variety of small animals, including beaver, raccoon, skunk, and squirrel, as well as models for fish and turtles. Prices range from as low as $16.77 for squirrel to as high as $247.86 for beaver. For information, write:

Tomahawk Live Trap Co.
Box 323
Tomahawk, WI 54487

Home Manufacture of Furs and Skins
Albert B. Farnham
1950/283 pp./$3

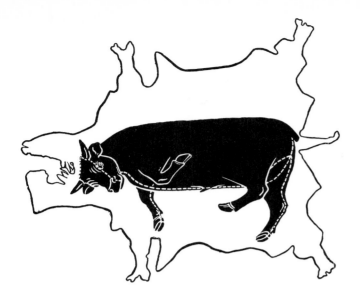

Illustration traces out the recommended pattern for skinning cattle (from *Home Tanning and Leather Making Guide*).

Home Tanning and Leather Making Guide
Albert B. Farnham
1950/176 pp./$2.25

A. R. Harding Publishing Co.
2878 E. Main St.
Columbus, OH 43209

These editions are reprints of two books originally published early in this century, but both are useful sources on the process of turning animal skins into furs and leather. The books deal with the small furbearers such as muskrat, raccoon, mink, marten, skunk, fox, otter, as well as cattle, horse, sheep, goat, and deer. Methods for skinning, cleaning, curing, tanning, and dyeing are described and illustrated in detail, with the necessary tools included. Also covered is the making of clothing and footwear with the furs and leather. This publisher—which also puts out *Fur-Fish-Game* magazine—sells a variety of books on trapping and hunting.

Brendan's Leather Book
Brendan Smith
1972/163 pp./$4.50
Bookpeople
2940 7th St.
Berkeley, CA 94710
    This introduction to leathercraft is a complete

guide for the beginner. After separate chapters on tools, selecting and working leather stock, hardware, and sewing technique, the author concentrates on the making of belts, sandals, and purses. However, what you can learn here could take you on to shoes, boots, and leather clothing. The author's instructions are illustrated by his own line drawings.

Drawing illustrates details in directions for making sandals (from *Brendan's Leather Book*).

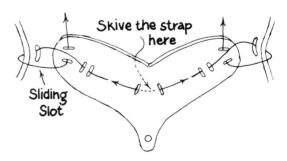

Craft Manual of North American Indian Footwear

George M. White
1969/71 pp./$3.25
G. M. White
Box 365
Ronan, MT 59864

This is a collection of over twenty different types of moccasins, with patterns and directions for making each of them. The different types range from ankle-high to what might be called boots. Some designs are simple, others more complex, but all of them show the possibilities for turning animal skin into footwear.

Woodland Ecology

Leon S. Minckler
1975, 1980/241 pp./$9.95
Syracuse University Press
1011 E. Water St.
Syracuse, NY 13210

A guide for the private owner of woodland, whether it be a few acres of trees or a few hundred acres of forest, this book is about living with woodland, as well as the sound management practices that can make it productive. If you are an owner or are thinking about becoming one, this book could be a valuable resource. Among its special sections is a sample timber-sale contract and a discussion of firewood production.

Knowing Your Trees

G. H. Collingwood and Warren D. Brush
Revised and Edited by Devereux Butcher
1978/389 pp./$9.50
American Forestry Association
1319 18th St., N.W.
Washington, DC 20036

A reference book to give you detailed help in identifying the trees of the United States organized by region, with mapping to show tree-species distribution. Text is combined with photographs to give you identification specifics.

The Maple Sugar Book

Helen and Scott Nearing
1950, 1970/273 pp./$5.95
Schocken Books, Inc.
200 Madison Ave.
New York, NY 10016

The authors of *Living the Good Life* tell how they farmed the sugar-maple trees of their Vermont homestead for a dependable cash crop.

This is an informal how-to manual that begins with a history of sugaring and covers the whole process of gathering the sap, making the syrup, and then making the sugar.

EQUIPMENT FOR MAPLE SUGARING

This firm manufactures the equipment for turning the sap from the sugar-maple tree into maple syrup and sugar. The evaporator is at the heart of the process. Along with it you use preheaters, gathering tanks, storage tanks, filters, buckets, thermometers, syrup containers—an investment of several hundred dollars. Write for catalog and the *Maple Sugar Makers' Guide,* an introduction to the equipment and its use:

Leader Evaporator Co., Inc.

25 Stowell St.
St. Albans, VT 05478

American Forests

$15/12 issues per year
American Forestry Association
1319 18th St., N.W.
Washington, DC 20036

If you are a stranger to the woods, here is a magazine that would give you some familiarity in a year of issues. Its article subjects vary widely from timbering to forest fires to nature studies, but its basic subject is the uses and conservation of our woodlands. If you contemplate buying woodland, this magazine could serve you well.

Ball Blue Book

1905, 1981/96 pp./$2.50
Ball Corp.
Box 2005
Muncie, IN 47302

In its thirtieth edition, this guide to home canning and freezing comes from the company that makes the jars and lids for the canning process. It is made up of individual sections on fruits, vegetables, meats, jams, pickles, and food freezing. There is a detailed guide to equipment for home canning and how to use it, and illustrations provide step-by-step directions throughout.

INSTRUCTIONS FOR USING TWO-PIECE VACUUM CAPS AND LIDS

1. Visually examine jars and sealing surfaces for nicks, cracks and sharp edges. Discard any damaged jars. Examine vacuum lids and screw bands and discard any that are bent, rusted or otherwise defective.

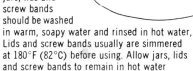

2. Follow manufacturer's directions for vacuum lids and screw bands. In general, jars, lids and screw bands should be washed in warm, soapy water and rinsed in hot water. Lids and screw bands usually are simmered at 180°F (82°C) before using. Allow jars, lids and screw bands to remain in hot water until needed.

3. Pack food into jar, leaving head space recommended in recipe. Eliminate air bubbles with a non-metallic kitchen utensil. Wipe away any food residue from top edge and threads of jar with a clean damp cloth.

4. Place lid on mouth of jar so that sealing compound rests on top edge.

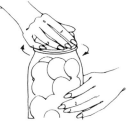

5. Screw the band down firmly, so that it is hand tight. Do not use jar wrench or other device to tighten the screw band.

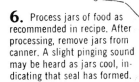

6. Process jars of food as recommended in recipe. After processing, remove jars from canner. A slight pinging sound may be heard as jars cool, indicating that seal has formed.

7. When jars are fully cooled, check the seal. The center of the lid should have been pulled down by vacuum, and will be

slightly concave. Remove screw bands. Store properly sealed jars in cool, dark, dry place.

8. To open, puncture the lid to break the vacuum and lift lid off. Discard lid; it is not reusable.

From: *Ball Blue Book,* by the Ball Corporation (Muncie, Ind: Ball Corp., 1981).

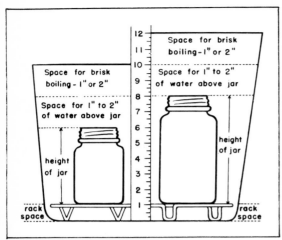

1

Home Canning and Preserving
Joan and Monte Burch
1977/240 pp./$10.50
Mary Ryan
Reston Publishing Co., Inc.
11480 Sunset Hills Rd.
Reston, VA 22090

This book is a prime source of know-how for preserving and storing foods of all kinds. It covers the canning, freezing, drying, and storing of fruits, vegetables, and meats. A separate chapter gives directions for drying, curing, and smoking meats. Illustrated with photos and drawings, the book gives do-it-yourself plans for making storage containers and preserving equipment.

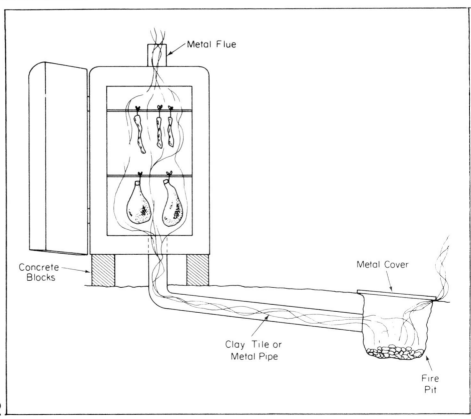

2

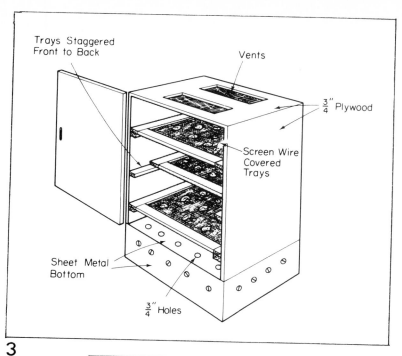

3

Trays Staggered Front to Back

Vents

$\frac{3}{4}''$ Plywood

Screen Wire Covered Trays

Sheet Metal Bottom

$\frac{3}{4}''$ Holes

4

Weighted Board Cover

Screen Wire

Soil

Hay

Drainage Ditch

Gravel

Four drawings from Home Canning and Preserving: 1, directions for water level in a canning container; 2, how to use an old refrigerator for smoking meats; 3, plan for building a stove-top dryer; 4, diagram shows pit storage of apples.

Kerr Home Canning and Freezing Book
1958, 1981/72 pp./$1
Kerr Glass Mfg. Corp.
Dept. CB-JL
Sand Springs, OK 74063

A standby how-to source for many years, this book is published by the company that manufactures the Kerr mason jars and lids. The book covers the canning and freezing of fruits, vegetables, meat and poultry, fish, jams and jellies, relishes. Especially useful is a five-page section with answers to frequently asked questions. The book's step-by-step directions are illustrated with photos and drawings.

Putting Food By
Ruth Hertzberg, Beatrice Vaughn, and Janet Greene
1973, 1975/500 pp./$10.95
Stephen Greene Press
Box 1000
Brattleboro, VT 05301

A thorough, detailed guide to preserving foods by canning, freezing, drying, salting, and smoking. In addition to canning meats of all kinds, also covered is the canning of fish and shellfish. And there are bonuses in the book: how to make soap, for instance, by using leftover fats, how to make sausages and how to preserve them. There is also a useful section on cutting up large portions of meat into proper cuts, illustrated with step-by-step photos. (When ordering from publisher, add $1 for postage and handling.)

Home Meat Curing
Morton Salt Co.
1980/42 pp./$2.95
Cumberland General Store
Route 3
Crossville, TN 38555

This how-to manual gives detailed directions for curing meats using salt in combination with various other ingredients. The book covers pork, beef, lamb, poultry, and wild game, and it includes instructions both for butchering animals and for cutting meats for curing. Photos and drawings illustrate the book throughout.

Stocking Up
Carol Hupping Stoner, Editor
1973, 1977/532 pp./$16.95
Rodale Press, Inc.
Organic Park
Emmaus, PA 18049

This comprehensive book is a how-to guide to all aspects of preserving food at home—whether you raise it yourself or buy it at the store. The book covers vegetables and fruits, dairy products, meats and fish, as well as nuts, seeds, and grains. Preserving methods range from canning and freezing to drying and smoking. Included are such processes as making jams and jellies, butter, cheeses, ice cream, and sausages. Directions are detailed, and the book is illustrated with charts, drawings, and photos.

FOOD STORAGE: BOOKS AND BOOKLETS THAT TELL HOW-TO

The Consumer Information Center, a federal agency, offers various books and booklets, some of them free. Here is a sampling:

Can Your Kitchen Pass the Food Storage Test?
1978/6 pp./free

Home Canning of Fruits and Vegetables
1979/32 pp./$1.50

Storing Vegetables and Fruits
1978/18 pp./$1.50

Write for catalog:

Consumer Information Center
Department DD
Pueblo, CO 81001

Dry and Save
Dora D. Flack
1976/118 pp./$3.95
Woodbridge Press
Box 6189
Santa Barbara, CA 93111

This guide to preserving fruits and vegetables

by drying is a thorough handbook of how-to directions. Various drying methods and equipment are covered, and there are detailed recipes for reconstituting dried foods and cooking them for the table. Included is a section on storing dehydrated foods. (If ordering from publisher, add $.75 for postage and handling.)

Garden Way's Guide to Food Drying
Phyllis Hobson
1980/216 pp./$5.95
Garden Way Publishing
1538 Ferry Rd.
Charlotte, VT 05445

How to use the three methods for drying foods: the oven, the sun, the dehydrator. The book mainly covers the drying of vegetables and fruits, but it also deals with meat, fish, eggs and dairy products, grains, herbs, mushrooms. There are recipes for cooking these dried foods, as well as information about dehydrators and a plan for building one yourself. (If ordering from publisher, add $1 for postage and handling.)

OTHER BOOKS FROM GARDEN WAY ON FOOD SUPPLY

Keeping the Harvest
Nancy Chioffi and Gretchen Mead
1976/216 pp./$7.95

Home Sausage Making
Charles Reavis
1981/128 pp./$6.95

The Canning, Freezing, Curing & Smoking of Meat, Fish & Game
Wilbur F. Eastman, Jr.
1975/220 pp./$5.95

Garden Way Publishing
1538 Ferry Rd.
Charlotte, VT 05445
(If ordering from publisher, add $1 for postage and handling.)

ELECTRIC FOOD DRYER: the Excalibur model 301 dehydrator features thermostatic control (80 to 140 degrees), see-through acrylic door, side-mounted fan. Price $149. (Stow-A-Way Industries, 166 Cushing Highway, Cohasset, MA 02025)

GRAIN MILL: the Marathon Uni-Mill, electrically powered and with both cutting blades and grinding stones, will handle wheat, rye, corn, soybeans to provide flour for bread and other food uses. Price $365. (Stow-A-Way Industries, 166 Cushing Highway, Cohasset, MA 02025)

DOUGH MIXER: a tool for kneading dough for bread making, this White Mountain unit is available in an electric model ($74.95) as well as one that is operated by hand ($39.95). (Stow-A-Way Industries, 166 Cushing Highway, Cohasset, MA 02025)

The Art of Home Cheesemaking
Anne Nilsson
1979/157 pp./$4.95
Woodbridge Press
Box 6189
Santa Barbara, CA 93111

A translation from Sweden, this how-to guide shows how to make cheeses of all kinds. Both hard and soft cheeses are covered, and included are directions for cheeses made from goat's and sheep's milk. Equipment and ingredients are thoroughly discussed, and step-by-step directions are illustrated with photos. (If ordering from publisher, add $.75 for postage and handling.)

buying or raising live animals, and by supplementing supply with game sources. This is the complete book on the subject, covering meats of all kinds, as well as poultry, fish, and game. Combining text, photos, and drawings, it explains all aspects: for instance, how to select for freshness when buying fish. Every kind of food-preservation process is presented, from canning and freezing to smoking, curing, and pickling.

MATERIAL BY USDA ON PROCESSING MEATS FOR HOME USE

Listed below are three booklets on processing meats for home use by the U.S. Department of Agriculture. For sale by the U.S. Government Printing Office, the booklets are a sampling of the variety of material from USDA:

Beef: Slaughtering, Cutting, Preserving and Cooking on the Farm
Farmers' Bulletin No. 2263
1977/68 pp./$2

Lamb: Slaughtering, Cutting, Preserving and Cooking on the Farm
Farmers' Bulletin No. 2264
1977/40 pp./$1.50

Pork: Slaughtering, Cutting, Preserving and Cooking on the Farm
Farmers' Bulletin No. 2265
1978/65 pp./$2.10

Superintendent of Documents
U.S. Government Printing Office
Washington, DC 20402

Better Than Store Bought
Helen Witty and Elizabeth Schneider Colchie
1979/325 pp./$13.95
Harper & Row
10 E. 53rd St.
New York, NY 10022
    A how-to book for making your own sausage, baking your own bread, mixing up your own ketchup. The authors provide detailed directions, and the categories covered include dairy products (cottage cheese, butter, ice cream, cream cheese), pickles and relishes, beverages, and desserts.

Butchering, Processing and Preservation of Meat
Frank G. Ashbrook
1955/318 pp./$5.95
Van Nostrand Reinhold Co.
Dept. RB
135 W. 50th St.
New York, NY 10020
    If you have the know-how and the facilities, you can reduce your costs for meats drastically by buying in quantity and when particular prices are at their lowest and then preserving the product, by

FOOD PROCESSOR FROM SUNBEAM

With the wide variety of food processors on the market, you have many models and features to choose from. At $78.95, the Sunbeam model 14–51, for instance, chops, slices, beats, shreds, grates, mixes, kneads, purees. You can use such a processor for preparing vegetables for canning, or for mixing dough for bread. See your local dealer or write for catalog:

Sunbeam Appliance Co.
5400 W. Roosevelt Rd.
Chicago, IL 60650

STEAM JUICER FOR FRUIT PRESERVING

Imported from Finland, the Mehu-Liisa steam juicer is made of stainless steel and comes in three models, starting at $79.50. It is designed to extract fruit juices for bottling or wine making, or for making jellies and syrups. The unit can also be used to steam vegetables before freezing. Ashdown House also publishes *Fruit Season: Suddenly It's Fun* ($2) as a handbook to accompany the steam juicer. The firm also sells the Little Harvey food dehydrator, as well as cookware related to food preserving. Write for literature:

Ashdown House
612 E. Pheasant Way
Bountiful, UT 84010

Better Beer and How to Brew It
M. R. Reese
1981/120 pp./$4.95
Garden Way Publishing
1538 Ferry Rd.
Charlotte, VT 05445

You start out with an investment of $20 to $50 for equipment. The ingredients for your first batch will cost $8 to $10. After 2½ hours of work and six to eight weeks of aging, you have your first five gallons of beer. The author gives instructions for brewing nineteen different beers and ales. And home brewing is legal: a 1979 change in federal law permits one person to make up to 100 gallons of beer each year, up to 200 if there is more than one person age eighteen in your household, though some states have more limiting regulations than this. (If ordering from publisher, add $1 for postage and handling.)

ICE CREAM FREEZER: for making ice cream the way it was done in times past—by hand—this White Mountain unit comes in three sizes: two-quart ($49.95), four-quart ($74.95), eight-quart ($149.15). (Stow-A-Way Industries, 166 Cushing Highway, Cohasset, MA 02025)

11 FOOD

Your Independence Garden for the 80's
Dick and Jan Raymond
1980/44 pp./$2
National Association for Gardening
180 Flynn Ave.
Burlington, VT 05401

A basic introduction for the new vegetable gardener: soils, fertilizers, seeds, techniques. The authors show how even the smallest growing space can put food on the table. The various common vegetables are discussed individually, and there are drawings to show the details of growing them.

SEED CATALOGS—WHERE GROWING FOOD BEGINS

Until you begin using seeds yielded by your own crops, you will have to buy your supply of seeds—as well as planting stock for trees—from gardening centers, nurseries, and mail-order catalogs and brochures. The catalogs can be an education; most of them give detailed information about the varieties of vegetables, fruit and nut trees, berries, and grape vines they sell. Below is a sampling of sources of seeds and nursery stock. Catalogs and brochures are free unless otherwise noted.

HENRY FIELD: fruit trees of all kinds, grape plantings, various tools and accessories:

Henry Field Seed and Nursery Co.
Shenandoah, IA 51602

GURNEY: wide variety of vegetables and fruit trees of all kinds:

Gurney Seed and Nursery Co.
Yankton, SD 57079

STARK BROTHERS: fruit and nut trees in a wide variety, strawberries and raspberries, vegetables, melons, pumpkins, peppers, grapes:

Stark Brothers' Nurseries and Orchards
Louisiana, MO 63353

MILLER: fruit and nut trees, berries, such specialties as hops, horseradish, rhubarb:

J. E. Miller Nurseries
Canandaigua, NY 14424

SHUMWAY: vegetables of all kinds, fruit trees, grapes, gardening accessories and supplies:

R. H. Shumway Seedsman
Box 777
Rockford, IL 61105

GARDENING AND THE GREAT DECESSION

The 1940s were the time of Victory Gardens, the 1980s became the decade of Survival Gardens. A political cartoonist syndicated in the daily newspapers gave the phenomenon its name, and it wasn't long before the federal government was using the term to promote its home-gardening program.

At first, only a small number of people participated—like those who preferred vine-ripened tomatoes to the tasteless mass-produced kind found in supermarkets.

But, little by little, the movement grew as hundreds of thousands of families were losing the race with inflation or, increasingly, had no incomes at all.

The predictions for the end of the recession were not encouraging and some economists and politicians tried to give it a new name: *decession.* But this hybrid combination of *recession* and *depression*—meant to somehow take some of the sting out of a 20 percent national unemployment rate—did not stick. People preferred the more familiar term *recession.*

By the latter part of the decade almost everyone had become a vegetable gardener—even people who could afford to buy all the produce they wanted.

The trouble was that food shortages had begun to become frequent. Agribusiness became

so big that it was almost the entire source of supply. There were some drought years, some years of extra-long winters, and some of the big corporations suddenly dropped out of the business of agribusiness. It took a season or two for crop production to adjust after one or two of a Big Three or Big Four went bankrupt.

Then there was drought and a dust bowl in the Midwest and on the high plains. One year the United States almost bought grain from the Russians—and the following year we did.

Vegetable gardening had become an established part of the curriculum in the public schools. First-graders all over the country were being taught how to tend compost heaps. Local governments maintained special departments to regulate gardening on vacant land. In the inner cities, planners and architects devised complex systems to provide gardening space.

There was talk that the president would establish a U.S. Department of Survival Gardening. The same political cartoonist who had given survival gardens their name did another lampoon: he showed a pair of grandparents telling a group of children about the times long ago when people bought all their vegetables in the stores. The cartoonist was quoted as saying that no federal department was needed: when people need food, vegetable gardening just grows up naturally . . .

REDWOOD CITY: vegetables, fruit and nut trees, garden and medicinal herbs (catalog $.50):

Redwood City Seed Co.
Box 361
Redwood City, CA 94064

MELLINGER'S: a wide variety of vegetables, fruit and nut trees, berries, grapes, and a selection of hand tools and greenhouse units:

Mellinger's, Inc.
2310 W. South Range Rd.
North Lima, OH 44452

BUTTERBROOKE: vegetables and herbs in a limited selection, but all organically grown:

Butterbrooke Farm
78 Barry Rd.
Oxford, CT 06483

ABUNDANT LIFE: vegetables and herbs, from a nonprofit foundation devoted to propagating seeds of the North Pacific Rim area (to order catalog send $2, for which you receive two successive annual editions):

Abundant Life Seed Foundation
Box 772
Port Townsend, WA 98368

JOHNNY'S: a wide variety of cooler-climate vegetables and herbs, gardening tools and accessories that feature wheeled hand-cultivating equipment:

Johnny's Selected Seeds
Albion, ME 04910

GRAHAM CENTER: this nonprofit organization publishes a directory of selected sources of fruit, nut, and vegetable seeds ($1):

Seed Directory
Frank Porter Graham Center
Rte. 9, Box 95
Wadesboro, NC 28170

KITAZAWA: vegetable seeds, primarily of Japanese and Chinese varieties:

Kitazawa Seed Co.
356 W. Taylor St.
San Jose, CA 95110

SEED SAVERS: this is a co-op devoted to preserving "heirloom" vegetable varieties: you become a member for $3, which entitles you to a yearbook listing all the members and the seed varieties they have for exchange (for $1 a nonmember can buy a sample of seeds, propagate them, and then offer them in the yearbook as a member):

Seed Savers Exchange
Rural Rte. 2
Princeton, MO 64673

HORTICULTURAL: mild and hot chiles, sweet and hot peppers, for those who want to grow their own spices:

Horticultural Enterprises
Box 340082
Dallas, TX 75234

VITA GREEN: specializes in organically grown seeds of all kinds, shipped in sealed cans ($2) or packages ($1), as well as organic soil conditioners:

Vita Green Farms
Box 879
Vista, CA 92083

GREENE HERB GARDENS: devoted to herbs and the seeds for growing them—for a listing (plus a packet of angelica seeds) send $1:

Greene Herb Gardens
Greene, RI 02827

RICHTERS: specializing in seeds for herbs, gourmet vegetables (such as Jerusalem artichoke, amaranth, oriental cucumber, fennel), catalog ($1):

Richters
Goodwood, Ontario
Canada LOC 1AO

SANCTUARY: traditional varieties, untreated and many organically grown, for vegetables, culinary and medicinal herbs:

Sanctuary Seeds
2388 W. 4th St.
Vancouver, B.C.
Canada V6K 1P1

Organic Gardening
$10/12 issues per year
Rodale Press, Inc.
Organic Park
Emmaus, PA 18049
    Here is a way to keep up to date on gardening in general and organic methods in particular. This magazine covers all the aspects of planting, growing, and harvesting, with seasonal advice for the gardener. The ads are especially valuable for shopping for tools, equipment, supplies, and seeds.

COOPERATIVE EXTENSION: FREE INFORMATION FOR PRODUCING YOUR OWN FOOD SUPPLY

A branch of the U.S. Department of Agriculture which functions nationwide under state supervision at the county level, the Cooperative Extension Service offers information and education in a wide range of areas from gardening and farming to natural resources and home economics. To learn about local services, contact the Extension office in your community.

Agriculture in the City
1976/71 pp./$2.50
Earthwork
3410 19th St.
San Francisco, CA 94110
A report on an urban-gardening project in Santa Barbara, this book offers guidance for both beginners and experienced gardeners.

Down-to-Earth Vegetable Gardening Know-How
Dick Raymond
1975/160 pp./$7.95
Garden Way Publishing
1538 Ferry Rd.
Charlotte, VT 05445
A basic book on growing vegetables, with the emphasis on answering all the questions that both new and experienced gardeners come up with. There are 150 illustrations to show you the way to food crops that you can grow in your backyard. (If ordering from publisher, add $1 for postage and handling.)

The Complete Vegetable Gardener's Sourcebook
Duane Newcomb
1980/340 pp./$9.95
Avon Books
959 8th Ave.
New York, NY 10019
Everything is covered in this big book: soil, seeds, tools, supplies, watering, pest management. There are chapters on hand tools as well as power tools, with listings of manufacturers. The chapter on vegetable varieties presents 159 pages, with information on growing seasons, characteristics, and seed sources. The book is illustrated with photos, drawings, and charts.

RAISING VEGETABLES: BOOKS AND BOOKLETS

The consumer Information Center, a federal agency, offers various books and booklets, some of them free. Here is a sampling:

Organic Gardening
1977/6 pp./free

Mini-Gardens for Vegetables
1976/12 pp./$1.50

Year-Round Gardening with a Greenhouse
1978/8 pp./free

Write for catalog:
Consumer Information Center
Department DD
Pueblo, CO 81001

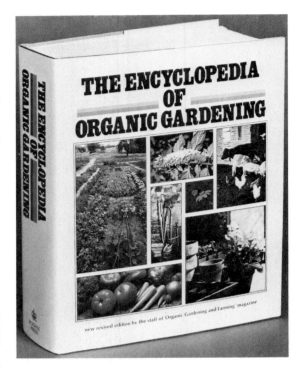

The Encyclopedia of Organic Gardening
Staff of *Organic Gardening* Magazine
1959, 1978/1,236 pp./$21.95
Rodale Press, Inc.
Organic Park
Emmaus, PA 18049
Beginning with the *A*'s, you can read at length about acidity-alkalinity in soils, and turning to the *Z*'s, you can learn about zucchini. In between, this encyclopedia presents over two thousand entries having to do with things that grow, including bees, farm animals, and fruit trees. The book's title does not do it justice. It deals with far more than gardening and much more than the organic approach, and it is a prime resource for self-sufficiency. There are photos and drawings throughout.

How to Grow More Vegetables
John Jeavons
1974, 1979/115 pp./$5.95
Ten Speed Press
Box 7123
Berkeley, CA 94707

This book is a sound introduction to the "biodynamic/French intensive" method of organic gardening. The emphasis is on making maximum use of the growing space, and there are step-by-step directions for conditioning soil, planning and seeding the garden plot, combining various vegetables and herbs in companion planting for optimum yield. Drawings illustrate the book in detail.

The Organic Method Primer
Bargyla and Gylver Rateaver
1973/257 pp./$10
Bargyla Rateaver
Pauma Valley, CA 92061

The authors are authorities in this field and their book is a sound starting point for learning about the organic method of gardening and farming. All aspects of the method are detailed, from soil conditioning and fertilizing to the use of compost and mulches. Included are chapters on seeds, planting, watering, pest and disease control, harvesting and storage, equipment, and marketing of crops.

Whole Grains
Sara Pitzer
1981/172 pp./$7.95
Garden Way Publishing
1538 Ferry Rd.
Charlotte, VT 05445

How to grow, harvest, store, grind, and cook your own grain crops for a family food supply. Covered are wheat, barley, millet, rye, buckwheat, oats, triticale, corn, and rice. The author maintains that it takes only one-tenth of an acre to raise 200 pounds of wheat, enough for a daily loaf of bread. (If ordering from publisher, add $1 for postage and handling.)

OTHER BOOKS FROM GARDEN WAY ON GROWING YOUR OWN FOOD

Vegetable Garden Handbook
Roger Griffith
1974/120 pp./$4.95

Nuts for the Food Gardener
Louise Riotte
1975/192 pp./$4.95

Growing and Using Herbs Successfully
Betty E. M. Jacobs
1976/240 pp./$6.95

Fruits and Berries for the Home Garden
Lewis Hill
1980/288 pp./$6.95

Success with Small Food Gardens
Louise Riotte
1977/196 pp./$5.95

Let It Rot! (The Gardener's Guide to Compost ing)
Stu Campbell
1974/152 pp./$4.95

The Mulch Book
Stu Campbell
1973/131 pp./$4.95

Growing and Saving Vegetable Seeds
Marc Rogers
1978/144 pp./$4.95

Making the Weather Work For You
James J. Rahn
1979/224 pp./$7.95

Garden Way Publishing
1538 Ferry Rd.
Charlotte, VT 05445
(If ordering from publisher, add $1 for postage
and handling.)

BULLETINS FROM GARDEN WAY ON GROWING YOUR OWN FOOD

Grow the Best Strawberries
Bulletin A–1/32 pp. /$1.50

Potatoes, Sweet and Irish
Bulletin A–4/32 pp./$1.50

Planning Your Dwarf Fruit Orchard
Bulletin A–7/32 pp./$1.50

Improving Your Soil
Bulletin A–20/32 pp./$1.50

**What Every Gardener Should Know
    about Earthworms**
Bulletin A–21/32 pp./$1.50

Grow the Best Tomatoes
Bulletin A–27/32 pp./$1.50

Building & Using Cold Frames & Hot Beds
Bulletin A–39/32 pp./$1.50

Fertilizers for Free
Bulletin A–44/32 pp./$1.50

Gardening Answers
Bulletin A–49/32 pp./$1.50

Great Grapes! Grow the Best Ever
Bulletin A–53/32 pp. /$1.50

Pruning Trees, Shrubs and Vines
Bulletin A–54/32 pp./$1.50

Attracting Birds for a Pest-Free Garden
Bulletin A–64/32 pp./$1.50

Grow the Best Corn
Bulletin A–68/32 pp./$1.50

Drought Gardening
Bulletin A–73/32 pp./$1.50

Garden Way Publishing
1538 Ferry Rd.
Charlotte, VT 05445
(If ordering from publisher, add $1 for postage
and handling.)

GARDENING TOOLS AND ACCESSORIES

This forty-seven-page catalog carries hand tools
and accessories of all kinds for the gardener.
There are hoes, nozzles, pruners, weeders, rakes,
books, trowels, planting accessories. Write for
catalog ($.50):

Walter F. Nicke
Box 667G
Hudson, NY 12534

**From the Walter F. Nicke catalog: heavy-duty digger
trowels, priced from $1.95 up.**

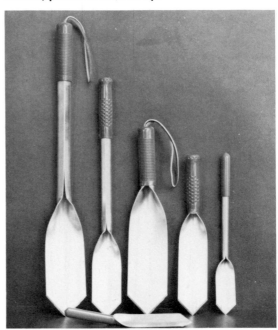

Jiffy-Pot seed starters from Carefree Garden Products.

VEGETABLE-GARDENING ACCESSORIES

Carefree Garden Products makes the small peat-fiber containers that you use to start seeds indoors for later transplanting in your garden—the roots of your tomato plants grow right through the peat and into the ground. Other products include plastic containers for "tub-farming"—raising vegetables in your home or apartment. Prices vary. You can find these products at a local retailer or write for literature:

Carefree Garden Products
Box 338
West Chicago, IL 60185

HAND TOOLS FOR GARDEN AND FARM

Under the brand names Green Thumb, Yard 'N Garden, Flex-Beam, and Farm King, Union Fork and Hoe markets hundreds of hand tools for the garden and farm. The line includes hoes, shovels, spades, post-hole diggers, augers, rakes, garden trowels, pruning shears and saws, wheelbarrows, fruit harvesters, spading and hay forks, mattocks, picks, wedges, mauls, sledges, crow and wrecking bars. See your local retailer or write for product and dealer information:

Union Fork and Hoe Co.
500 Dublin Ave.
Columbus, OH 43216

GARDEN TOOLS FROM AMES

Ames is one of the fine old names in garden tools. They sell through dealers, and prices will vary, but the quality is reliable. Write for literature and dealer information:

Ames
Box 1774
Parkersburg, WV 26101

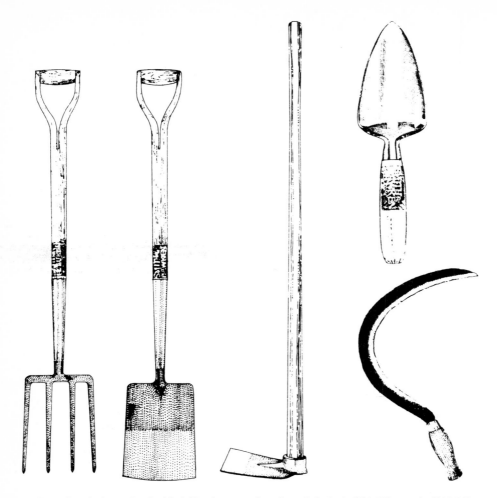

A sampling of tools from the Smith & Hawken catalog, from left: fork ($31.60), spade ($33.90), grub hoe ($19.50), sickle ($22.60), and trowel ($19.90).

SMITH & HAWKEN GARDEN TOOLS

The Smith & Hawken catalog presents a line of imported tools with a reputation for quality and durability: rakes, hoes, shovels, forks, spades, and garden trowels and forks. The prices are on the higher side. Write for catalog:

Smith & Hawken Tool Co.
68 Homer Ave.
Dept. 084
Palo Alto, CA 94301

GARDEN AND FIELD HOES BY SCOVIL

Their reputation for durability makes the Scovil hoes a good investment at about $8 each. They are forged from a single piece of high-carbon steel tempered to hold its cutting edge and not shatter on rocks. Several blade shapes are offered, including a grub design. The hoes are sold at many garden centers. For information, write:

The Samoa Corp.
Scovil Hoe Co.
Box 328
Locust Valley, NY 11560

TOOLS FOR YOUR VEGETABLE GARDEN

This mail-order source offers such things as a hand-operated compost shredder ($95), soil-testing kit ($11.95), and a composting bin in two sizes ($49.50 and $64.95) made of vinyl-covered sheet metal. Write for catalog:

Brookstone
127 Vose Farm Rd.
Peterborough, NH 03458

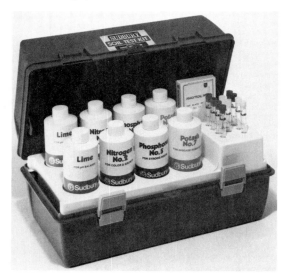

SOIL TESTING: KEEPING PLANT ROOTS WELL FED

Even if your county agricultural extension agent offers it as a free service, you may very well prefer to do your own soil testing on the spot. The purpose is to measure acidity-alkalinity levels (pH), as well as nitrogen, phosphorus, and potash levels—which all affect plant-root nutrition. This firm sells a variety of soil-testing kits: from $12.99 for a basic unit in a cardboard box, to $69.99 for a cased kit with more sophisticated elements, to a professional kit for $159.99. See your garden-supply dealer, or write for information:

Sudbury Laboratory, Inc.
572 Dutton Rd.
Sudbury, MA 01776

Photo at left shows Sudbury model A soil-testing kit, $69.99. Photo at right shows model D kit, $12.99.

Carrots Love Tomatoes

Louise Riotte
1976/240 pp./$5.95
Garden Way Publishing
1538 Ferry Rd.
Charlotte, VT 05445

Subtitled *Secrets of Companion Planting for Successful Gardening*, this book explains how specific plants can help other plants by deterrring bugs and weeds, and by building soil. By teaming up your vegetables and fruits in the right partnerships, you can increase your harvests. (If ordering from publisher, add $1 for postage and handling.)

Rodale's Color Handbook of Garden Insects

Anna Carr
1979/241 pp./$14.95
Rodale Press, Inc.
Organic Park
Emmaus, PA 18049

The author estimates that in one square yard of the soil and plants in your garden there are over two thousand insects of all kinds and sizes, ranging from the microscopic to such relative giants as beetles and butterflies. Her book tells and shows you how to identify them, understand their places in the food chain, and control those that jeopardize your crops. The book is illustrated with over three hundred color photographs of insects in the egg, larval, pupal, and adult stages.

The Bug Book

John and Helen Philbrick
1974/128 pp./$4.95
Garden Way Publishing
1538 Ferry Rd.
Charlotte, VT 05445

This book presents over one hundred bugs, illustrated and described with the types of damage they can do to your vegetables and fruits, as well as preventive measures and natural remedies. All the remedy recipes are nontoxic approaches to insect control. (If ordering from publisher, add $1 for postage and handling.)

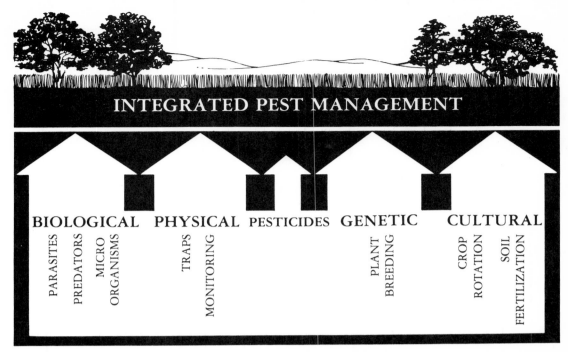

INTEGRATED PEST MANAGEMENT

BIOLOGICAL PHYSICAL PESTICIDES GENETIC CULTURAL

PARASITES PREDATORS MICRO ORGANISMS TRAPS MONITORING PLANT BREEDING CROP ROTATION SOIL FERTILIZATION

Illustration indicates various insect-control measures other than chemical insecticides (from *The Least Is Best Pesticide Strategy*).

The Least Is Best Pesticide Strategy
Jerome Goldstein, Editor
1978/205 pp./$6.95
J.G. Press
Box 351
Emmaus, PA 18049

If you are going to grow your own food you may be wondering about pesticide sprays. This book—a collection of articles and research reports—will tell you about "Integrated Pest Management," an approach aimed at minimizing or eliminating use of pesticides. IPM uses such means as insect traps, both to contain pests and to identify specific threats to vegetables and fruits so that only necessary chemical spraying is done. Other tactics include plant breeding, crop rotation, and soil fertilization to counter the effects of insects.

Weeds—Guardians of the Soil
Joseph A. Cocannouer
1950/179 pp./$4.95
Devin-Adair Co.
143 Sound Beach Ave.
Old Greenwich, CT 06870

If you are going to be a gardener or farmer, you should get to know the weeds as well as the grains and vegetables. The author explains how weeds play their part in producing crops by bringing minerals up from subsoil to topsoil, by conditioning the soil, and by storing nutrients. The emphasis is on the *controlled* use of weeds to get the maximum yield from the soil.

Ecology of Compost
Daniel L. Dindal
1972/12 pp./$.25

TRASH CAN~
COMPOST CONTAINER
FOR AREAS WITH
LIMITED SPACE.

AIR

WITH A DOUBLE BIN, MATERIALS
MAY BE TRANSFERRED FROM ONE SIDE
TO THE OTHER. THIS STIMULATES
AERATION.

BINS MAY BE CONSTRUCTED
WITH BRICKS OR CEMENT BLOCKS.
PERMIT AIRFLOW BY LEAVING
OPENINGS AROUND BOTTOM.
LEAVE ONE SIDE OPEN FOR EASY
ACCESS TO COMPOST.

AIR

Three ways to contain a compost pile (from *Ecology of Compost*).

Office of Public Service
and Continuing Education
State University of New York
College of Environmental Science & Forestry
Syracuse, NY 13210

This pamphlet is a brief but complete introduction to the subject of compost. It explains how to make it, how it works, and how to use it as a fertilizer that actually puts waste material to productive new use.

Compost

H. H. Koepf
1968/18 pp./$1.50
Bio-Dynamic Literature
Box 253
Wyoming, RI 02898

This booklet concisely explains compost, how it is made, what it does for a growing crop, the various materials that can be used, and exactly how to go about the process, with some basic explanation of the chemistry and biology involved. The booklet is a publication of the Bio-Dynamic Farming and Gardening Association, a group devoted to the bio-dynamic approach to agriculture—a form of organic farming with particular stress on composting methods.

ROTO-HOE SHREDDERS FOR MULCH AND COMPOST

If you cultivate a large area and use mulch or compost on it, a shredding machine could be an efficient investment. The Roto-Hoe Co. sells five models, ranging from 3½ h.p. to 8 h.p. at prices from $269 to $599. The machines are built to chew up vines, corncobs, flower stems, weeds, kitchen garbage, hay, leaves, small branches, tree prunings. The firm's model 550, with 6-h.p. engine at $399, has a thirteen-inch loading throat at the top as well as a side feed. Roto-Hoe also sells a line of rotary tillers. Write for literature and prices:

The Roto-Hoe Co.
Newbury, OH 44065

The Roto-Hoe model 550 large-capacity shredder.

The World of the Soil

Sir E. John Russell
1957/285 pp./$1.95
Franklin Watts, Inc.
730 5th Ave.
New York, NY 10019

You may want to wait until after you have planted and harvested your first vegetable crop before you leisurely take up this study. It is a book of science about the soil—what it is made up of, the life in it, its fertility for growing plants—but it is easy reading written for the layperson. The setting for the book is England, but the soil varieties represented there are all to be found in the United States.

Hydro-Story

Charles E. Sherman and Hap Brenizer
1976/95 pp./$4.95
Nolo Press
Box 544
Occidental, CA 95465

Hydroponics is a growing method in which vegetables draw their nutrients not from the soil, but from a water solution fed into a "growing medium" such as sand, gravel, or mineral or organic material. The authors explain how the method works and how you can make it work for you. One advantage of hydroponics is that high yields can be produced in small spaces: indoors, outdoors, in a greenhouse, on your porch, in your window box. There are photos and drawings to show how it is done, information about suppliers, as well as tips on growing individual vegetables.

Many a modern worker, dependent on wage or salary, lodged in city flat or closely built-up suburb and held to the daily grind by family demands or other complicating circumstances, has watched for a chance to escape the cramping limitations of his surroundings, to take his life into his own hands and live it in the country, in a decent, simple, kindly way.

Helen and Scott Nearing, *Living the Good Life* (New York: Schocken, 1970).

Discovering Hydroponic Gardening

Alexandra and John Dickerman
1975/143 pp./$3.95
Woodbridge Press
Box 6189
Santa Barbara, CA 93111

An introduction for beginners to growing vegetables hydroponically, both indoors and outdoors. The authors present clear explanations of soilless growing methods and show how to produce year-round vegetable crops in limited space. The detailed how-to directions are illustrated with photos and drawings, and a listing of sources of equipment and supplies is included. (If ordering from publisher, add $.75 for postage and handling.)

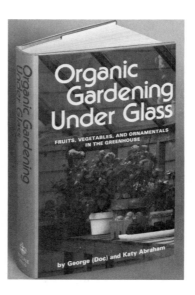

Organic Gardening Under Glass

George and Katy Abraham
1975/308 pp./$10.95
Rodale Press, Inc.
Organic Park
Emmaus, PA 18049

Devoted largely to methods of growing vegetables, fruits, and ornamentals indoors, this book will show you the possibilities and practicalities of gardening in greenhouses. Included are designs for homemade and minigreenhouses, with several ideas for window units that you can build yourself or buy from manufacturers. The book is illustrated with both drawings and photos.

HOW TO FEED A TOMATO PLANT—
THE HYDROPONIC WAY

If you find the idea of growing fresh vegetables in a hydroponic garden on your porch appealing, you may now be puzzling over how the "hydro" part of the process works.

There are several methods for feeding a vegetable the liquid nutrient solution that goes into the medium which supports the plant.

One of the most common methods is to flood the growing medium (sand, gravel, or other material) with nutrient solution one or more times a day. After the plant roots have been fed, the solution is drained back into a reservoir and held for the next feeding. In between feedings, the roots have access to the oxygen in the drained growing medium. A container with a plastic tube can be used to fill and drain the growing tray by gravity, or a pump and automatic timer can be set up.

Another method is to place the container of nutrient solution below the growing tray: synthetic-fiber wicks feed the solution up into the growing medium and the plant roots.

Two other methods require mechanical devices. One is to keep the nutrient solution continuously in the growing medium while providing oxygen for the roots with an air pump. The other method is drip irrigation, in which the solution is fed into the growing medium in a steady and controlled quantity.

Gardening Under Lights
1980/64 pp./$2.25
Brooklyn Botanic Gardens
1000 Washington Ave.
Brooklyn, NY 11225

Raising a food crop under fluorescent light would produce very costly peas and carrots. But this method is practical for starting your own seedlings for outdoor planting, particularly if you want to raise vegetable varieties not available locally. This handbook is concerned with growing plants and flowers under artificial light, but it covers the method thoroughly for anyone who wants to grow vegetable seedlings.

The Complete Greenhouse Book
Peter Clegg and Derry Watkins
1978/288 pp./$10.95
Garden Way Publishing
1538 Ferry Rd.
Charlotte, VT 05445

How to build and use all kinds of greenhouses, ranging from traditional structures to solar designs. Architect Clegg and gardener Watkins provide building plans and details as well as instruction in the use of greenhouses for growing food crops. Included is a window greenhouse, as

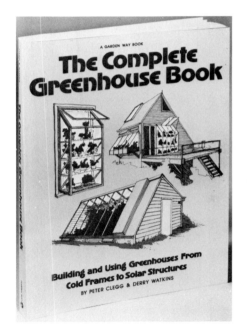

well as other small units which will work in limited space and make year-round gardening possible even for apartment dwellers. (If ordering from publisher, add $1 for postage and handling.)

OTHER BOOKS FROM GARDEN WAY ON GREENHOUSES AND THEIR USES

Building and Using Our Sunheated Greenhouse
Helen and Scott Nearing
1977/156 pp./$7.95

Building and Using a Solar-Heated Geodesic Greenhouse
John Fontanetta and Al Heller
1979/208 pp./$9.95

Garden Way Publishing
1538 Ferry Rd.
Charlotte, VT 05445
(If ordering from publisher, add $1 for postage and handling.)

General Viticulture
A. J. Winkler et al.
1974/710 pp./$27.50
University of California Press
2223 Fulton St.
Berkeley, CA 94720

This very big reference book tells everything you need to know about raising wine and table grapes, including details for turning your grapes into raisins. The book comes from a state with a reputation for know-how in grape growing, and while it is directed chiefly to large-scale production, it offers sound instruction for the small-scale grower as well.

A subsistence homestead was established, paying its own way and yielding a modest but adequate surplus. About three-quarters of the goods and services we consumed were the direct result of our own efforts. Thus we made ourselves independent of the labor market and largely independent of the commodity markets. In short, we had an economic unit which depression could affect but little and which could survive the gradual dissolution of [the] United States economy.

Helen and Scott Nearing, *Living the Good Life* (New York: Schocken, 1970).

Growing and Cooking Your Own Mushrooms
Jo Mueller
1976/180 pp./$6.95
Garden Way Publishing
1538 Ferry Rd.
Charlotte, VT 05445

The author shows how small-scale mushroom growing works, using a small cellar or outbuilding. She reports on methods that she has developed herself. Included is a section on the drying, freezing, and canning of mushrooms. (If ordering from publisher, add $1 for postage and handling.)

Growing Wild Mushrooms
Bob Harris
1976, 1978/88 pp./$4.50
Bookpeople
2940 7th St.
Berkeley, CA 94710

This guide for beginners can take you beyond identifying mushrooms for collecting in the woods: you find the edible species and then grow it at home, either in indoor bottle gardens or indoor/outdoor compost gardens. The how-to directions are thorough and illustrated with photos and drawings. In the interest of complete coverage, the author includes mushrooms of the genus *Psilocybe* and the genus *Panaeolus*, which are restricted by law because of their hallucinogenic chemical content.

MAINLINE ROTARY TILLER

If your vegetable garden grows in size, you may need some mechanical help. The Mainline rotary tillers come in models 715, 725, and 735, with 8 and 10 h.p. gasoline and diesel engines, at prices ranging from $1,195 to $2,466. These walking tractors are convertible for a variety of uses with such attachments as sickle bar, mulching bar, grain grinder, compost shredder, furrower, potato digger, cultivator, disc, snow thrower, dozer blade, hydraulic log splitter, dump cart, sprayer, and a high-capacity gear pump. Write for catalog:

Mainline Rotary Tillers
Central States Distributors
Box 348
London, OH 43140

Mainline rotary tiller model 725, $1,445.

ROTO-HOE TILLING MACHINES

In gardening or small-scale farming, a gas-powered rotary tiller can substitute for a tractor and plow. The Roto-Hoe Company makes four models, three of which are designed for use with various attachments, such as tillers, furrowers, cultivators, and shredders. Prices for the multipurpose units range up to several hundred dollars, depending on which attachments are included in the rig. One model, the Single Purpose Tiller, is available in 3^1/$_2$ h.p. for $295 or 5 h.p. for $322.50: the unit has two speeds forward, slow for spring tilling and fast for year-round cultivating. The firm also sells a line of shredders for making mulch and compost cuttings. Write for literature and prices:

The Roto-Hoe Co.
Newbury, OH 44065

Arise, come, hasten, let us abandon the city to merchants, attorneys, brokers, usurers, tax-gatherers, scriveners, doctors, perfumers, butchers, cooks, bakers and tailors, alchemists, painters, mimes, dancers, lute-players, quacks, panderers, thieves, criminals, adulterers, parasites, foreigners, swindlers and jesters, gluttons who with scent alert catch the odor of the market place, for whom that is the only bliss, whose mouths are agape for that alone.

Francesco Petrarch, *De Vita Solitaria* (1356) (Quoted by Helen and Scott Nearing, *Living the Good Life* [New York: Schocken, 1970].)

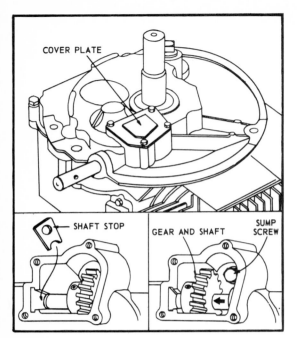

Part of directions for disassembly of a Briggs & Stratton engine (from *Small Air Cooled Engines Service Manual*).

Small Air Cooled Engines Service Manual
1981/336 pp./$9.95
Technical Publications Division
Intertec Publishing Corp.
Box 12901
Overland Park, KS 66212
This manual covers engines of less than fifteen-cubic-inch displacement: twenty-five different makes, with over five hundred basic model types. With this guide, you have the technical directions for maintenance and repair of your Rototiller, garden tractor, water pump, and a variety of other gasoline-engine equipment. Step-by-step directions are combined with exploded-view drawings.

The spirit of self-help is the root of all genuine growth in the individual; and, exhibited in the lives of many, it constitutes the true source of national vigor and strength.

Samuel Smiles, *Self-Help* (1859)

TROY-BILT ROTOTILLER

This line of Rototillers is designed for plowing and cultivating open ground, as well as plowing under crop residues for compost. They have rear-mounted tillers and come in two sizes and several models, ranging from about $600 to upwards of $1,000. With 14½-inch tilling width, the smaller machine, the Pony, is 5 h.p. The larger 20-inch size comes in a Horse model at 6 h.p., as well as a Professional model in 7 and 8 h.p. versions. Optional accessories include furrower and dozer/snow blade. The firm sells a 112-page book ($2), *The Joy of Gardening the Troy-Bilt Way,* which gives case-report accounts of Rototiller applications. Write for catalog:

Troy-Bilt Tillers
Garden Way Mfg. Co., Inc.
102nd St. & 9th Ave.
Troy, NY 12180

The Troy-Bilt catalog cover illustrates uses of its roto-tiller units.

Photo shows Horse model Troy-Bilt roto tiller.

Useful Arts are sometimes lost for want of being put into Writing. Tradition is a very slippery Tenure, and a slender Pin to bear any great Weight for a long Time. . . . Whoever has made any observation or Discoveries, altho' it be but a Hint, and looks like a small Matter, yet if pursued and improved, may be of publick Service. . . . I am sure I should have been glad of such an History of Facts (as imperfect as it is). It would have afforded me Light, Courage and Instruction.

Jared Eliot, *Essays upon Field-Husbandry in New-England* (1760) (Quoted by Helen and Scott Nearing, *Living the Good Life* [New York: Schocken, 1970].)

JARI SICKLE-BAR MOWING MACHINES

Jari makes its sickle-bar mowers in two models: the 3 h.p. Chief and the 5 h.p. Monarch, both self-propelled. Sickle bars are available in cutting widths from sixteen inches to sixty inches. The unit is designed to mow through heavy brush, cutting saplings over an inch thick, or for use on grass, hay, grain. Prices are in the $500-to-$700 range. Write for literature with price and dealer information:

Jari Division
Box 2075
Mankato, MN 56001

The Jari five-horsepower Monarch sickle-bar mower.

SICKLE-BAR MOWING MACHINE

The Kinco sickle-bar mower, a self-propelled walking unit powered by a 3½-h.p. gas engine, is the kind of machine that would be useful on a small farm for such jobs as clearing brush on land to be planted. A sickle bar of this kind operates in the same way a tractor-drawn mower does, laying down the cut material evenly and thus making it efficient for harvesting small crops of grain and hay. With a cutting width of thirty-eight inches, the Kinco unit sells for $680. For information, write:

Kinco Manufacturing
170 North Pascal St.
St. Paul, MN 55104

A CART FOR MANY USES

This two-wheel cart, with axle placement designed to balance heavy loads, will haul garden crops, building materials, firewood. It has rubber tires and comes in three sizes, the largest of which sells for upwards of $150 and has a 400-pound capacity. Write for catalog:

Garden Way Research
133 Ferry Rd.
Charlotte, VT 05445

The Garden Way cart model 26 has 400-pound capacity.

12
DO-IT-YOURSELF SKILLS

The Integral Urban House
Farallones Institute
1979/494 pp./$12.95
Sierra Club Books
Box 3886 Rincon Annex
San Francisco, CA 94119

The premise of this book is that a self-sufficient way of life is as practical inside the city as it is in the suburbs or the countryside. With clear text and numerous detailed illustrations, this book demonstrates its point with how-to material on everything from raising vegetables, small livestock (rabbits, chickens), and food fish in a city setting, to energy-conserving design of living space, application of solar energy, and management of such urban "wildlife" as rats and roaches. Throughout the book, the emphasis is on how to make the most efficient use of the limited space available to city dwellers. The many contributors to this book are scientists, designers, horticulturists, and technicians associated with the Farallones Institute. (If ordering from publisher, add $1.75 for postage and handling.)

More Other Homes and Garbage
Jim Leckie, Gil Masters, Harry
  Whitehouse, and Lily Young
1975, 1981/374 pp./$14.95
Sierra Club Books
Box 3886 Rincon Annex
San Francisco, CA 94119

Don't let this title confuse you. This book is all

about all the ways of applying the new and different "appropriate" technologies to self-sufficient use of energy and resources. The authors, who teach engineering, have translated sophisticated scientific and engineering concepts into language for laymen. Their text, combined with illustrations of all kinds, presents a treasury of knowledge. It is about the home—where to site it and how to heat it and light it with solar energy; how to insulate and ventilate it; how to generate electricity from wind, water, and sun (photovoltaic) power; and how to deal with waste-handling and water-supply systems. It is also about raising vegetables and grains, livestock, food fish—all on a small, self-sufficient scale. (If ordering from publisher, add $1.75 for postage and handling.)

CARL HELDMANN

Be Your Own House Contractor
Carl Heldmann
1981/144 pp./$6.95
Garden Way Publishing
1538 Ferry Rd.
Charlotte, VT 05445
　　Subtitled *How to Save 25 Percent without Lifting a Hammer,* this book tells how to arrange your own financing, estimate your costs, buy supplies at discounts, and how to find, judge, and hire subcontractors. (If ordering from publisher, add $1 for postage and handling.)

What is a weed? A plant whose virtues have not yet been discovered.

Ralph Waldo Emerson, *Fortune of the Republic* (1878)

House Form and Culture
Amos Rapoport
1969/150 pp./$8.95
Prentice-Hall, Inc.
Englewood Cliffs, NJ 07632
　　This book will give you food for thought about the housing we live in—how we build and where we site our dwellings. It will also give you a variety of ideas for survival shelter. The book is a study in cultural geography, and it surveys all of the different kinds of dwellings that humankind—present and past—calls home. A chapter on construction materials and design is particularly useful, and there are clear drawings throughout the book.

**Illustrated Handbook
of Vernacular Architecture**
R. W. Brunskill
1971, 1978/249 pp./$17.50
Merrimack Book Service
99 Main St.
Salem, NH 03079
　　This book from Britain is a text for architectural research, but not about churches, mansions, or public buildings. Instead, it studies surviving "vernacular" or "everyday" buildings: houses, barns, mills, inns. The structures date back

Everyone can't move to the country or there won't be a country any more, and besides, if people move to the country with their urban consciousness, the country will be transformed into the city just as happened with the suburbs. The challenge is to make cities ecologically stable and healthy places to live.

Bill and Helga Olkowski, quoted in introduction to, Farallones Institute, *The Integral Urban House* (San Francisco: Sierra Club Books, 1979).

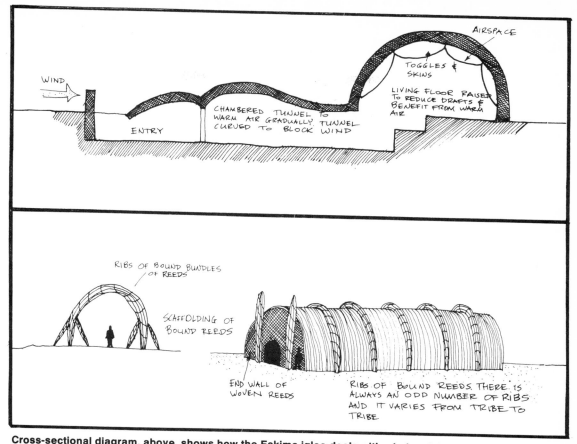

Cross-sectional diagram, above, shows how the Eskimo igloo deals with wind and draft. Drawing, below, illustrates how marsh dwellers of Iraq make use of reeds in dwelling (from *House Form and Culture*).

through the centuries and—except for a handful of American examples—are all in Britain. But this book is an excellent resource for the layperson for learning how buildings were constructed in earlier times. It covers designs, materials, and construction methods, and is illustrated with both photos and line drawings.

HOUSING: BOOKS AND BOOKLETS

The Consumer Information Center, a federal agency, offers various books and booklets, some of them free. Here is a sampling:

Remodeling a House—Will It Be Worthwhile?
1978/9 pp./free

New Life for Old Dwellings
1979/95 pp./$4

Can I Really Get Free or Cheap Public Land?
1980/12 pp./free

Write for catalog:

Consumer Information Center
Department DD
Pueblo, CO 81001

The Owner-Built Home

Ken Kern
1972, 1975/374 pp./$7.95
Charles Scribner's Sons
579 5th Ave.
New York, NY 10017

Owning your own home has long been a large part of the American Dream, but before you set out to build a house for yourself—or even have it built for you—read this book. The goal of the author, an architect, is to help you think out everything that is involved in the process before you start. One piece of advice, for instance: build in stages and pay as you go, instead of borrowing money at the cost of interest payments (a total, over a long mortgage period, that will be more than the amount of money you got from the bank to start with). The book covers every aspect of building a home: site, design, materials, construction, skills, tools, heating, plumbing, wiring. The book is illustrated extensively with drawings.

Build Your Own Low-Cost Home

L. O. Anderson and Harold F. Zornig
1972/204 pp./$6.95
Dover Publications, Inc.
180 Varick St.
New York, NY 10014

This book is a gem—a collection of complete working drawings and specifications for eleven houses—for people who would want to build their way out of the economic bind and into a home of their own. It is a big book (eleven inches by sixteen inches), with clear text and drawings, and it offers a bonus. Included is a fifty-six-page Construction Manual, presented in the same large format, which shows the excellent drawings of detail in a large scale. The only element which is noticeably missing is the application of solar energy (developed since the book was published), but any of these plans could be adapted for solar installations.

THREE BOOKS ABOUT BUILDING YOUR OWN HOUSE

The Healthy House

Ken Kern
1978/180 pp./$5.75

An evaluation of hazardous design, construction and building material in use in modern dwellings.

The Owner-Builder and the Code

Ken Kern, Ted Kogon, and Bob Thallon
1976/192 pp./$5

About dealing with your local building code when you are building your own house.

The Work Book
Ken Kern and Evelyn Turner
1979/316 pp./$7.95

The personal experience of building your own house: twenty owner-builders tell how it affected them and their families.

Owner-Builder Publications
Box 817
North Fork, CA 93643

DO-IT-YOURSELF BUILDING SKILLS: SUNSET BOOKS

Basic Carpentry Illustrated
1972/88 pp./$4.95

Basic Home Repairs Illustrated
1971, 1980/96 pp./$4.95

Basic Home Wiring Illustrated
1977/88 pp./$3.95

Basic Plumbing Illustrated
1975/88 pp./$3.95

Basic Masonry Illustrated
1981/96 pp./$4.95

Sunset Books
Mail Order
Willow & Middlefield Roads
Menlo Park, CA 94025

How to Remodel Buildings
Donald R. Brann
1978/258 pp./$5.95
Easi-Bild Directions Simplified, Inc.
Box 215
Briarcliff Manor, NY 10510
   This book shows how to restore and remodel old dwellings for new use—even those that may appear beyond repair. Drawings and photos illustrate step-by-step directions that cover the

Illustration shows use of solid bridging between joists to restore old floors (from *How to Remodel Buildings*).

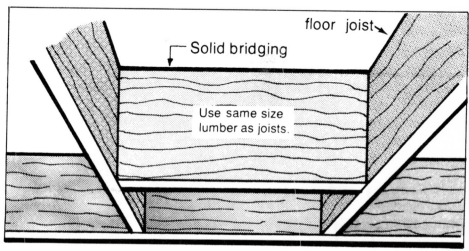

skills, tools, and materials needed for carpentry, plumbing, masonry, floorings. There are sections on the repair and replacement of structural elements, as well as on the creation of new living space by partitioning.

The Old-House Journal

$16/12 issues per year
The Old-House Journal Corp.
69A Seventh Ave.
Brooklyn, NY 11217

If you are buying an old house in a rural village—or an old house in the inner city—here is a magazine that could give you a great deal of help in restoring a building. This firm also publishes an annual catalog ($9.95) of products and services involved in the process of restoration.

Wood-Frame House Construction

L. O. Anderson
1970, 1975/223 pp./$4.25
(S/N 001–000–03528–2)
Superintendent of Documents
U.S. Government Printing Office
Washington, DC 20402

The clear and detailed drawings in this book make it an especially valuable resource for the do-it-yourself builder. Prepared by the Forest Products Laboratory of the Forest Service, U.S. Department of Agriculture, the book covers all of the basics, including such aspects as concrete and masonry (foundation walls and piers, concrete floor slabs), roofing, insulation, plumbing installation, sheet-metal work, painting, chimneys and fireplaces, and concrete walks and driveways. There are separate chapters on protection against decay, termites, and fire, as well as on methods for reducing costs, and maintenance and repair.

There is a time in every man's education when he arrives at the conviction . . . that he must take himself for better, for worse, as his portion; that though the wide universe is full of good, no kernel of nourishing corn can come to him but through his toil bestowed on that plot of ground which is given to him to till . . . and none but he knows what that is which he can do, nor does he know until he has tried.

Ralph Waldo Emerson, *Self-Reliance* (Reading, Pa.: Spencer Press, 1936).

INSPECTING AN OLD HOUSE FOR DECAY AND INSECT DAMAGE

Look for decay in any part of the house where wood has remained wet for a time, such as close to the ground.

Decayed wood can be identified by its loss of sheen, abnormal color, and sometimes fungal growth on the surface. A test for extent of decay is to prod the wood with a sharp tool to see if it mars easily. Pry out a splinter. If toughness has been reduced, the wood may break across the grain with little splintering and lift out with little resistance. Sound wood will lift out as one or two relatively long slivers, and breaks are splintery.

Termite damage is sometimes harder to spot. Look on foundation walls for earthen tubes. The tubes are evidence of subterranean termites, which use them as runways from soil to the wood above. These termites follow the grain of the wood as they eat their way through, leaving galleries surrounded by an outer shell of sound wood.

By contrast, nonsubterranean termites, which are found only in warm coastal areas, eat freely across the wood grain. The nonsubterranean type requires no connection to the ground.

If any termites are in evidence, get the opinion of a professional exterminator.

From: *Living on a Few Acres,* by the U.S. Department of Agriculture (Washington, D.C.: U.S. Government Printing Office, 1978).

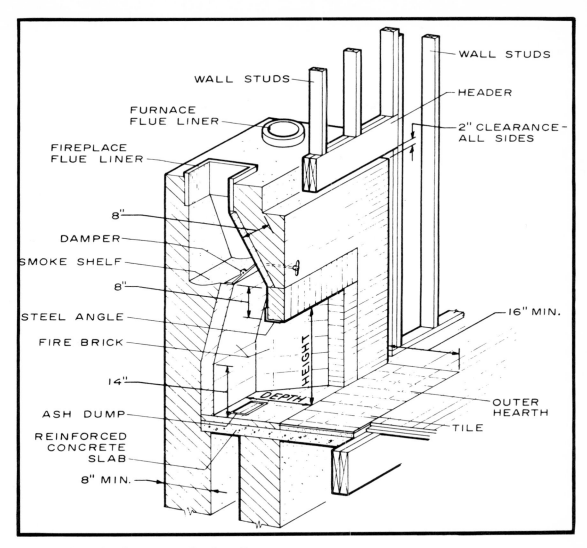

WALL STUDS

WALL STUDS

FURNACE
FLUE LINER

HEADER

2" CLEARANCE-
ALL SIDES

FIREPLACE
FLUE LINER

8"

DAMPER

SMOKE SHELF

8"

STEEL ANGLE

FIRE BRICK

HEIGHT

16" MIN.

14"

DEPTH

ASH DUMP

OUTER
HEARTH

REINFORCED
CONCRETE
SLAB

TILE

8" MIN.

Drawing gives plan for masonry fireplace (from
***Wood-Frame House Construction*).**

PLYWOOD AND ITS USES

Plywood is a building material with many applications, from sheathing for a house to uses in fine
woodworking. This association offers a variety of
publications, including an encyclopedia that

illustrates how-to details for working with plywood. Write for publications index:

Publications Dept.
American Plywood Assn.
Box 11700
Tacoma, WA 98411

Building Construction Illustrated
Francis D. K. Ching
1975/314 pp./$11.95
Van Nostrand Reinhold Co.
Dept. RB
135 W. 50th St.
New York, NY 10020

Written by an architect for use by architects and builders, this book illustrates everything having to do with construction, in precise line-drawing detail. The text, in fact, is secondary. Whether you are building, repairing, or remodeling, this reference source will tell you exactly where to put the nail or screw, how wide to set the studs, the size and number of rafters in the roof. Nothing seems to be left out—not chimneys, nor stucco, nor fireplaces, nor ladders—and all of the building materials are covered as well.

Your Engineered House
Rex Roberts
1964/237 pp./$8.95
M. Evans & Co., Inc.
216 E. 49th St.
New York, NY 10017

The author is an engineer, but this is not a technical manual. Instead, it is a book for the layperson, about thinking out the siting and building of a house. The idea is to get the most house for the least money. The author takes you through the whole process: finding the right land, choosing a design that suits both your needs and the site, and using the right construction methods and materials. Throughout, the emphasis is on the sensible and the usable. The book was written before energy became a crisis, and so there is nothing here about solar applications—but everything else applies. The author's many sketches make the thinking-out approach clear and easy to follow. If you are going to build, buy, expand, or rebuild a house, this book is a good starting place.

> People are always blaming their circumstances for what they are. I don't believe in circumstances. The people who get on in this world are the people who get up and look for the circumstances they want, and, if they can't find them, make them.
>
> **George Bernard Shaw,** *Mrs. Warren's Profession* (1893)

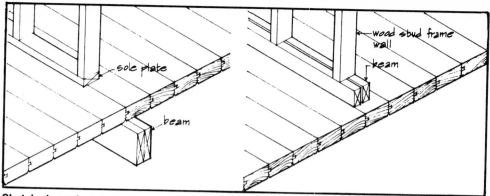

Sketch shows how partitions parallel to floor planking may be supported by beams below or above the planking (from *Building Construction Illustrated*).

THE AFFORDABLE HOUSE

The American Dream of the family-owned home began to take its late-twentieth-century form toward the end of the 1980s. Instead of buying ready-built houses, families increasingly built their own. Or at least they did a large part of the job themselves, contracting out the excavation or foundation or plumbing and heating installation.

For decades, the single-family dwelling had been a mass-production commodity, priced by a manufacturing and marketing process that was inflated with profits for everyone but the consumer. The land speculator took a profit, the building contractors took theirs, the developer marked up the price of the total package, and then the real estate sales commission was added on to that.

And there was the profit taking of the mortgage lenders. Interest rates began soaring in the 1970s, and by 1980 the private single-family home was out of reach for many American families.

The shift to the family-built home developed slowly at first. Banks were reluctant to lend the money, having dealt with professionals for decades. But the demand grew. Amateurs who had learned how to hammer and nail and construct wood-frame porches were learning how to build wood-frame houses.

The fashion changed. Where building your own house had once been considered extraordinary, it now became commonplace. More and more people learned that the house they couldn't afford to buy was a house they *could* afford to build. There was no other way. Too many people were insisting on doing it themselves, and the bank money flowed to the new market for it.

By 1995 the ready-built house was considered a luxury, and some of those who could afford them even wondered whether they were missing out on something by not building themselves.

MATERIAL BY THE USDA ON DO-IT-YOURSELF PROJECTS

Listed below are three do-it-yourself booklets by the U.S. Department of Agriculture. All three give detailed and illustrated directions for making things for self-sufficiency. For sale by the U.S. Government Printing Office, the booklets are a sampling of the variety of material from the USDA:

House Construction: How to Reduce Costs
Home and Garden Bulletin No. 168
1969, 1977/16 pp./$1.50

Fireplaces and Chimneys
Farmers' Bulletin No. 1889
1963, 1971/24 pp./$1.50

Storing Vegetables and Fruits: In Basements, Cellars, Outbuildings and Pits
Home and Garden Bulletin No. 119
1970, 1978/18 pp./$2

Superintendent of Documents
U.S. Government Printing Office
Washington, DC 20402

GARDEN WAY BOOKS ON BUILDING

Low-Cost Green Lumber Construction
Leigh Seddon
1981/176 pp./$8.95

Build Your Own Low-Cost Log Home
Roger Hand
1977/208 pp./$8.95

HOME-BUILDING PRACTICES THAT SAVE WORK AND MONEY

• Grade and stone the driveway before you start construction of the house. It will be convenient for making deliveries of materials and for getting to and from the site in bad weather.
• Place all utilities before you pour the concrete slab in slab-on-grade construction.
• Install all utilities before you enclose and finish walls and floors.
• Place drains and sewers before you pour the foundation footings.
• Fabricate trusses and gable ends on the ground where a jig can be used to speed up the job and improve workmanship.
• Build the wall panels on the platform of the house.
• Omit non-load-bearing partitions until after you finish the floors and ceilings. You can then install the flooring and ceiling in two or more rooms at one time and save some cutting and fitting of materials.
• In crawl-space construction, floor joists generally span about half the width of the house with the ends near the center of the house supported by a beam. Shorter spans will allow the use of smaller joists. Support the joists with two or three beams. However, don't spend more on beams than you save on joists.
• In concrete-slab construction, increase the thickness of the slab under load-bearing walls instead of pouring separate footings.

From: *House Construction: How to Reduce Costs,* Home and Garden Bulletin No. 168, by the U.S. Department of Agriculture (Washington, D.C.: U.S. Government Printing Office, 1977).

Homemade
Ken Braren and Roger Griffith
1977/176 pp./$5.95

Build Your Own Stone House
Karl and Sue Schwenke
1975/156 pp./$5.95

Garden Way Publishing
1538 Ferry Rd.
Charlotte, VT 05445
(If ordering from publisher, add $1 for postage and handling.)

The Way Things Work, Vol. 2
1967, 1971/591 pp./$16.95

Simon and Schuster
1230 Avenue of the Americas
New York, NY 10020

These two volumes are an encyclopedia of all the major mechanisms in our technology, from eyeglasses and flush toilets to computers and rocket engines. There are several hundred items here: each thing, machine, process, system is illustrated with line drawings on the right-hand page and explained in text on the left.

The Way Things Work, Vol. 1
1963, 1967/590 pp./$16.95

CURVED-CLAW NAIL HAMMER: BASIC TOOL FOR YOUR CARPENTRY KIT

The curved-claw nail hammer is the tool to use for nailing and nail-pulling. Its usual bell-faced (slightly convex) striking surface minimizes marring when nails are driven flush, reduces nail deflection from off-angle blows. Hammer weights, based on head weight, are commonly 7 ounces for very light work, 13, 16, and 20 ounces for general carpentry. Ripping hammers (with straight claws) are designed for rough work and dismantling, as in opening crates, where the straight claws fit more readily between boards for prying. Their usual weight is 20 ounces, 28 or 32 ounces for heavy-duty work. In either type, the head should be drop-forged steel rather than brittle cast iron. The handle should be steel or fiberglass if the hammer must withstand excessive heat or humidity. To avoid dangerous chipping, strike nails or other objects squarely.

In nailing, grasp the hammer near the end of the handle. Hold the nail between thumb and forefinger of your left hand and tap it lightly until it stands up in the wood. Then take your fingers away and drive the nail. To avoid marring a surface when pulling nails, place a thin piece of wood under the hammer head. (A thicker block gives you better leverage on long nails.) A ball peen hammer (not a claw hammer) is best for metal work; using a nail hammer to strike metals harder than its face can damage it and is likelier to cause dangerous chipping.

From: *Complete Do-It-Yourself Manual,* by the editors of *Reader's Digest* (Pleasantville, N.Y.: Reader's Digest, 1973).

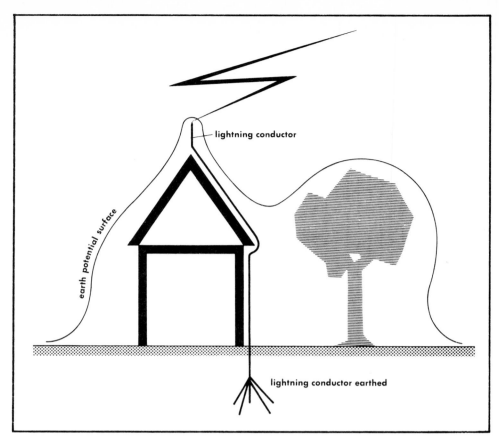

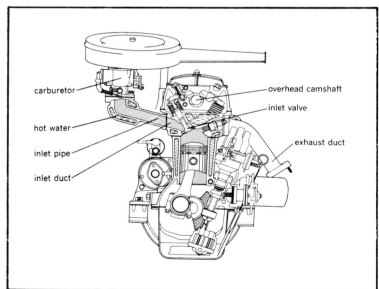

Upper drawing diagrams the function of a lightning rod, lower drawing shows basic components of a four-cylinder gasoline engine (from Vol. 1 and Vol. 2, respectively, of *The Way Things Work*).

Complete Do-It-Yourself Manual
1973/600 pp./$16.95
Reader's Digest
Pleasantville, NY 10570

This large-format book is a comprehensive guide to do-it-yourself tools and skills, illustrated with step-by-step photos and drawings throughout. The book covers hand and power tools; fasteners, hardware, and adhesives; all kinds of interior and exterior repairs; plumbing, electrical wiring, heating, and air conditioning; working with metals, wood, brick, stone, and concrete. (If ordering from publisher, add $1.55 for postage and handling.)

Fix-It-Yourself Manual
1977/480 pp./$16.98
Reader's Digest
Pleasantville, NY 10570

A complete guide to fixing anything and everything in and around your home: furniture, typewriter, plumbing, electrical appliances, automobile, lawn mower, bicycle, fishing tackle, flashlights, and lanterns. The sections on appliances, for instance, include everything from your toaster to your TV set. Photos and detailed drawings illustrate the step-by-step directions. (If ordering from publisher, add $1.32 for postage and handling.)

Formulas, Methods, Tips and Data for Home and Workshop
Kenneth M. Swezey and Robert Scharff
1969, 1979/670 pp./$15.95
Harper & Row
10 E. 53rd St.
New York, NY 10022

A collection of hundreds of items of know-how that make it a most valuable resource for do-it-yourself self-sufficiency. It deals with woods, paints, metalworking, masonry, plastering, home heating and cooling, glues, cleaning agents, gardening. The book is a storehouse of information for getting things done, made, or fixed.

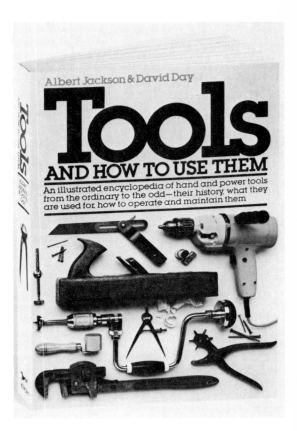

Albert Jackson & David Day

Tools
AND HOW TO USE THEM
An illustrated encyclopedia of hand and power tools from the ordinary to the odd—their history, what they are used for, how to operate and maintain them

Most of the luxuries, and many of the so-called comforts, of life are not only not indispensable, but positive hindrances to the elevation of mankind.

Henry David Thoreau, *Walden* (1854)

Tools and How to Use Them
Albert Jackson and David Day
1978/352 pp./$9.95
Alfred A. Knopf, Inc.
201 E. 50th St.
New York, NY 10022

Over five hundred tools of all kinds are presented in this encyclopedia explaining their origins, workings, and uses. Over a thousand two-color drawings illustrate hand and power tools ranging from the common screwdriver to complex and specialized equipment.

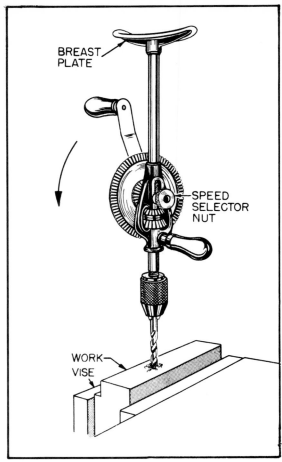

Tools and Their Uses

Bureau of Naval Personnel
1971, 1973/179 pp./$2.75
Dover Publications, Inc.
180 Varick St.
New York, NY 10014

This U.S. Navy training manual is a concise but detailed introduction to all of the basic tools. Covered are hand, power, and measuring tools, as well as the range of fastening devices, such as nails, screws, and bolts. Also covered are grinding and metal-cutting equipment and their use. The book is illustrated throughout with drawings, photos, and step-by-step directions.

Handtool Handbook for Woodworking

R.J. DeCristoforo
1977/184 pp./$5.95
HP Books
Box 5367
Tucson, AZ 85703

This manual explains and describes everything you need to know for a start in woodworking with hand tools. There are sections on the types and uses of saws, hammers, chisels, planes, as well as on selecting woods, fasteners, and glues. With several hundred photos and line drawings, the directions are clear and step-by-step. There are also plans for making a workbench, as well as some beginning building projects.

Drawing at top illustrates use of a breast drill, illustration at bottom shows use of a screw-pitch gauge (from _Tools and Their Uses_).

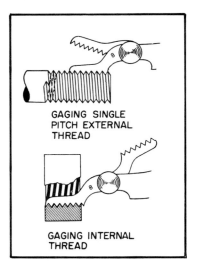

Mechanix Illustrated
$11.94/12 issues per year
1515 Broadway
New York, NY 10036

Popular Mechanics
$9.97/12 issues per year
224 W. 57th st.
New York, NY 10019

Learning how to do it yourself requires accumulating both skills and information. These magazines can give you a monthly selection of how-to material. The publications carry articles and columns on a variety of topics: cars and auto repair and maintenance, carpentry and woodworking, various fix-it-yourself skills and methods, energy uses in the home. Detailed tips, directions, and building plans are included.

The Complete Home Carpenter
George Daniels
1972, 1976/222 pp./$16.50
Bobbs-Merrill Co., Inc.
4300 W. 62nd St.
Indianapolis, IN 46268

Written for the beginner or advanced carpenter, this book justifies its title with over forty projects of all kinds, combined with special sections of basic how-to instructions for everything from driving a nail to fine woodworking. All the related tools and materials are covered in detail. Throughout, the instructions, project plans, and tools are illustrated with drawings and photos, most of them in color. Among the step-by-step project plans are various items of household furniture, kitchen-cupboard units, the repair of sash and casement windows, the building of doors, and the building of mansard and hipped roofs.

Modern Carpentry
Willis H. Wagner
1969, 1979/480 pp./$14
Goodheart-Willcox Co., Inc.
125 W. Taft Dr.
South Holland, IL 60473

Designed for use in school and apprentice-training programs, this textbook presents the skills, tools, and materials of carpentry in thorough detail. Drawings and photos illustrate instructional material that covers residential and commercial building. There are chapters on every aspect of carpentry: footings and foundations, framing, roofing, windows and doors, insulation, wall and ceiling finish, stairs. Also covered are plans, specifications, codes.

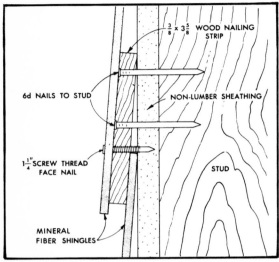

Drawing illustrates typical application of siding over composition sheathing (from *Modern Carpentry*).

Building for Self-Sufficiency
Robin Clarke
1976/296 pp./$5.95
Universe Books
318 Park Ave. S.
New York, NY 10016
   Here is a book to start with as a guide to learning do-it-yourself skills. The author is British, and here and there you must translate words or spellings to our usage, but it is clear reading and the numerous drawings make the text even clearer. This is a book of basics about making, building, repairing, and maintaining anything and everything: tools, materials, carpentry, plumbing, heat-

ing, solar energy, wind-power energy, and food supply. A separate chapter about building your own house is a particularly valuable piece of reading.

FURNITURE: TOOLS FOR FINE WOODWORKING

Frog Tool is a mail-order source offering precision craft tools for woodworking: chisels of all kinds, wood-carving knives, rasps, rifflers, files, mallets, gouges, veneering and doweling tools, taps and dies, drills, planes, measuring tools, saws, screwdrivers, clamps. Also available is a line of furniture plans, and there is an extensive listing of books on woodcraft: furniture making, carving, musical instruments, carpentry, blacksmithing, knife making, log-cabin building, boat building. Write for catalog ($1.25):

Frog Tool Co., Ltd.
700 W. Jackson Blvd.
Chicago, IL 60606

The Furniture Maker's Handbook
Editors of Family Handyman Magazine
1958, 1977/281 pp./$15.95
Charles Scribner's Sons
579 5th Ave.
New York, NY 10017
   This how-to-manual will guide you not only in making furniture, but also in repairing what you already have. The book covers tools, materials, designs, and methods, with over three hundred photos and drawings and complete step-by-step directions.

The Modern Blacksmith
Alexander G. Weygers
1974/96 pp./$6.95
Van Nostrand Reinhold Co.
Dept. RB
135 W. 50th St.
New York, NY 10020
   Making things by hand out of steel has a long history, but basic blacksmithing has changed little over the centuries. One difference the author points out is the wide availability of scrapped steel, from which tools and all manner of things can be forged. Along with giving an introduction

to the skills and tools of this craft, the author presents detailed and illustrated instructions for making such things as door latches, shovels, wrenches, and pliers. Included are the basics for tempering steel.

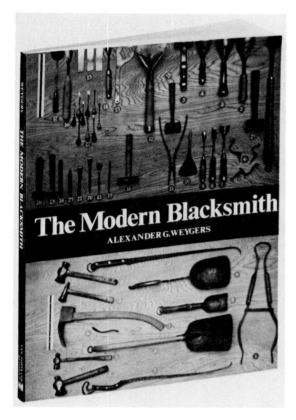

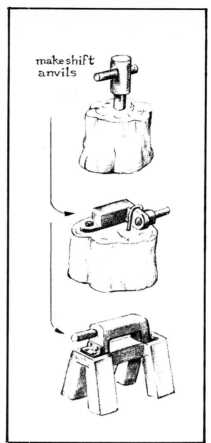

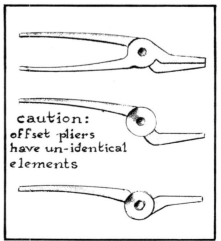

Drawings at top show possibilities for makeshift anvils, illustration at bottom shows details from directions for forging a pair of pliers (from *The Modern Blacksmith*).

CROSSCUT SAW: THE BEGINNING OF YOUR CARPENTRY KIT

The crosscut saw—as the name says—is designed for cutting *across* the grain of the wood. Its teeth are shaped to cut like sharp-pointed knives so they sever wood fibers rather than tear them. If the experienced cabinetmaker or carpenter had to limit himself to one saw, he would probably choose the crosscut design because it comes closest to being all-purpose. It does the optimum job across the grain and when used at an angle to the grain as in miter cuts. It does a respectable job when used *with* the grain although it would lose a speed race if competing with a ripsaw. It is the best saw to use on plywoods because its smaller teeth do minimum damage to surface veneers. For similar reasons, it is a wise choice for cutting hardboards, particle boards and the like.

Average blade-lengths are 16, 20, 24 or 26 inches with PPI (points per inch) running from 7 to 12. The lower the PPI number, the faster the cut, but you pay for speed in cut-quality. More teeth make smoother cuts—a fact that applies generally to all saws.

Blade length also affects speed because you must take shorter strokes with shorter blades. Short saws are good convenience items for working in tight areas, storing in a small tool box, or holding in a tote box for on-location work. Although 24 and 26 inches are the most popular lengths, remember that saw quality has nothing to do with its size.

From: *Handtool Handbook for Woodworking,* by R. J. De Cristoforo (Tucson, Ariz.: HP Books, 1977).

The Making of Tools
Alexander G. Weygers
1973/93 pp./$6.95
Van Nostrand Reinhold Co.
Dept. RB
135 W. 50th St.
New York, NY 10020

This book is a companion to *The Modern Blacksmith,* by the same author. Here he goes beyond the forging of steel and further into the use of the various power tools: drill press, grinder, buffer, sander. Using precise line drawings for step-by-step illustration, he shows how to make a variety of tools: hammers, chisels, screwdrivers, cutting tools.

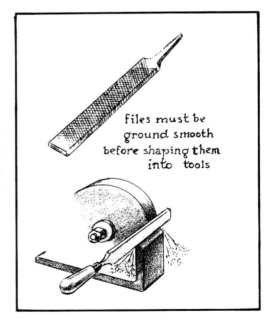

Files must be ground smooth before shaping them into tools

Drawing shows details from directions for making tools from old files (from *The Making of Tools*).

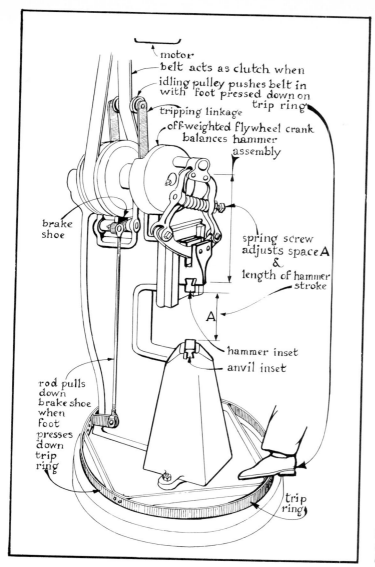

motor

belt acts as clutch when
idling pulley pushes belt in
with foot pressed down on
trip ring

tripping linkage

off-weighted flywheel crank
balances hammer
assembly

brake
shoe

spring screw
adjusts space A
&
length of hammer
stroke

A

hammer inset

anvil inset

rod pulls
down
brake shoe
when
foot
presses
down
trip
ring

trip
ring

Drawing shows the basic components of the triphammer (from *The Recycling, Use and Repair of Tools*).

The Recycling, Use and Repair of Tools
Alexander G. Weygers
1978/112 pp./$6.95
Van Nostrand Reinhold Co.
Dept. RB
135 W. 50th St.
New York, NY 10020
    How to set up a combination machine shop and smithy for a variety of work with steel, using scrap metal. Separate chapters, for instance, give directions for making a pump to recycle waste water, to recycle and operate a metal-turning lathe, and to operate the trip-hammer for forging. Step-by-step drawings illustrate the instructions.

PYRAMID FOUNDRY SETS

If you want to set up a small-scale foundry operation to make such things as metal parts, here is a line of sets for making metal castings in sand molds. There are five models, ranging in furnace capacity from three pounds to fifty-three pounds and in price from $172 to $315. Each set comes with furnace chamber and lid, electric motor, blower-mixer, blower tube, flexible hose, crucible tongs, flask and sand to match size of furnace, flour silica, and silicon-carbide crucible. An instruction booklet explains furnace operation and the method for making molds for metal castings. Write for brochure:

Pyramid Products Co.
3736 S. 7th Ave.
Phoenix, AZ 85041

STANLEY HAND TOOLS

This firm is one of the best-known names in the field. It markets a full line from screwdrivers, hammers, and saws to levels, planes, chisels, and cutting tools of all kinds. The firm's products are sold under the Stanley name as well as such other brand names as Handyman, Thrifty, and Workmaster. See your local hardware store or write for dealer information:

Stanley Tools
195 Lake St.
New Britain, CT 06050

BLACK & DECKER: TOOLS AND A WORKBENCH TO USE THEM ON

This firm's line of power tools is well known and varied: drills, circular saws, jigsaws, grinders. But one of its best-known products is its Workmate line of folding portable workbenches. These units are ideal for the do-it-yourselfer. They store in a minimum of space and come in several models for varied uses. See your local retailer or write for catalog:

Black & Decker, Inc.
701 E. Joppa Rd.
Towson, MD 21204

Structures: Or Why Things Don't Fall Down
J. E. Gordon
1978/395 pp./$8.95
Da Capo Press, Inc.
233 Spring St.
New York, NY 10013

This book is about how and why materials and structures—both in nature and manmade—hold together, work, and endure. It is the "engineering" in things—from earthworms to suspension bridges. The author is an engineer, but his writing and drawings are presented in elementary, commonsense style, with just a minimum of essential mathematics. If you want to make and build things, this is the kind of book that can set your thinking straight.

SEARS: STANDBY SOURCE OF TOOLS

The Sears *Craftsman Tools* catalog presents almost one-hundred-fifty pages of hand and power tools of all kinds. It is difficult to think of anything that is missing from this collection of things to use in building, making, repairing, and maintaining. Included is such equipment as portable kerosene heaters and portable generators. Write for catalog:

Sears, Roebuck and Co.
Sears Tower
Chicago, IL 60684

A MAIL-ORDER SOURCE FOR TOOLS AND HARDWARE

In its 200-page catalog, U.S. General Supply sells tools and hardware of all kinds and at discount prices. The variety includes: power tools, tools for carpentry and automobile maintenance and repair, chain saws. You'll find many of the well-known brand names here: Black & Decker, Stanley, Skil, Channellock. You can use the catalog for shopping by mail or to scout your options before you go to a local retailer. Write for catalog ($1):

U.S. General Supply Corp.
100 Commercial St.
Plainview, NY 11803

handled include Rockwell, Milwaukee, Bosch, Makita, Stanley, Skil. Write:

Whole Earth Access
2990 7th St.
Berkeley, CA 94710

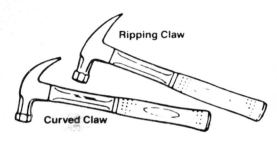

From the Whole Earth Access catalog, drawing shows two types of hammer claws.

HEAVY-DUTY ELECTRIC TOOLS

Milwaukee Electric Tools specializes in heavy-duty tools for contractors and industry, but the piece of equipment you are looking for could be in this company's line. The firm sells drills of all kinds: band, jig, and circular saws; sanders and grinders. Write for the company's catalog with its listing of local distributors:

Milwaukee Electric Tool Corp.
13135 W. Lisbon Rd.
Brookfield, WI 53005

A MAIL-ORDER CATALOG FOR SELF-SUFFICIENCY TOOLS

Whole Earth Access offers hand and power tools, as well as tools and equipment for gardening, food preparation, and alternative energy. Its 250-page catalog ($3) presents background material on the uses of its offerings. Power tools

SMALL ENGINES: BOOKS FROM AAVIM

Care and Operation of Small Engines, Vol. 1
1979/152 pp./$6.95

Maintenance and Repair of Small Engines, Vol. 2
1979/202 pp./$8.95

American Association for Vocational Instructional
   Materials
120 Engineering Center
Athens, GA 30602
(When ordering from publisher, add $1 for postage and handling; catalog available.)

Home and Workshop Guide to Glues and Adhesives
George Daniels
1979/120 pp./$4.95
Harper & Row
10 E. 53rd St.
New York, NY 10022
   A thorough introduction to the wide range of glues and adhesives on the market, their brand names, characteristics, and uses. Included are products that work with wood, metal, glass, plastic. The book is illustrated with photos and drawings.

147

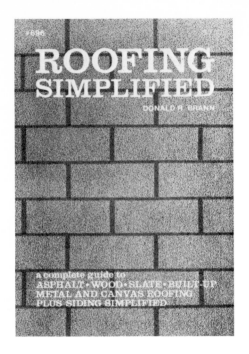

and tools. Covered are asphalt, wood, and slate shingles, including step-by-step directions. There are directions for the use of scaffolds, as well as sections on special installations, house siding, gutters and leaders, and roofing repairs.

Slate Roofs
National Slate Association
1926/84 pp./$7.25
Vermont Structural Slate Co., Inc.
Fair Haven, VT 05743
Slate is not a common roof material in these times, but it remains one of the most durable ways to keep the rain out. This book gives the details of working with slate, showing how to do it in photos and drawings. A possibility to consider: you might be able to salvage slate from an old building in your area and put it on your own roof.

Wiring Simplified
H. P. Richter and W. C. Schwan
1959, 1981/160 pp./$2.50
Park Publishing, Inc.
1999 Shepard Rd.
St. Paul, MN 55116
This book, based on the 1981 National Electri-

Roofing Simplified
Donald R. Brann
1979/130 pp./$3.50
Easi-Bild Directions Simplified, Inc.
Box 215
Briarcliff Manor, NY 10510
An introduction to roofing methods, materials,

Illustration shows position of base flashing installation when shingling around a chimney (from *Roofing Simplified*).

BASE FLASHING

cal Code, is for the person who wants to learn the skills of installing electrical wiring. It begins with chapters on the basics of electricity and wiring, and then takes the reader through the illustrated details of various installations.

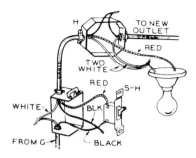

Drawing diagrams a method for adding an outlet beyond an existing outlet (from *Wiring Simplified*).

Practical Electrical Wiring
H. P. Richter and W. C. Schwan
1981/645 pp./$22.50
Park Publishing, Inc.
1999 Shepard Rd.
St. Paul, MN 55116
This book covers residential, farm, and industrial electrical wiring. From the same authors and publisher as *Wiring Simplified,* it is a much larger reference manual. Like the smaller book, it is designed to start a beginner in wiring—but at the same time it will serve the worker more advanced in skill.

Maintaining the Lighting and Wiring System
AAVIM
1980/80 pp./$5.50
American Association for Vocational
  Instructional Materials
120 Engineering Center
Athens, GA 30602
A how-to book that gives illustrated directions for replacing cords, plugs, sockets, fuses, circuit breakers, switches, light fixtures. (When ordering from publisher, add $1 for postage and handling.)

The Complete Handbook of Electrical & House Wiring
S. Blackwell Duncan
1977/473 pp./$6.95
TAB Books, Inc.
Blue Ridge Summit, PA 17214
This manual for the do-it-yourself electrician covers initial installation, modification, or rewiring

in the home and repair of appliances. The author begins with the basics of electricity, deals with code requirements in detail, and discusses all of the fundamentals. Products, materials, tools, and how-to directions are all illustrated with both photos and drawings.

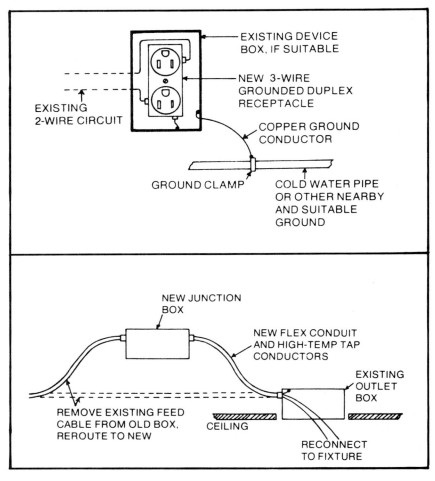

Upper drawing illustrates directions for replacement of existing two-wire receptacle with grounding receptacle and ground connector, lower drawing diagrams installation of a new junction box and tap conductors at an existing fixture outlet (from *The Complete Handbook of Electrical & House Wiring*).

It is a comfortable feeling to know that you stand on your own ground. Land is about the only thing that can't fly away.

Anthony Trollope, *The Last Chronicle of Barset* (about 1850)

OTHER BOOKS FROM TAB ON WIRING

Electrical Wiring Handbook
Edward L. Safford, Jr.
1981/432 pp./$10.95

The Master Handbook of Electrical Wiring
Art Margolis
1980/401 pp./$9.95

Write for book catalog:

TAB Books, Inc.
Blue Ridge Summit, PA 17214

How to Be Your Own Home Electrician
George Daniels
1965, 1973/144 pp./$3.95

Home Guide to Plumbing, Heating and Air Conditioning
George Daniels
1967, 1973/186 pp./$3.95

Harper & Row
10 E. 53rd St.
New York, NY 10022

Concise, detailed, and illustrated with photos and drawings, these two books could be your starting point for self-sufficiency with the machinery in your home. One will help you with your household wiring and the motors of your appliances, the other will guide you with your plumbing system and the heating and cooling of your home.

The Illustrated Home Electronics Fix-It Book
Homer L. Davidson
1982/368 pp./$12.95
TAB Books, Inc.
Blue Ridge Summit, PA 17214
    This illustrated guide to fixing your TV set, radio, stereo, electronic game or what have you could save you costly repair bills. Beginning with an explanation of the necessary tools, each chapter presents repair solutions for major problems of specific electronic units.

The Complete Handbook of Plumbing
Robert E. Morgan
1982/400 pp./$11.95
TAB Books, Inc.
Blue Ridge Summit, PA 17214
    A comprehensive manual for do-it-yourself plumbing explaining the fundamentals of the home plumbing system, with details on tools, materials, and techniques. The illustrated directions cover installation, modification and repair of water supply, sewage disposal, and such units as sinks, drains, toilets, and faucets.

USING A CLOSET AUGER TO UNPLUG YOUR CLOGGED TOILET

All toilet bowls have traps within their porcelain base. The flow of water and soil out of a toilet bowl is up and then down. In some designs the flow is up the front of the bowl. In others the flow of soil is up and then down the rear of the bowl. Generally you can determine this direction by examination. In order to clear an obstruction in the toilet bowl's trap you must guide the snake up and over by hand.

    The alternative approach is to use a closet auger, which is a short length of snake fastened to a handle and positioned within a bent length of tube. The tube enables you to direct the snake where you wish without placing your hands in the water and to get it past the lip without problems.

The auger tube holding the snake is directed upwards into the trap. The auger handle, which is attached to the short snake, is turned while the snake end is urged forward. One can attempt to hook the obstruction on the end of the snake and pull it backwards and out, and one can hope to push the obstruction clear and into the straight section of the drain, where, again, hopefully, it will continue on and out. As the trap portion of the toilet system is the most constricted and difficult to pass, this is where most foreign materials get stuck. Therefore, once clear of the trap, chances are the obstruction will pass out.

From: *Do-It-Yourself Plumbing*, by Max Alth (New York: Harper & Row, 1975).

Do-It-Yourself Plumbing
Max Alth
1975/301 pp./$13.95
Harper & Row
10 E. 53rd St.
New York, NY 10022

If you want to be your own plumber, this is the kind of book that will get you started. The author explains the home plumbing system and the tools and techniques you need for tending it. There are separate chapters on pipes and fittings and how to cut and join them, on faucets, valves, toilets, drains, steam and hot-water systems, septic tanks. Step-by-step directions are illustrated with both photos and drawings.

The Toilet Book
Helen McKenna
1975/80 pp./$3
Bookpeople
2940 7th St.
Berkeley, CA 94710

The next time you reach for the phone to call in your highly paid plumber, stop, and read this book instead. It tells how your flush toilet works and how to fix it, with numerous drawings for step-by-step illustration. The author believes that anyone can fix a toilet, and she tells how with a sense of humor that takes much of the pain out of the work.

Building the Timber Frame House
Tedd Benson and James Gruber
1980/211 pp./$12.95
Charles Scribner's Sons
579 5th Ave.
New York, NY 10017

Those old barns you see still standing after 100 and even 200 years were timber-frame constructions. In recent times, we have learned to live with the stud-framing method: based on the two by four, which, in fact, has been steadily reduced in size and now is closer to one inch by three inches in dimensions. Stud-framing construction is cheaper and faster, of course, but a timber-frame building can last for centuries. A key factor in this contrast is the joiner's craft: making the mortises and tenons that bind the timber members together. This craft, it turns out, is by no means a lost art, and this book reports on the revival of timber-framing construction. The authors present skills, tools, designs, and construction methods, with a combination of drawings and photos to show exactly how the work is done.

FOR OWNER-BUILDERS: BRUINER HOUSE PLANS

This firm sells hundreds of house designs. Its catalogs are listed below: when you make a

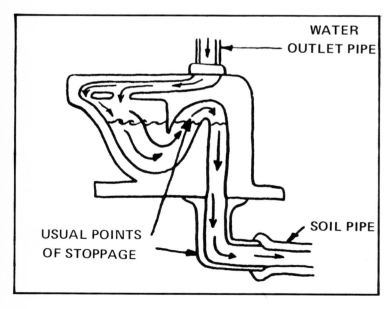

WATER
OUTLET PIPE

USUAL POINTS
OF STOPPAGE

SOIL PIPE

Cross section of a toilet bowl shows usual points of stoppage (from *The Toilet Book*).

choice from a catalog, you buy the construction blueprints at prices from $60 to upwards of $100:

160 Homes for Hillsides ($2)

350 Custom Trend Homes ($2)

Over 250 One and Two Story Homes ($3)

180 Duplex Income Homes ($4)

Over 290 Plans for Sloping and View Sites, Vol. 1 ($3)

300 Plans for Sloping and View Sites, Vol. 2 ($3.50)

L. M. Bruiner & Associates, Inc.
1304 S.W. Bertha Blvd.
Portland, OR 97219

Kit Houses by Mail
Brad McDole and Chris Jerome
1979, 1982/206 pp./$9.95
The Stonesong Press, Inc.
Hearst Books
224 W. 57th St.
New York, NY 10019
    The authors present details and specifications for over fifty vacation and year-round homes available as kits. These are "manufactured" houses that are delivered to your building site as precut and preassembled structural units. You either put the house up yourself, hire others, or turn the whole job over to a contractor. The kits range from small to large houses, at varying prices. The authors show specific costs, and the book is illustrated with photos and floor-plan drawings.

If you do not think about the future, you cannot have one.

John Galsworthy, *Swan Song* (1928)

We live in a nation that demands an electric toothbrush and worries about nuclear waste disposal. We cannot have it both ways. Continuing on our present course invites the bureaucratic nightmare of gas rationing, a loosening of environmental protections, a serious loss of jobs, and increased environmental hazards from nuclear wastes, coal production and breeder reactors.

Shawn Buckley, *Sun Up to Sun Down— Understanding Solar Energy* (New York: McGraw-Hill, 1979).

BUILDING PLANS FOR THREE ENERGY-EFFICIENT HOUSES

Miller Solsearch offers complete building plans for three houses which are designed with solar and other features for reducing energy use. The Conserver One has been contractor built for $35,000 (1978), the Conserver Two for $38,000 (1979), and the Conserver Three for $40,000 (1980). A single set of plans is $50, a set of three sets is $75. Write for free illustrated brochures:

Miller Solsearch
Box 1869
Charlottetown, P.E.I.
Canada C1A 1H9

How to Build a Low-Cost House of Stone
Lewis and Sharon Watson
1978/96 pp./$6
Stonehouse Publications
Box 4104
Sweet, ID 83670
    The authors built their own house, and this book is as much a how-to-do-it manual as it is a personal account of their experience. The house is constructed with formed stone walls, a method in which a wooden form is set up, gathered stones are arranged in the form, and then concrete is poured into the form to fill the space and bind the wall. The method is fully explained with drawings and photos, and they not only describe alternate techniques, but also discuss their mistakes and

From the Miller Solsearch brochures: top left and right, Conserver One, Conserver Two; bottom, Conserver Three.

what they learned. If you contemplate building your house—even if not of stone—this book would be a useful introduction to the prospects. The Watsons' experience developed into a new way of life for them: they now operate a mail-order business from their home, selling their own book as well as other books for owner-builders. Write for their catalog ($.50).

Cross-sectional view of stone wall and house structure (from *How to Build a Low-Cost House of Stone*).

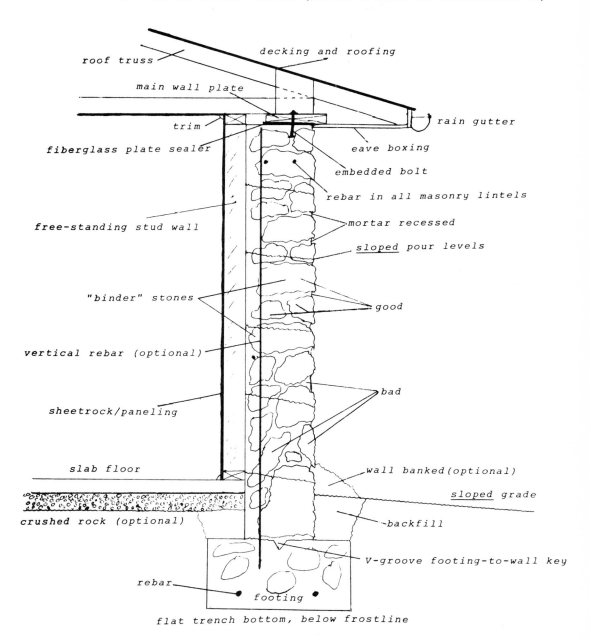

Modern Masonry

Clois E. Kicklighter
1980/256 pp./$10.64
Goodheart-Willcox Co., Inc.
123 W. Taft Dr.
South Holland, IL 60473

A textbook on working with brick, block, and stone, prepared for students in school and apprentice-training programs. It covers all aspects of masonry, beginning with the building materials themselves and progressing through construction fundamentals to such subjects as mathematics and blueprint reading. The details of the work are illustrated in step-by-step photos and drawings.

Bricklaying Simplified

Donald R. Brann
1979/146 pp./$5.95
Easi-Bild Directions Simplified, Inc.
Box 215
Briarcliff Manor, NY 10510

All phases of bricklaying, from mixing mortar and selecting bricks to building house walls and backyard barbecues, are covered. The how-to directions are illustrated with photos and drawings, and the uses and techniques of the bricklayer's tools are fully explained.

The recommended method for beveling a bed joint (from Bricklaying Simplified).

Stone Masonry

Ken Kern, Steve Magers, and Lou Penfield
1976, 1980/192 pp./$11.95
Charles Scribner's Sons
579 5th Ave.
New York, NY 10017

This how-to manual for building with stone begins with the nature of the material itself, selecting it, and collecting it. The three main masonry methods are covered thoroughly: laid, faced, and formed construction. Along with step-by-step directions for building house walls, the authors explain how to build steps, floors, arches, fireplaces. Drawings and photos are combined to illustrate the book.

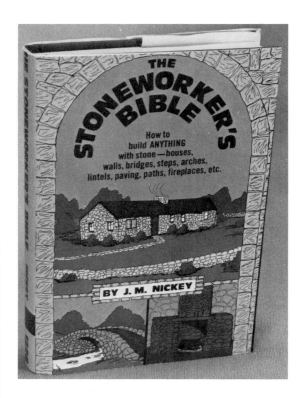

The Stoneworker's Bible

J. M. Nickey
1979/294 pp./$15.95
TAB Books, Inc.
Blue Ridge Summit, PA 17214

All of the basics of stone masonry (tools, techniques, and materials) with step-by-step how-to illustrations. Diagramed plans for specific projects are included.

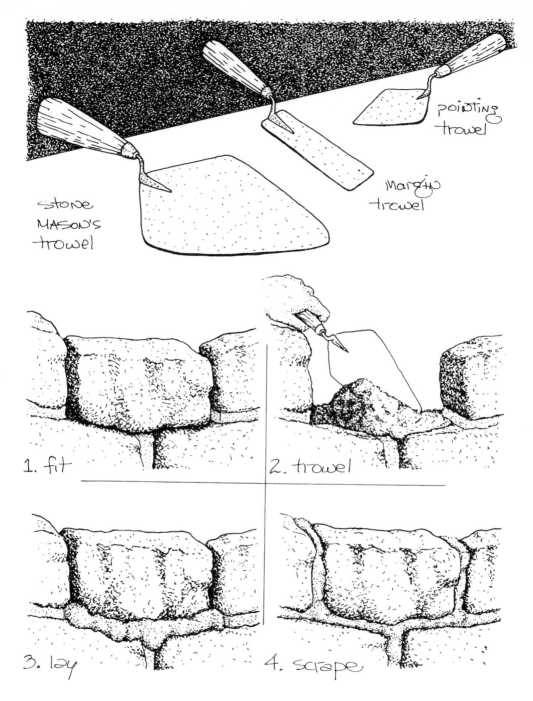

pointing
trowel

margin
trowel

stone
MASON'S
trowel

1. fit

2. trowel

3. lay

4. scrape

Sketches illustrate basic tools, above, and steps, below, in laying stone with mortar (from *Stone Masonry*).

Concrete, Masonry and Brickwork
U.S. Dept. of the Army
1970, 1975/199 pp./$4
Dover Publications, Inc.
180 Varick St.
New York, NY 10014

This U.S. Army training manual covers its subject thoroughly, with drawings and photos to illustrate the how-to step-by-step directions. Tools and techniques are explained throughout.

TOOLS FOR THE "TROWEL TRADES"

Goldblatt Tool specializes in trowels for work with concrete, masonry, plastering, laying floor tile. But the firm's ninety-one-page catalog goes far beyond this specialty: there are concrete- and mortar-mixing machines, related tools, carpenter's tools, scaffolding, spraying equipment of several kinds, and tools for work with drywall and wallpaper and carpeting. Write for catalog:

Goldblatt Tool Co.
Box 2334
Kansas City, KS 66110

Adobe: Build It Yourself
Paul Graham McHenry, Jr.
1973/157 pp./$8.95
University of Arizona Press
Box 3398
Tucson, AZ 85722

The mud brick has a history in dry-climate areas that goes back thousands of years. The author, a designer-builder, starts with that history and then takes you through the whole process of building your own adobe house. Everything is covered, including the plumbing and bathroom fixtures, with photos and drawings for illustration.

Adobe Architecture
Myrtle and Wilfred Stedman
1975/42 pp./$4.25

Adobe Remodeling
Myrtle Stedman
1976/31 pp./$3.95

Adobe Fireplaces
Myrtle Stedman
1974, 1977/16 pp./$2.50

Sunstone Press
Box 2321
Santa Fe, NM 87501

These three large-format booklets will give you a thorough introduction to the use of the adobe brick in home building. The book on architecture includes both floor plans and construction details, as well as instruction in how to make the bricks yourself. The remodeling book covers structural details and such aspects as mending adobe plaster. The drawings in the fireplace book give specific plans for the elements of design and construction.

Low-Cost Pole Building Construction
Ralph Wolfe with Doug Merrilees and Evelyn Loveday
1973/176 pp./$9.95
Garden Way Publishing
1538 Ferry Rd.
Charlotte, VT 05445

The pole construction method is easy to visualize: picture a standing network of telephone poles, each set deep in the ground, and a build-

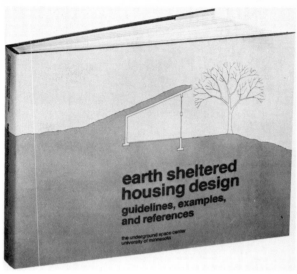

aspects as energy use, waterproofing and insulation, building-code and zoning ordinance considerations, legal and financial questions.

ing hung on this network. The poles support roof and floors, and they are the framework for the walls. The authors show how it works and how to do it, with plans for houses, cottages, barns, sheds. Also covered: choosing poles, preservative wood treatments. (If ordering from publisher, add $1 for postage and handling.)

Earth Sheltered Housing Design
Underground Space Center,
University of Minnesota
1979/318 pp./$10.95
Van Nostrand Reinhold Co.
Dept. RB
135 W. 50th St.
New York, NY 10020
    Despite all of its practical advantages, the earth-sheltered house remains an exotic form until you read a book like this one. The book is the work of several architects and engineers and it shows—with text, drawings, and photos—how underground houses are designed and constructed. Included in this coverage are such

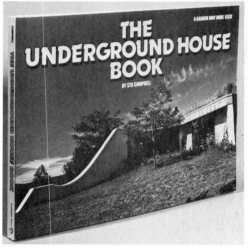

The Underground House Book
Stu Campbell
1980/208 pp./$10.95
Garden Way Publishing
1538 Ferry Rd.
Charlotte, VT 05445
    The author estimates that an "earth-sheltered"

house costs about 10 percent more to build but that it can produce energy savings of 50 to 75 percent per year. He covers the subject of underground houses thoroughly, including: site planning, building codes and zoning, soil and excavation, landscaping, water factors, heating and cooling, ventilation, condensation, and humidity control. There are 105 diagrams and thirty-five photos. (If ordering from publisher, add $1 for postage and handling.)

The $50 & Up Underground House Book
Mike Oehler
1978/112 pp./$7.95
Mole Publishing Co.
Rte. 1, Box 618BM
Bonners Ferry, ID 83805
  The author recounts his personal experiences in building underground houses. He shows the inexpensive ways to build these dwellings. There are photos, drawings, and house designs, but the approach aims at encouraging building ideas in the reader. In a separate chapter, the author discusses twenty-three advantages of underground houses, some of which are: no foundation and less building material; warm in winter and cool in summer; shelter from atmospheric radiation and fallout; concealment and defensibility; closer to water source and natural insulation of water pipes. (When ordering from publisher, add $1 for postage and handling.)

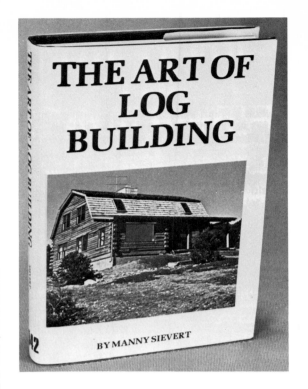

Solar offers the best means to get us through this century. It fosters energy conservation and self-reliance. Solar will create a new industry and thousands of new jobs. If we made solar and other renewable energy sources a national priority, we could meet 25 percent of our energy needs with these alternative sources by the year 2000. Without a commitment to develop and commercialize solar, this nation's energy future is bleak.

Shawn Buckley, *Sun Up to Sun Down — Understanding Solar Energy* (New York: McGraw-Hill, 1979).

The Art of Log Building
Manny Sievert
1981/304 pp./$17.95
TAB Books, Inc.
Blue Ridge Summit, PA 17214
  The author covers log structures of all kinds, built from scratch or from kits. The book emphasizes basics for beginners, and includes the step-by-step process of felling, curing, shaping, and preserving logs for building. The construction process includes the necessary tools, as well as all of the basics of log-building methods and joints. The how-to illustrations include diagramed details.

Building a Log House in Alaska
Axel R. Carlson
1970, 1977/80 pp./$2.50
Cooperative Extension Service
University of Alaska
303 Tanana Dr., Rm. WW6A
Fairbanks, AK 99701
  With this book as your guide, you can build a

year-round log house anywhere that you have a supply of logs. It is an excellent source, illustrated with numerous step-by-step line drawings. It covers the various construction methods, explains tools and skills, and details design elements. The book also illustrates three log-house designs, complete building plans for which are available for purchase.

Drawing illustrates steps in chinkless log-house wall construction (from *Building a Log House in Alaska*). Cooperative Extension Service, University of Alaska).

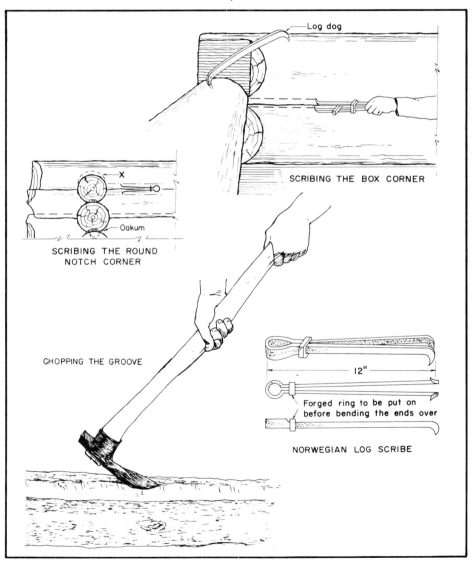

Log dog

SCRIBING THE BOX CORNER

X

Oakum

SCRIBING THE ROUND NOTCH CORNER

CHOPPING THE GROOVE

12"

Forged ring to be put on before bending the ends over

NORWEGIAN LOG SCRIBE

Building with Logs
B. Allan Mackie
1974, 1979/91 pp./$12

Log House Plans
B. Allan Mackie
1979/169 pp./$12

Log House Publishing Co., Ltd.
Box 1205
Prince George, B.C.
Canada V2L 4V3

These two books provide a basic how-to text for building with logs. They are illustrated with photos and drawings, and the book of plans presents thirty-seven designs. The publisher is also associated with a school for log building and offers a free brochure for the program. (When ordering books from the publisher from the United States, add $1 — $1.50 if ordering both — for postage and handling.)

KITS FOR DESIGNING AND BUILDING YOUR OWN LOG HOUSE

Green Mountain Cabins offers a designing service as well as a materials-package selection for building your own log house. The company sells "log" packages and "shell" packages, to be trucked to your building site. A log package includes all of the basic structural materials plus windows and doors, while a shell package adds such materials as joists, porch components, and roofing. Logs are precut and are erected with the firm's patented Arrowspline device used to align and seal the logs together. Among the stock house designs available are the four-bedroom Stowe model ($12,531 for log package, $18,349 for full-shell package), and the Tisbury, a three-bedroom model with built-in two-story greenhouse for passive solar heating (log package, $17,767, shell package, $27,842). Aside from the stock designs, the firm will sell you its kit called "Designing Your Own Green Mountain Log Home" ($4.50), with materials from which you can specify a customized house. Write for free brochure:

Green Mountain Cabins, Inc.
Box 190, Dept. BMC
Chester, VT 05143

The Dome Builder's Handbook
John Prenis, Editor
1973/107 pp./$6
Running Press
125 S. 22nd St.
Philadelphia, PA 19103
This collection of over twenty articles by indi-

From Green Mountain Cabins: the Tisbury model log house.

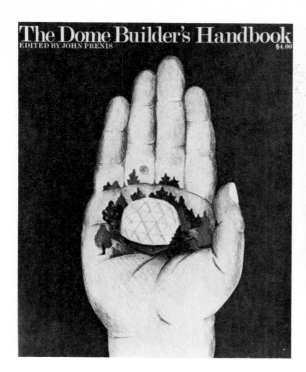

The Dome Builder's Handbook
EDITED BY JOHN PRENIS $4.00

HOW TO INSULATE YOUR HOME AND SAVE FUEL
Prepared by the U.S. Department of Housing & Urban Development

vidual authors will give you a thorough introduction to the dome as a dwelling. The book covers theory and design, as well as materials and construction details, and it is illustrated with both photos and drawings. (If ordering from publisher, add $.50 for postage and handling.)

Dome Builder's Handbook No. 2
William Yarnall
1978/126 pp./$6.95
Running Press
125 S. 22nd St.
Philadelphia, PA 19103

After an introduction to the basics of domes, the author sets out to help you consider whether the form is right for you as a dwelling. From there, he explains how a dome is constructed. The focus is on how to build it yourself, and there are architectural drawings for several dome designs. The book is illustrated with photos in both color and black-and-white, showing examples of buildings under construction and in use. (If ordering from publisher, add $.25 for postage and handling.)

How to Insulate Your Home and Save Fuel
U.S. Dept. of Housing
and Urban Development
1975, 1977/72 pp./$2
Dover Publications, Inc.
180 Varick St.
New York, NY 10014

Illustrated with step-by-step drawings, this useful book shows in detail how to save money by keeping furnace heat in during the winter and by keeping outside heat outside during the summer. Charts help you calculate your fuel savings with the dollars you invest in various kinds of insulation. Included are insulation of walls, unfinished areas, basements, and crawl spaces, as well as use of storm windows and doors and the caulking and weather stripping of windows and doors. The how-to directions provide details on the use of tools and materials.

Movable Insulation
William K. Langdon
1980/379 pp./$14.95
Rodale Press, Inc.
Organic Park
Emmaus, PA 18049

The idea of movable insulation is to let the heat in when you want it and keep it there when it wants to get out. The means are shades and shutters of various kinds, and this book explains all,

163

including how to make them yourself, with extensive drawings, photos, and charts. Materials and equipment are covered, with listings of specifications and manufacturers.

ENERGY CONSERVATION WITH A TURBINE VENTILATOR

An unventilated attic can cause problems and costs. Summer heat radiates down into living areas, putting a strain on air-conditioning if you have it or on you if you don't. Winter moisture can damage rafters and wiring and reduce the efficiency of insulation. One solution is the turbine ventilator: it uses zero energy, its fins catching even a breeze to spin the turbine and take air out of the attic. The Whirlybird made by Lomanco is an example of this kind of unit. The firm also sells various other items for the home: louvers, vent units, and shutters, as well as fans and powered ventilators. Write for brochures and dealer information:

Lomanco, Inc.
Box 519
Jacksonville, AR 72076

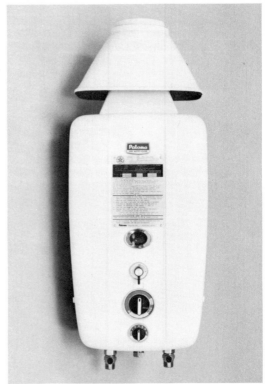

Paloma Constant Flow water heater.

A WATER HEATER FOR SAVING FUEL COSTS IN THE HOME

This firm's Constant Flo water heaters are designed to cut fuel costs by one-fourth. They are tankless and heat water only as it is used, operating on either LP or natural gas. The suitcase-size unit is hung on a wall, and the water supply flows through it to be heated at an automatically controlled temperature and volume. Several models are available, with varying output capacities. For literature and information on dealers and prices, write:

Paloma Industries, Inc.
241 James St.
Bensenville, IL 60106

How to Cut Your Electric Bill and Install Your Own Emergency Power System
Edward A. Lacy
1978/140 pp./$5.95
TAB Books, Inc.
Blue Ridge Summit, PA 17214
This manual on electrical use in the home explains how the power system works and the various steps you can take to cut your costs. The author details the workings of lighting, heating, air-conditioning, and other appliance systems and shows how energy can be conserved and how needs can be reduced by such means as home insulation. Emergency lighting and standby and portable generators, with examples of equipment on the market, are discussed. The book is illustrated with photos, drawings, and charts.

USDA FACT SHEETS: FREE INFORMATION FOR SELF-SUFFICIENCY

The U.S. Department of Agriculture publishes a variety of information in the form of Fact Sheets. These two-page and four-page publications are available free to the public, subject to supply. Below is a sampling:

- **How to Save Money with Storm Doors and Windows** (AFS–2–3–1)
- **Tips on Financing Home Weatherization** (AFS–2–3–3)
- **Landscaping to Cut Fuel Costs** (AFS–2–3–5)
- **How to Determine Your Insulation Needs** (AFS–2–3–8)
- **How to Install Insulation for Ceilings** (AFS–2–3–10)
- **How to Install Insulation for Walls** (AFS–2–3–11)
- **How to Install Insulation for the Floor and Basement** (AFS–2–3–12)
- **Locating New Home Sites to Save Fuel** (AFS–2–3–15)

U.S. Dept. of Agriculture
Governmental and Public Affairs
Washington, DC 20250

Superhouse
Don Metz
1981/224 pp./$12.95
Garden Way Publishing
1538 Ferry Rd.
Charlotte, VT 05445

An update on energy-saving houses, this book covers earth-sheltered, double-envelope, and super-insulated designs and seeks to produce a "Superhouse Hybrid" that combines the best elements of these designs. (If ordering from publisher, add $1 for postage and handling.)

HOW WINDBREAKS OF TREES AND SHRUBS CAN CUT YOUR WINTER HEATING BILL

An unprotected home loses much more heat on a cold windy day than on an equally cold still day. Well-located trees and shrubs can intercept the wind and cut your heat loss.

Up to one-third of the heat loss from a building may escape through the walls and roof by conduction. Wind increases the convective air currents along outside walls and the roof, thus increasing the heat loss.

Infiltration of air leakage can account for as much as one-third of heating losses in some buildings. Cold outside air flows in through cracks around windows and doors, and even through the pores in walls. This produces drafts that may cause you to overcompensate by raising the thermostat to unreasonable levels just to maintain a modicum of comfort. Both windbreaks and foundation plantings can cut down this penetrating power of the wind.

Studies of windbreaks show that they can reduce winter fuel consumption by 10 to 30 percent.

One study in Nebraska compared the fuel requirements of identical test houses which maintained a constant inside temperature of 70 degrees F. The house protected by a windbreak used 23 percent less fuel.

In one month, an exposed electrically heated house in South Dakota used 443 kilowatt-hours to maintain an inside temperature of 70 degrees F. An identical house sheltered by a windbreak used only 270 kilowatt-hours. The difference in average energy requirements for the whole winter was 34 percent.

The amount of money saved by a windbreak around a home will vary depending on the climate of the area, location of the home, and what the house is built of. A well-weatherized house with adequate ventilation, caulking, and weather stripping won't benefit from windbreaks nearly as much as a poorly weatherized house.

From: *Landscaping to Cut Fuel Costs*, Fact Sheet AFS-2-3-5, by the U.S. Department of Agriculture (Washington, D.C.: U.S. Government Printing Office, 1981).

Superinsulated Houses and Double-Envelope Houses

William A. Shurcliff
1981/182 pp./$12
William A. Shurcliff
19 Appleton St.
Cambridge, MA 02138

If you are considering building—or rebuilding—a house to avoid the high costs of energy for heat and light, this book is one of the prime sources of information. In a superinsulated house, the insulation is so thorough and the building so airtight that almost all the heating comes from passive solar energy, electrical usage, and body temperature. The double-envelope house design is basically a house built with a second housing surrounding it and with a consequent insulating air space: such a design also incorporates a solar greenhouse on the south side to provide heat. The author gives specific design examples and covers such factors as humidity, ventilation, and construction. Line drawings illustrate the book.

HEAT-EXCHANGE VENTILATORS

As you insulate and seal off a house to conserve energy by keeping the heated or cooled air in, the contained air can become unacceptably stale. The solution is to bring in fresh air from the outside: but this air must then be heated or cooled, adding to the load on the system. The solution is a heat-exchange ventilator of the Lossnay type, which conducts air flow through a system of treated-paper plates and fins: to precool and dehumidify fresh air in the summer, and preheat and humidify the fresh air in the winter. Mitsubishi sells a line of Lossnay ventilators with window models that begin at prices upwards of $100. Write for literature:

Mitsubishi Electric Sales America, Inc.
3030 E. Victoria St.
Compton, CA 90221

The Master Handbook of All Home Heating Systems

Billy L. Price and James T. Price
1979/352 pp./$12.95
TAB Books, Inc.
Blue Ridge Summit, PA 17214

This book covers oil, gas, electric, steam, wood, and coal heating systems. The text and illustrations present how-to directions for installation and maintenance as well as tune-up and repair. The authors offer techniques for increasing fuel efficiency, as well as making furnace-fuel conversions to cut heating costs.

HEATING WITH WASTE OIL

The search for less costly energy sources takes many paths. This one involves waste petroleum products. If you have a source of cheap waste crankcase oil, consider the Kutrieb CTB–87 Incinerator. The heating unit costs $898, is rated to deliver 87,000 Btu.'s of heat per hour, and has been tested to meet Environmental Protection Agency emission standards. The unit is 39½ inches high, 19 wide, 30 long, and weighs 170 pounds. Like other Kutrieb units, it was designed for commercial and industrial installations where waste oil is produced on the site. But if you can get the oil to your home, here's a possibility for cheap heat. Literature available:

Kutrieb Corp.
430 Phillip St.
Chetek, WI 54728

Kutrieb CTB-87 waste-oil incinerator.

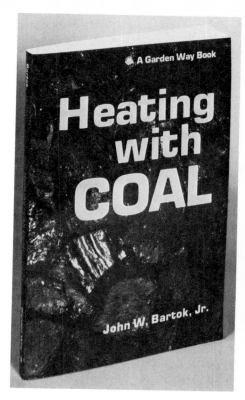

Heating with Coal
John W. Bartok, Jr.
1980/192 pp./$6.95
Garden Way Publishing
1538 Ferry Rd.
Charlotte, VT 05445

How much could you save on your heating bill by switching to coal? The author explains how to estimate your coal-burning cost effectiveness, and beyond that question to how to choose the coal stove or furnace that is right for your heating needs. A complete listing of available stoves and furnaces is included. (If ordering from publisher, add $1 for postage and handling.)

Wood Heat
John Vivian
1978/428 pp./$9.95
Rodale Press, Inc.
Organic Park
Emmaus, PA 18049

A complete book on heating—and cook-ing—with a wood fire. Beginning with an introduction to the history, economics, and practicalities of the use of wood as fuel, the book covers everything involved: fireplaces, stoves, ovens, flue systems, installation and maintenance, and safety. There are chapters on wood selection and supply, and cooking in the fireplace and on the stove top. Especially valuable is a listing of manufacturers of equipment and supplies, as well as other reading on the subject. The book is illustrated throughout with clear drawings, as well as photos, that include step-by-step do-it-yourself directions.

Woodstove Directory
1980, 1982/360 pp./$2.95
Energy Communications Press
Box 4474
Manchester, NH 03108

This big directory covers both wood-burning

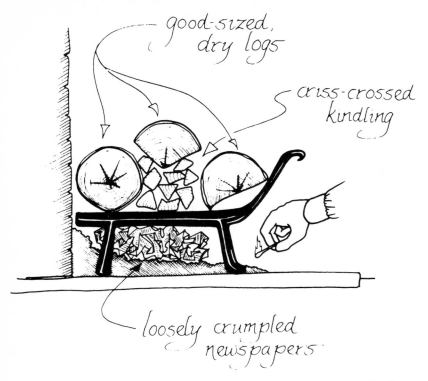

good-sized,
dry logs

criss-crossed
kindling

loosely crumpled
newspapers

Illustration shows basic method for starting a fireplace fire (from _Wood Heat_).

and coal-burning stoves, as well as accessories of all kinds, including those for fireplaces. There are hundreds of photos and diagrams to illustrate what appears to be a complete listing of every product in this field. The directory presents manufacturer descriptions of the products, with addresses, and includes as well a listing of retailers, state by state. Other features of the book are a listing of chimney sweeps and a selection of how-to articles. If you are thinking about switching to wood or coal, this is an information source to start with. (When ordering from publisher, add $.55 for postage and handling.)

AN OIL-BARREL WOODSTOVE

A do-it-yourself kit that consists of a door assembly, stovepipe flange, and legs assembly; all you

need is a fifty-five-gallon oil barrel to produce a stove. The kit costs about $60. Write for information:

Enderes Tool Co., Inc.
Box 691
Albert Lea, MN 56007

A MAIL-ORDER SOURCE FOR WOOD- AND COAL-BURNING STOVES, RANGES, AND FURNACES

Lehman Hardware handles over a hundred different models of stoves, ranges, and furnaces for use with wood or coal, some of them made in the

168

The Enderes barrel-stove kit consists of door assembly, stovepipe flange, and legs assembly: you supply the barrel.

United States and some of them imported. Write for the *Non-Electric* catalog ($2) and the *Cooking Range* catalog ($1):

Lehman Hardware & Appliances, Inc.
Box 41
Kidron, OH 44636

ELMIRA WOOD/COAL-BURNING COOKING RANGES

Pacific Lamp & Stove sells the Oval and Julia model cooking ranges made in Canada by Elmira Stove Works. Both models are airtight designs for both cooking and heating. The oval sells for $2,195, and the less ornate Julia for $1,750. The units come with solid-copper hot-water reservoirs with 7.8-gallon capacity, and an optional water jacket ($99) can be used to hook into the home plumbing system to provide hot water. Grates are available for conversion to coal for both the Oval ($100) and the Julia ($70). Write for information:

Pacific Lamp & Stove Co.
Box 30610
Seattle, WA 98103

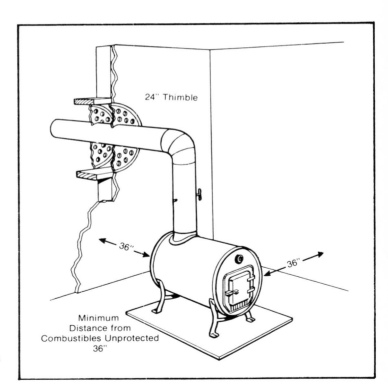

Illustration shows safety standards for use of Enderes barrel stove.

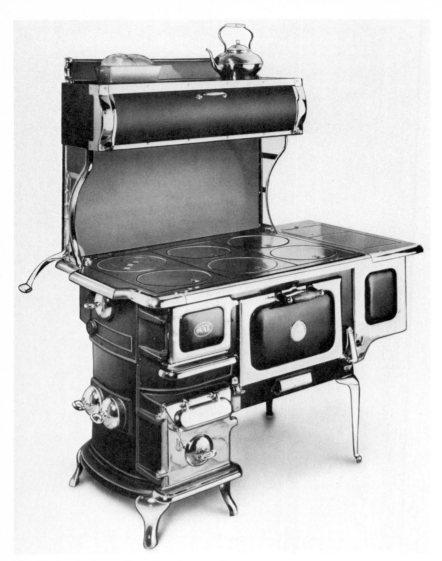

The Elmira Oval wood/coal-burning cooking range ($2,195), sold by Pacific Lamp & Stove Company.

STOVES FOR BURNING WOOD OR COAL

Vermont Castings manufactures three cast-iron stove models: the Defiant, the Resolute, and the Vigilant. The Defiant is a wood-burner, for $650. The Resolute—in versions from $470 to $695—comes in wood or coal types, with a conversion kit available ($180) for the wood type. The Vigilant is also for wood or coal, $550 to $795, and also has a conversion kit ($195) for the wood

Defiant wood stove, $650
(photo used with permission
from Vermont Castings, Inc.).

type. The stove design uses horizontal combustion (rather than updraft combustion) based on an automatic thermostat which controls oxygen level to provide efficient burning of volatile gases from wood or coal. The firm also sells stove accessories. Write for information packet, which includes a manual that is a useful introduction to wood and coal stoves:

Vermont Castings, Inc.
Prince St.
Randolph, VT 05060

WOOD STOVES OF IRON AND STEEL— AND MASONRY

Maine Wood Heat sells a line of American-made and imported stoves and is also a prime source of information. It handles such makes as Monarch, Olympic, Franco Belge, Jotul, and Tirol, and its *Quality Wood Cookstove Catalog and Review* ($1 plus $.50 postage) discusses the stoves in detail. The firm also publishes the *Masonry Stove Guild Newsletter,* the first four issues ($5) of which are an introduction to these built-in, brickwork stoves for heating and cooking.

Maine Wood Heat Co.
RFD 1, Box 38
Norridgewock, ME 04957

Wood Stoves
Ole Wik
1977/194 pp./$5.95
Alaska Northwest Publishing Co.
Fulfillment Office
130 Second Ave. South
Edmonds, WA 98020
　　Subtitled *How to Make and Use Them,* almost half of this book is devoted to making wood stoves out of such raw material as oil barrels. The author covers use from all angles: fuel supply, stove selection, safety, types of stoves, accessories. The chapters on making stoves give step-by-step directions, with line drawings that show the various designs clearly. A listing of manufacturers indicates the types of stoves that each carries.

Wood Furnaces & Boilers
Bulletin A-25/32 pp./$1.50
Garden Way Publishing
1538 Ferry Rd.
Charlotte, VT 05445
　　Authority Larry Gay explains and evaluates the various types of wood-burning furnaces and boilers available, including units that combine wood with gas or oil capability. The bulletin is illustrated with drawings, and a listing of manufacturers is included. (If ordering from publisher, add $1 for postage and handling.)

Woodstove Cookery
Jane Cooper
1977/208 pp./$5.95
Garden Way Publishing
1538 Ferry Rd.
Charlotte, VT 05445
　　Cooking on a wood stove is not at all the same

Woodstove Cookery

AT HOME ON THE RANGE

Jane Cooper

as cooking on the gas or electric range—there's no knob to turn to control the intensity of the heat. Know-how is required, and here's the book to help you acquire it. In fact, with their slow, even heat, wood stoves can produce cooking results that a gas or electric range cannot. The author gives directions, recipes, and tips from firsthand experience. (If ordering from publisher, add $1 for postage and handling.)

The Hunter combination furnace has separate oil and wood combustion chambers (from *Wood Furnaces & Boilers*).

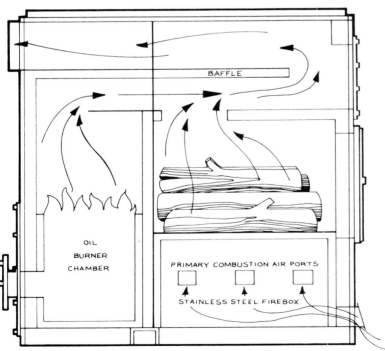

BAFFLE

OIL BURNER CHAMBER

PRIMARY COMBUSTION AIR PORTS

STAINLESS STEEL FIREBOX

Fireplaces

Ken Kern and Steve Mager
1978/200 pp./$7.95
Owner-Builder Publications
Box 817
North Fork, CA 93643

Step-by-step directions for building heat-radiating, air-circulating, or water-circulating fireplaces.

Adobe Fireplaces

Myrtle Stedman
1974, 1977/16 pp./$2.50
Sunstone Press
Box 2321
Santa Fe, NM 87501

This large-format booklet presents designs and ideas for several fireplaces. The drawings give specific plans for the elements of design and construction.

Firewood

M. Michaelson
1978/159 pp./$2.95
Gabriel Books
Box 224
Mankato, MN 56001

This field guide to identifying the trees of the United States opens with an introduction that clearly explains the heat-producing characteristics and differences among the species. Hickory, for instance, yields about the same amount of Btu.'s per pound as aspen, but hickory is twice as dense and weighs twice as much (and a cord of it can give off about as much heat as a ton of coal). The guide provides identification characteristics—such as shape, bark, leaves, and buds—for both summer and winter phases.

Wood Energy

Mary Twitchell
1978/144 pp./$7.95
Garden Way Publishing
1538 Ferry Rd.
Charlotte, VT 05445

Along with covering wood-burning furnaces and boilers, this book reports on the newly available combination furnaces: either wood or coal, or wood combined with oil or gas. Catalog sections present the available wood stoves. Covered are such subjects as stove installation, firewood, the best use of existing fireplaces, and a look into the future of wood energy with wood chips and compressed pellets. (If ordering from publisher, add $1 for postage and handling.)

A MACHINE FOR SPLITTING FIREWOOD

The Bark-Buster is an auger-type wood-splitter that could make your woodpile bigger with less work. There are four models: one is a unit that

HEAT VALUES AND WEIGHTS OF COMMON FIREWOODS IN THE UNITED STATES

WOOD	Millions of BTUs per cord	Pounds of wood per cord
Hickory	25	4600
Oak, white	23	4400
Beech	22	4000
Maple, sugar	21	4000
Oak, red	21	3900
Birch, yellow	21	3900
Pine, yellow	21	3700
Ash, white	20	3800
Maple, red	19	3400
Tamarack	19	
Birch, paper	18	3400
Fir, Douglas	18	2900
Pine, pitch	18	3200
Pine, Norway	18	2800
Birch, gray	18	3500
Elm	18	3200
Spruce, red	15	2600
Hemlock	15	2600
Balsam	14	2200
Pine, white	14	2700
Aspen	13	2200
Basswood	11	

From: *Firewood*, by M. Michaelson (Mankato, Minn: Gabriel Books, 1978).

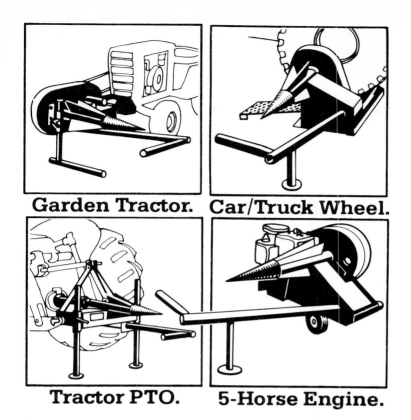

Garden Tractor.   Car/Truck Wheel.

Tractor PTO.   5-Horse Engine.

Drawing shows how the four Bark-Buster woodsplitter models work.

attaches to the wheel of your car or truck; with the wheel up off the ground, spin your wheel and you spin the auger. Another model operates with a 5-h.p. engine of its own, and the two other models are linked up with a farm or garden tractor. Prices range upward from about $400. Write for literature and dealer information:

Bark-Buster, Inc.
14125 21st St. N.
Minneapolis, MN 55441

TOOLS FOR SPLITTING FIREWOOD

By Hand & Foot offers several American-made and imported tools collected in a system for firewood splitting. The splitting ax—or maul—is

$26, and there is a handle guard for $2.90. Also offered: steel wedge, $12.20, wood-and-steel wedge, $17.40, and froe (a type of steel wedge, mounted on a handle), $37.50. The company also sells a two-wheeled cart designed for hauling firewood. Write for brochure and prices:

By Hand & Foot, Ltd.
Box 611
Brattleboro, VT 05301

Splitting Firewood
David Tresemer
1981/142 pp./$6.50
By Hand & Foot, Ltd.
Box 611
Brattleboro, VT 05301
    If you do become a wood-burner and wood-

splitter, you will find that the presumably elementary task of making firewood is not always so simple. This author has made a study of the subject, testing the various tools—both hand and mechanical—and techniques that are in use. He delves into some history, as well as some of the science of firewood. Illustrated with line drawings, the book could make your work both easier and more interesting.

Handmade Hot Water Systems

Art Sussman and Richard Frazier
1978/91 pp./$4.95
Garcia River Press
Box 527
Point Arena, CA 95468

The authors tell—and show—you how to turn your wood-burning stove or fireplace into a hot-water source. They also give directions for building your own solar collectors for heating water. Further, they explain how to combine the two systems for a year-round hot-water supply: solar in summer, wood-burning in winter. Included are detailed directions for fabricating such components as the water coils for your wood stove (you twist the copper pipe—filled with sand to prevent crimping—around a jig made of logs to shape the coil). The line drawings illustrate the detailed directions clearly.

WOOD-BURNING WATER HEATER

With a fourteen-gallon capacity, the Magamex is

Drawing details a wood stove water heater (Drawing by Pam Brazier, from *Handmade Hot Water Systems*).

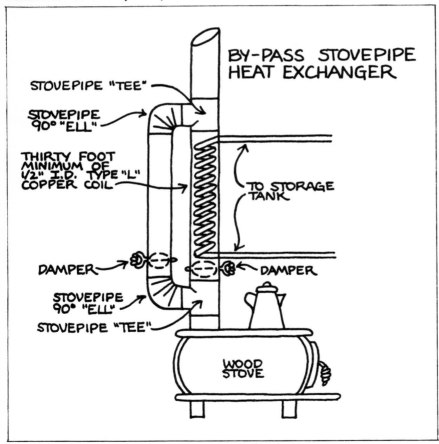

designed to provide a continuous flow of hot water for as long as the wood fire is maintained. The unit is manufactured in Mexico, but it is compatible with plumbing in this country. The heater is priced at $265, but at current utility rates it should pay for itself in several months. Write for literature:

New Atlantis Enterprises
535 Cordova Rd.
Suite 244
Santa Fe, NM 87501

A MAIL-ORDER SOURCE FOR NONELECTRIC TOOLS AND EQUIPMENT

Lehman Hardware began as a retailer serving a large Amish and Swiss Mennonite farming community and since has expanded into a mail-order outlet specializing in nonpowered tools and equipment of various kinds. The firm's catalogs show kitchenware, kerosene lamps, things for the farm, kerosene and LP gas refrigerators, as well as an extensive line of wood- and coal-burning stoves. Write for the *Non-Electric* catalog ($2) and the *Cooking Range* catalog ($1):

Lehman Hardware & Appliances, Inc.
Box 41
Kidron, OH 44636

**Chain Saws: Buying, Using,
Maintaining, Repairing**
Robert A. Ouellette
1981/144 pp./$6.95
TAB Books, Inc.
Blue Ridge Summit, PA 17214

This is a combination buyer's guide and user's manual that covers the major brands on the market, evaluating units from such makers as Poulan, Homelite, McCulloch, and Stihl. The author deals with saw operation in the woods and at the

All my previous attempts at being a handyman ended up with ill-fitting doors, wobbles, squeaks, and a sort of prefabricated finish which now seems to be the hallmark of the do-it-yourselfer. At Eithin, with time, the proper tools, and at least one person around who knew more than I did, I found all this vanished. Concrete-mixing, drain-laying, carpentry, joinery, roofing, plumbing, wiring, guttering, rendering, farming, and even vehicle maintenance soon became part of the daily life. And we did them well. So, I suspect, can everyone else. Yet in our society there is a mystique attached to such crafts which leads 95 per cent of us to declare ourselves incapable of them. This is profoundly untrue.

Robin Clarke, *Building for Self-Sufficiency* (New York: Universe Books, 1977).

woodpile, as well as saw maintenance and troubleshooting, with how-to illustrations.

Chain Saw Service Manual
1980/320 pp./$8.95
Technical Publications Division
Intertec Publishing Corp.
Box 12901
Overland Park, KS 66212

This manual is one of several from its publisher covering various small equipment. It is a guide to maintenance and repair of the major brands of chain saws. Illustrated directions show how to tear down, repair, reassemble, and adjust, with specific troubleshooting procedures, including both engine and chain maintenance.

Directions for proper adjustment (at right) in chain-saw guide groove (from *Chain Saw Service Manual*).

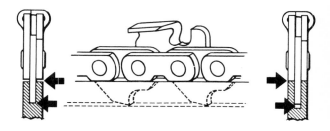

LUMBERING WITH A PORTABLE CHAIN-SAW MILL

The chain saw will not only cut a tree down for you, you can also use it on logs to mill lumber for your house or barn, or for sale. What you need is a portable mill, a rig to which you attach one or two chain saws. Sperber makes four models, priced about $500 and somewhat higher. The model 34, which uses two chain saws, will mill boards up to thirty-four inches wide. Write for literature:

Sperber Tool Works, Inc.
Box 1224
West Caldwell, NJ 07006

GRANBERG CHAIN-SAW MILLS

This firm makes several units for transforming your chain saw into a sawmill. The G-555 Mini-Mill

sells for $64.95. The G-776 Mark III Alaskan, with larger capacity, ranges in price from $124.95 to $190.95 and in size from twenty-four inches to fifty-six inches. The firm also sells manual and electric chain-saw sharpeners, as well as other accessories. Write for catalog:

Granberg Industries, Inc.
200 S. Garrard Blvd.
Richmond, CA 94804

A MAIL-ORDER SOURCE FOR TOOLS FOR THE WOODS

Bailey's is a discount mail-order firm that sells equipment and supplies to loggers. Its catalog lists everything from chain saws to gasoline-powered generators to hand tools to work clothes to various accessories. If you cut your own firewood, there is a large selection of wedges made

Sperber model 34 portable chain-saw mill in operation.

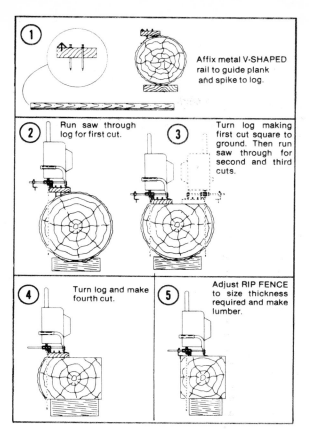

1. Affix metal V-SHAPED rail to guide plank and spike to log.

2. Run saw through log for first cut.

3. Turn log making first cut square to ground. Then run saw through for second and third cuts.

4. Turn log and make fourth cut.

5. Adjust RIP FENCE to size thickness required and make lumber.

of plastic and aluminum in a wide range of sizes at prices from $2 to $12. Write for catalog ($1):

Bailey's, Inc.
Box 550
Laytonville, CA 95454

Professional Timber Falling
D. Douglas Dent
1974/181 pp./$10.95
D. Douglas Dent
Box 905
Beaverton, OR 97005

This book is about the right way and the safe way to fall trees. Whether you are cutting trees for firewood, for lumber to build with, or as a means of earning a living, this is a manual for doing the job. The directions are detailed with drawings

Illustration shows steps in use of Granberg Mini-Mill to saw lumber from log with chain saw (from Granberg brochure).

Photo shows Granberg Mark III Alaskan chain-saw mill in operation.

and photos and cover the use of tools and safety equipment and the falling of trees and bucking them into logs. The author pays particular attention to the use of the chain saw.

Planning for an Individual Water System
AAVIM
1973/156 pp./$6.95
American Association for Vocational Instructional
  Materials
120 Engineering Center
Athens, GA 30602
    Developed in cooperation with the U.S. Department of Agriculture and the Environmental Protection Agency, this book presents all of the basics involved in a water-supply system for home or farm. Sections cover supply assessment, water conditioning for safe use, pumping, piping, electrical installation. The drawings are particularly clear and detailed. (When ordering from publisher, add $1 for postage and handling.)

WELL WATER: POWERED PUMPS, WINDMILLS, HAND PUMPS

In addition to powered water pumps of all kinds, this firm sells both windmills and hand pumps, both of which free you from dependence on electrical or fuel sources. A Dempster six-foot-size mill assembly, complete with pumping engine, costs $775; a twenty-two foot tower adds $655 to the basic cost of the system. With intervening sizes ranging upward, the largest-capacity system is a fourteen-foot windmill, $4,860, combined with a forty-foot tower, $2,140. The firm's hand pumps, designed for use with or without a windmill, come in two models, each with two options, priced from $175.60 to $200.15. Write:

Dempster Industries, Inc.
Box 848
Beatrice, NE 68310

Drawing shows a use of a wedge in falling a tree (from *Professional Timber Falling*).

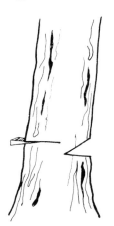
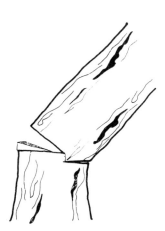

From Dempster Industries: above, fourteen-foot size windmill assembly, below, one of hand-pump models.

HYDRAULIC RAMS: PUTTING PHYSICS TO WORK TO PUMP YOUR WATER

If you have a usable natural water supply close by that can be dammed to provide a head of pressure, but an intervening lower elevation requires pumping to get the water to your tap, you should investigate the hydraulic ram pump. This mechanism employs the pressure of the water coming down a pipe from the source; it then can pump the water back up to a higher elevation. This firm manufactures ram pumps with a variety of capacities and prices. The Davey rams ($192 to $309) have capacities ranging from 3 quarts to 2 gallons per minute up to 6 to 14 gallons per minute; they are designed to use a water-supply head of 3 to 20 feet and deliver to elevations of five to ten times the head, to a maximum of 100 feet. The SU series of rams, with capacities from 3 to 10 gallons per minute to 75 to 350 gallons per minute, range in price from $538 to $3,353. Write:

Rife Hydraulic Engine Mfg. Co.
Box 415
Andover, NJ 07821

A Rife hydraulic ram pump in the SU series.

From the Rife catalog: drawing diagrams how hydraulic ram pumps water from supply source up to use point.

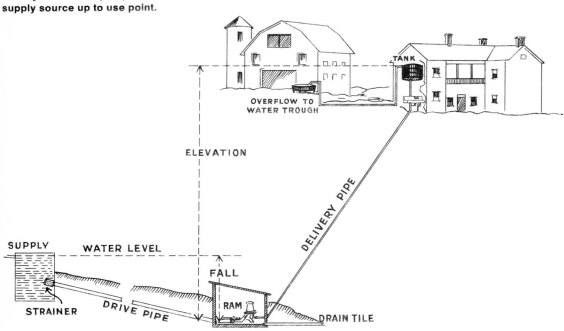

HOW TO DRILL YOUR OWN WATER WELL

If you have no dependable water supply, or the one you have is too costly, here is a do-it-yourself way to drill your own well. The Hydra-Drill can be operated hand held or mounted on a power mast. While the three-horsepower engine turns the drill stem, water pumps into the unit (either from an available pumped supply or from an auxiliary pump) to cool and lubricate the drilling bit and to flush out the cuttings. A basic assembly including ten five-foot drill-stem sections (to get you down into the ground fifty feet) costs $545. You might drill your own well and then pay off your cost by drilling wells for others. Write for literature, including the booklet *How to Drill Your Own Water Well:*

Deeprock Manufacturing Co.
Box 1
Opelika, AL 36802

The Hydra-Drill, shown mounted on a power mast.

HAND-OPERATED CLOTHES WASHER AND WRINGER

The James washer is operated by moving a long handle back and forth in a pendulum arc. The Lovell wringer attaches to the washer and operates with a hand crank. The washer tub is made of stainless steel and has a capacity of up to six large bed sheets. This is the way that Grandma washed clothes, but it is a method that not only uses zero electricity, but also conserves water. Washer, $114.90. Wringer, $59.90. Write for information.

S & H Metal Products
RR 1, Box 57
Topeka, IN 46571

FROM SWEDEN: A TOILET THAT SAVES WATER AND DOLLARS

A standard water-closet toilet, using five gallons of water per flush and flushed sixteen times per

The three-liter If ö: Cascade toilet.

day, will use almost thirty thousand gallons in a year. By comparison, the three-liter Ifö Cascade toilet will use less than five thousand gallons. The water-bill savings result from the efficiency of the Cascade's design and its higher pressure "cascade" flush. Imported from Sweden, the toilet is priced at $368 in white, or $433 in colors. Matching wash basins, pedestals, and bidets by the same manufacturer are also available. Write for literature:

Western Builders Co-op
2150 Pine Drive
Prescott, AZ 86301

The Toilet Papers
Sim Van der Ryn
1978/124 pp./$4.95
Capra Press
Box 2068
Santa Barbara, CA 93120

If you are perplexed by the water cost of your flush toilet, you may already have put bricks in the water closet to reduce the flow volume. Or you may be thinking about the composting toilet— and beyond. In any case, this is a book to turn to if you want to learn about toilets: their history and variations around the world, past and present, and the alternatives to waste-handling systems now in general use. The author, an architect, tells all— including how to build your own composting privy, as well as a variety of gray-water systems. The book is illustrated with photographs, drawings, and detailed building plans.

A TOILET THAT MAKES COMPOST

While a unit like the Ifö Cascade reduces the use of flush water drastically, the Carousel Compost Toilet eliminates water supply completely. And it yields a bonus of compost, which can be used to condition soil when buried under twelve inches of cover. The Carousel takes its name from its waste container, which is divided into four sections that are rotated at six-month intervals. An aerobic process converts the body waste to carbon dioxide and water vapor—which goes out through a vent pipe—and a residue of compost material. The unit comes in two sizes, the larger of which is designed to serve an average family of four on a year-round basis. Priced at upwards of $1,000 or $1,500, the Carousel is a considerable investment, but there are potential dollar savings. Where a septic system is used, the dry composting toilet can reduce the size of the leach field by as much as 50 percent, or in an existing system solve developing capacity problems. And there is the savings in plumbing installation and the water supply itself, as well as the value of the compost material. The unit has the approval of the National Sanitation Foundation. Write for literature and prices:

Enviroscope Corp.
711 W. 17th St., Unit F–8
Costa Mesa, CA 92627

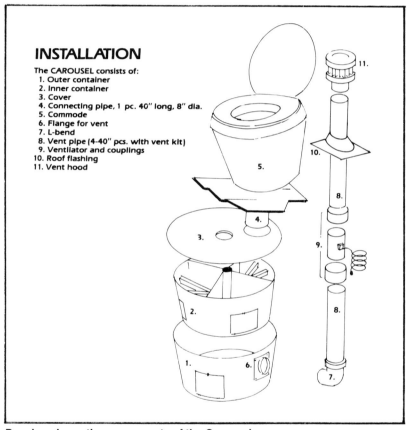

INSTALLATION

The CAROUSEL consists of:
1. Outer container
2. Inner container
3. Cover
4. Connecting pipe, 1 pc. 40" long, 8" dia.
5. Commode
6. Flange for vent
7. L-bend
8. Vent pipe (4-40" pcs. with vent kit)
9. Ventilator and couplings
10. Roof flashing
11. Vent hood

Drawing shows the components of the Carousel Compost Toilet.

Goodbye to the Flush Toilet
Carol Hupping Stoner, Editor
1977/285 pp./$6.95
Rodale Press, Inc.
Organic Park
Emmaus, PA 18049
   A book about the waterless toilet, which pro-

duces compost fertilizer for your garden instead of water bills and clogged pipes and septic fields. The various composting-toilet designs are reviewed, with illustrated explanations of how they work.

Septic Tank Practices
Peter Warshall
1973, 1979/177 pp./$3.95
Doubleday & Co., Inc.
245 Park Ave.
New York, NY 10017

The septic-tank-drain-field system of homesite sewage treatment got a bad name in recent decades, and the current trend has been toward large centralized sewage-treatment systems. The author makes a convincing case for going back the other way. In the process, he explains how septic systems work and how they can be made to work most efficiently in soils appropriate for their use. The text is illustrated extensively with drawings and diagrams.

Excreta Disposal for Rural Areas and Small Communities
Edmund G. Wagner and J. N. Lanoix
1958/187 pp./$5
WHO Publications Center
49 Sheridan Ave.
Albany, NY 12210

Prepared for the World Health Organization by two engineer authors, this manual covers methods, designs, materials, and equipment that range from a large variety of privies to cesspool and septic systems. Emphasis is placed on means for protecting water supply from pollution. The text is clear reading for the layperson, and the book is illustrated throughout by numerous drawings. (WHO publishes a variety of books on water supply, waste management, public health: write for a book listing.)

How to Make Your Car Last a Lifetime
Bob Fendell
1981/189 pp./$7.95
Holt, Rinehart & Winston
521 5th Ave.
New York, NY 10175

The author maintains that there is no recent American-made car that cannot last at least 150,000 miles and that some may be capable of going double that mileage. He tells how to evaluate your present car to determine if it is worth keeping, or how to select a new car for long life, and explains the ways of driving your car that will extend its life. The major portion of the book is devoted to basic maintenance, with clear explanation of the workings of an automobile, including an illustrated appendix that details a car's operating systems. Also covered: modifying for maximum efficiency; refurbishing; and dealing with service-station mechanics.

Why Trade It In?
George and Suzanne Fremon
1976, 1980/247 pp./$5.95
Liberty Publishing Co.
Box 298
Cockeysville, MD 21030

The premise of this book is that your car can serve you for as many as 300,000 miles or more, and that you don't have to be your own mechanic

10,000 MILES

Miles per Gallon **Price per Gallon**

Miles per Gallon	$1.00	$1.15	$1.25	$1.50	$1.75	$2.00	$2.25	$2.50
12	834	958	1042	1250	1458	1666	1874	2082
14	714	822	892	1072	1250	1428	1608	1786
16	624	718	782	938	1094	1250	1406	1562
18	556	638	694	834	972	1112	1250	1388
20	500	574	624	750	874	1000	1124	1250
22	454	522	568	682	796	910	1022	1136
24	416	480	520	624	730	834	938	1042
26	384	442	480	576	674	770	866	962
27.5	**364**	**418**	**455**	**545**	**636**	**727**	**818**	**909**
28	358	410	446	536	624	714	804	892
30	334	384	416	500	584	666	750	834
32	312	360	390	468	566	624	704	782
34	294	338	368	442	514	588	662	736
36	278	320	348	416	486	556	624	694
38	264	302	330	396	460	526	592	658
40	250	288	312	374	438	500	562	624
42	238	274	298	355	416	476	536	596
44	228	262	284	340	398	456	512	568
46	218	250	272	326	380	436	490	544
48	208	240	260	312	364	416	468	520
50	200	230	250	300	350	400	450	500

Chart indexes annual cost of gasoline, based on 10,000 miles of driving, and indicates dollar gains.

to get these years of use and the thousands of dollars that can be saved. The trick is preventive maintenance and effective service and repair by good mechanics. The authors explain how a car works in clear and simple terms, so that you can keep track of the maintenance and so that you can deal confidently with the carefully chosen mechanic. You regularly check such things as oil, coolant, tire pressure, and you spot potential trouble by knowing what to look and listen for—but your mechanic does the work. If you do want to learn to be your own mechanic, this book could be a good starting point for you.

The Inside Story: How You Can Save Fuel and Money with a Healthy Car
1980/40 pp./$1
Fram Corp.
Box 6346
Providence, RI 02940

Prepared by the engineering department of a manufacturer of automotive products, this booklet is a clear and concise guide for the car owner who wants to keep his or her vehicle running well and for a long time. The booklet explains each operating system separately, with drawings for illustration and with simple directions for service, maintenance, and checking for trouble.

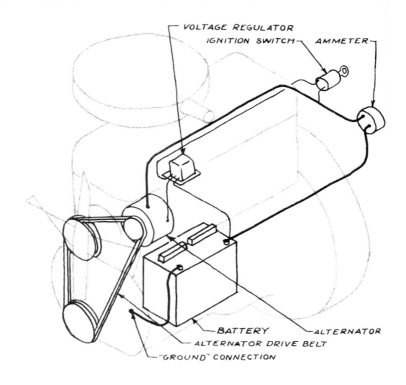

VOLTAGE REGULATOR
IGNITION SWITCH
AMMETER
BATTERY
ALTERNATOR
ALTERNATOR DRIVE BELT
"GROUND" CONNECTION

How to Talk About Your Starter Problems

1. When you turn the ignition key to "start," and you hear nothing but a click, tell your mechanic "The solenoid just goes click; the starter isn't cranking the engine."

2. When the starter goes "rumrumrumrum," but the engine won't start, say "The starter is working but the engine doesn't start."

3. When you hear a loud clashing noise, as of steel against steel, when you operate the starter, say "I've got a starter gear clash."

Sketch illustrates the electrical system. Below are tips for talking with mechanic about starting problems (from *Why Trade It In?*).

SERVICING YOUR CAR'S COOLING SYSTEM

Main Components	Component Function	Service Directions
RADIATOR COOLANT	Circulates through the cooling system, flowing through water jackets in the engine block. Consists of coolant (water and anti-freeze) to prevent winter freezing and summer boiling. Geographic location dictates correct coolant mixture.	Check the coolant level, when the engine is cold, every one to two months, and add a mixture of water and anti-freeze as needed to cover the pipes inside the radiator, or the level called for in your owner's manual. Drain and flush the system every 24,000 miles and add fresh coolant.
FAN BELT	A flexible drive belt that turns the radiator fan and water pump.	Check every other month to make sure belt is not too loose or tight. Replace if belt looks worn, frayed or shiny. Watch alternator light on dashboard which can indicate loose or broken fan belt.
RADIATOR HOSES	Transport coolant between the radiator and the engine.	Check condition of hoses every other month. Replace if they are cracked, brittle, bulgy or overly soft.

From: *The Inside Story: How You Can Save Fuel and Money with a Healthy Car*, by the Fram Corporation, (Providence, R.I.: Fram Corp., 1980).

Complete Car Care Manual
Wade A. Hoyt, Editor
1981/480 pp./$19.98
Reader's Digest
Pleasantville, NY 10570

Everything you need to know about your car: buying a new or used car, operating costs, driving methods for maximum economy. The book explains in detail how the various systems of the car work, and it shows how to maintain and repair them. Tools of all kinds are presented, with directions for their uses. Throughout the book, drawings and photos show each step along the way. Included is a separate seventy-two-page tune-up-data supplement. (If ordering from publisher, add $1.32 for postage and handling.)

DO-IT-YOURSELF AUTO MECHANICS: BOOKS, BOOKLETS

The Consumer Information Center, a federal agency, offers various books and booklets, some of them free. Here is a sampling:

The Backyard Mechanic, Vol. 1
1979/57 pp./$1.60

Common Sense in Buying a Used Car
1979/19 pp./free

Gasoline: More Miles Per Gallon
1977/9 pp./free

Write for catalog:

Consumer Information Center
Department DD
Pueblo, CO 81001

Feedstock	gallons/ton
whey, dry	95
Wheat	85
Corn	84
Buckwheat	83
Raisins	81
Grain sorgum	80
Rice, rough	80
Barley	79
Dates, dry	79
Rye	79
Prunes, dry	72
Molasses, blackstrap	70
Cane sorgum	70
Oats	64
Cellulose (pure)	62
Figs, dry	59
Wood & agricultural residue	47
Sweet potatoes	34
Yams	27
Potatoes	23
Sugar beets	22
Figs, fresh	21
Jerusalem artichokes	20
Pineapples	16
Sugar cane	15
Grapes	15
Apples	14
Apricots	14
Pears	12
Peaches	11
Plums	11
Carrots	10

Corn	2.6 gallons/bushel
Grain sorgum	2.6 gallons/bushel
Wheat	2.7 gallons/bushel
Barley	2.1 gallons/bushel
Potatoes	1.2 gallons/100 lbs.

Upper chart shows approximate alcohol yields from various feedstocks, in gallons per ton of feedstock; lower chart shows yields for five feedstocks, in gallons per bushel (from *How to Make Your Own Alcohol Fuels*).

THINGS FOR TENDING YOUR CAR

A mail-order source for tools and accessories for car maintenance: battery-booster cables, tire pumps, wrenches. A plastic drain-pan unit ($7.25) catches your waste crankcase oil or radiator coolant and at the same time is a container, with handle, to carry it away. Write for catalog:

Brookstone
127 Vose Farm Rd.
Peterborough, NH 03458

AUTO PARTS AND ACCESSORIES

This 242-page catalog offers products for tuning up your ignition system or overhauling your engine. The prices are at discount: shock absorbers (each) at $3.99, $5.98, $8.88. There are separate pages of items for four-wheel-drive vehicles: included are fiberglass or steel bodies and body parts for jeeps. There are tools and accessories of all kinds, as well as repair manuals in a long listing. Write for catalog ($1):

J. C. Whitney & Co.
Box 8410
Chicago, IL 60608

How to Make Your Own Alcohol Fuels
Larry W. Carley
1980/195 pp./$5.95
TAB Books Inc.
Blue Ride Summit, PA 17214

The author provides the basic background information for the home production and use of alcohol fuel. Here is how to design and build a still, as well as how to modify engines so that they will run on alcohol fuel. There are detailed drawings and listings of sources of equipment and supplies. (The author emphasizes that this book is about producing fuel alcohol only, not drinking alcohol: fuel alcohol can contain harmful or fatal contaminants, and the making of drinking alcohol requires a federal permit.)

Making Your Own Motor Fuel
Fred Stetson
1980/192 pp./$6.95
Garden Way Publishing
1538 Ferry Rd.
Charlotte, VT 05445

How to distill your own alcohol for blending to make gasohol. There are details for building and operating a fifty-five-gallon backyard still. An index lists suppliers of material and equipment, and procedures are included for licensing a still with the Bureau of Alcohol, Tobacco and Firearms. (If ordering from publisher, add $1 for postage and handling.)

13
ENERGY

How to Be Your Own Power Company
Jim Cullen and J. O. Bugental
1980/142 pp./$10.95
Van Nostrand Reinhold Co.
Dept. RB
135 W. 50th St.
New York, NY 10020

You can indeed be electrically self-sufficient, the author maintains—and he shows how in this clear, illustrated book with examples from his own experiences. What you do is generate your own electricity with an integrated system you can build yourself. Based on twelve-volt power, your system produces much of its capacity with the alternator in your car by storing electricity in auxiliary batteries that charge while you are using the vehicle: drive during the day, light your house during the night. The system is expandable: with water power from a small dam or with a windmill in your yard. To deal with the twelve-volt power, you use adapters and appliances that are available for twelve-volt current. Such a system can be set up to be completely independent, or it can be teamed with power from your utility company. Even on the smallest scale, your system could keep your lights burning when the next blackout comes by just switching on your storage batteries.

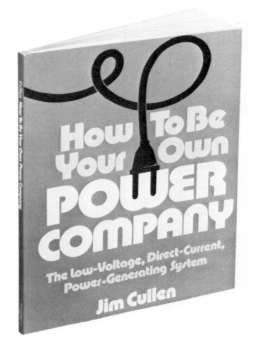

Harnessing Water Power for Home Energy

Dermot McGuigan
1978/112 pp./$4.95
Garden Way Publishing
1538 Ferry Rd.
Charlotte, VT 05445

If you have a stream, brook, or river near your door, you might want to consider generating your own electrical power. This book covers such subjects as: dams, fish passes, spillways, pipelines, waterwheels, impulse wheels, turbines, alternators, and costs, as well as other practical considerations such as potential legal problems. Included are descriptions of working installations and an index of equipment manufacturers. (If ordering from publisher, add $1 for postage and handling.)

HOMEMADE HYDROELECTRIC POWER

It can be done. If you have a stream with the right kind of water flow—and if you have the capital to invest—you could become your own power company. This firm offers the small hydro turbines that can do it. Ask for *Pamphlet A,* which explains what is involved: you fill out its form with data about your water flow and your power plans, and the firm will report back to you. Write:

James Leffel & Co.
426 East St.
Springfield, OH 45501

How to Make Home Electricity from Wind, Water & Sunshine

John A. Keucken
1979/252 pp./$10.95
TAB Books, Inc.
Blue Ridge Summit, PA 17214

Presenting both the fundamentals of electrical power in the home and the specifics of alternate-energy applications, this book is a useful starting point for the beginner. The author covers wind power, water power, and the use of solar cells and collectors for generating current, as well as various methods for storing electrical power. Illustrations accompany the how-to text.

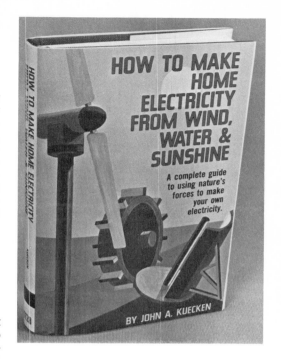

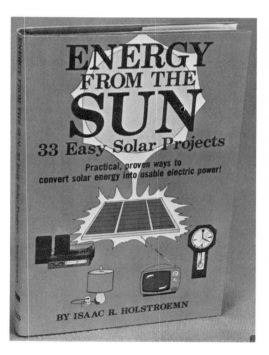

Energy from the Sun—33 Easy Solar Projects
Isaac R. Holstroemn
1981/182 pp./$10.95
TAB Books, Inc.
Blue Ridge Summit, PA 17214

A thorough introduction to the basics of producing solar electric power beginning with an explanation of the makeup of light and its use with the photovoltaic cell and other methods for converting sunlight to electrical energy. All of the tools, instruments, and materials involved, as well as the special techniques employed, are discussed. The author's do-it-yourself projects are small-scale mechanisms—a solar-powered TV unit, radios, an alarm clock that will sound when the sun rises—all of which are designed to turn theory into practical operation. The book is illustrated throughout with detailed line drawings as well as photos.

WINDS OF CHANGE

The predictions did not lie at all in this case. When all the existing nuclear-power facilities were shut down by federal law, the energy crisis became supercritical.

The sudden loss of this large proportion of the country's electrical-power capacity brought brownouts, blackouts, and new highs in utility bills for the consumer.

Legislation for the shutdown came quickly, in response to almost unanimous public outcry. The historic Three-Mile Island accident had been frightening, but this second near meltdown (known as Three Mile Island Two) terrified the population.

With utilities struggling to recoup their losses, the price of electricity went up and up. Consumer conservation redoubled, and the utility companies raised prices further to maintain their profit margins. Manufacturing and service industries were severely affected as their power costs rose. They raised prices accordingly, further unbalancing the economy.

The consequences of the end of nuclear-generated electricity were many.

Coal, once an economical home-heating fuel, became as expensive as the oil it replaced when the utilities further increased their exclusive use of it to make up for the lost nuclear capacity. For a while, it looked as if wood would become the home-heating fuel of choice, but when its use doubled, and then doubled again, prices skyrocketed.

Just as Americans were ready to give up completely on the idea of cheap energy, sunlight and the wind turned out to be the solutions for home heating and lighting and appliances—not cheap, but affordable. During the 1980s, the technology of solar heating and wind-generated electricity had developed rapidly. Now the new demand for these energy resources expanded their use radically during the short span of five years.

By the end of this period of adjustment there were solar collectors everywhere. Roof units were the most obvious: they became part of the scenery, and you saw them wherever you traveled. But there were also the ground arrays in backyards, and the efficient portable window models, which became more common than the air conditioners of the past.

But it was the family wind turbine that produced the most dramatic change in the look of America. Solar collectors seemed to blend in, while wind turbines stuck out. Soon the family spinner was as firmly established an institution as the family car. In the most up-to-date models, the installation was usually located at the opposite end of the roof from the TV antenna. It powered the television set, of course, as well as the lights, washing machine, and other appliances.

It wasn't long before the wind-turbine industry got into the business of styling. You could buy colonial models, featuring quaint wrought-iron weather vanes or sleek, modern ones available in a selection of decorator colors.

Who would have thought it? Back then, at the beginning of the 1980s . . .

OTHER BOOKS FROM TAB ON SOLAR ENERGY AND ITS USES

Build-It Book of Solar Heating Projects
William M. Foster
1980/196 pp./$5.95

How to Make Your Own Solar Electricity
John W. Stewart
1980/168 pp./$5.95

Making & Using Electricity from the Sun
Technical Staff of the Solarex Corp.
1980/144 pp./$5.95

Adding Solar Heat to Your Home
Robert W. Adams
1981/280 pp./$7.95

Write for book catalog:

TAB Books, Inc.
Blue Ridge Summit, Pa 17214

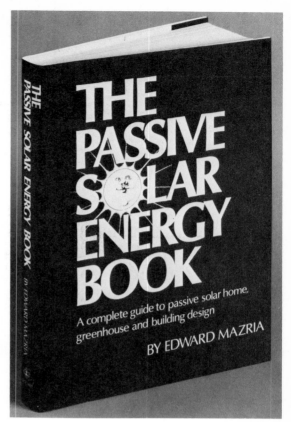

Sun Up to Sun Down—Understanding Solar Energy
Shawn Buckley
1979/166 pp./$6.95
McGraw-Hill Book Co.
1221 Avenue of the Americas
New York, NY 10020

Here is the book that takes the mystery out of solar energy. The author, an engineer, combines his clear text with a stream of simple line drawings to explain it, once and for all: conduction, convection, radiation, thermal storage, passive and active systems, collectors, beadwall, direct gain, diode function, heat exchanger, preheater, thermosyphon, retrofit. Everything is here— pumps, pipes, valves, controls.

The Passive Solar Energy Book
Edward Mazria
1979/435 pp./$14.95
Rodale Press, Inc.
Organic Park
Emmaus, PA 18049

To understand solar energy as a practical and economical home-heating source, it is essential to understand the difference between active and passive systems. *Active* means that other sources

of energy are involved—to run fans, pumps, controls. *Passive* means the system sustains itself—collects the heat from sunlight, stores it, and circulates it by "natural" means. The author, an architect, explains all—in terms a layperson can follow, and with directions and designs that can be used by the do-it-yourselfer. Extensive drawings and photos illustrate the book throughout.

SOLAR EQUIPMENT AND ACCESSORIES

The Solar Components catalog contains sixty-seven pages of products and information for solar applications. There are solar collectors, collector covers, energy-conservation devices, fixed and movable insulations, circulation devices, control equipment, hot-water storage containers. Write for catalog ($3):

Solar Components Corp.
Box 237
Manchester, NH 03105

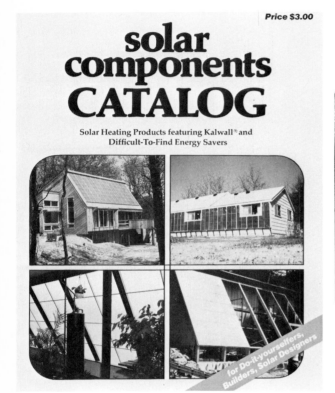

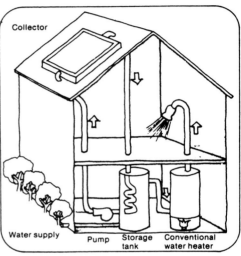

From the Solar Components catalog: drawing illustrates how a solar hot-water heater works in combination with a conventional water heater.

We can reduce or remove the mystery about toilets by understanding how they work. Aside from confronting our mysteries, we can *sometimes* save ourselves the miseries of plumbing disasters and the money that would be spent on plumbing bills. . . . If we learn what the parts in a toilet are supposed to do, then we know a lot. With mechanical problems, once we know what is right, the way things are supposed to work, then we can know how wrong they are when something happens.

Helen McKenna, *The Toilet Book* (San Diego: A Harmless Flirtation with Wealth, 1976).

Build Your Own Solar Water Heater
Stu Campbell with Doug Taff
1978/120 pp./$7.95
Garden Way Publishing
1538 Ferry Rd.
Charlotte, VT 05445
A handbook of plans and directions, this book stresses workable systems that can be built with off-the-shelf plumbing components available locally. The systems can be mixed and matched according to individual needs, and costs are calculated, including pay-back time for your investment. The authors estimate that up to 80 percent of your domestic hot-water costs can be eliminated. (If ordering from publisher, add $1 for postage and handling.)

Thermal Shutters & Shades
William A. Shurcliff
1980/238 pp./$13.95
Brick House Publishing Co., Inc.

34 Essex St.
Andover, MA 01810

Over one hundred uses of shutters and shades to reduce heat loss through windows. These are do-it-yourself ideas, illustrated with drawings. They range from simple adaptations of the common window shade to more elaborate uses of such material as rigid foam. Included are listings of manufacturer sources of materials and hardware.

I had other things which my eye was more upon: as, first, tools to work with on shore; and it was after long searching that I found out the carpenter's chest, which was indeed a very useful prize to me, and much more valuable than a ship-load of gold would have been at that time. I got it down to my raft, even whole as it was, without losing time to look into it, for I knew in general what it contained.

My next care was for some ammunition and arms. There were two very good fowling-pieces in the great cabin, and two pistols; these I secured first, with some powderhorns, and a small bag of shot, and two old rusty swords.

Daniel Defoe, *Robinson Crusoe* (New York: Macmillan, 1962).

SOME COMMON SOLAR-HEATING TERMS

- Active System: a system which uses powered pump or fan to transfer solar heat.
- Passive System: a system which relies on the natural flow of solar heat.
- Solar Collector: the device which catches sunlight and its heat for use in the system.
- Thermosyphon: the process of circulation in which heated water or air rises and is replaced by cooler water or air.
- Retrofit: the installation of a solar system in an existing house.
- Beadwall: a system used with a glassed area of a south-facing wall—sunlight passes in through two layers of glass, the space between which is fan-pumped full of styrofoam beads at night to become an insulator to prevent heat loss.
- Drumwall: a heat-storage system using water-filled drums positioned inside the glassed area of a south-facing wall.
- Trombe Wall: a system in which a masonry wall is positioned immediately inside a glassed area of south-facing wall—the masonry absorbs solar heat, and openings in the top and bottom of the masonry wall produce air circulation.

From Zomeworks: drawing illustrates use of Big Fin collector in solar water-heating system.

ZOMEWORKS: SOLAR-ENERGY AND ENERGY-CONSERVING APPLICATIONS

Zomeworks markets a variety of solar products, ranging from collectors to heat exchangers, reflector-shades, movable insulation, and skylids. The emphasis is on passive solar systems, and the firm sells do-it-yourself plans for several applications. Write for literature:

Zomeworks
Box 712
Albuquerque, NM 87103

Heat Pumps
Dermot McGuigan
1981/160 pp./$6.95
Garden Way Publishing
1538 Ferry Rd.
Charlotte, VT 05445

A heat pump does not produce heat—instead, it moves existing "environmental" heat into your house from such sources as solar systems, well water, seawater, lakes and ponds, and the earth below the frost line. In the summer, you reverse the pump to move the heat out of your house for cooling. The author explains how they work, how much they cost with various heat sources, and he includes a complete catalog of air-source and water-source heat pumps. (If ordering from publisher, add $1 for postage and handling.)

EQUIPMENT FOR SOLAR APPLICATIONS

This firm manufactures the components of refrigerant-charged solar systems: collectors, heat exchangers, duct coils, pumps, and accessories.

Write for catalog:

Refrigeration Research, Inc.
Solar Div.
Box 869
Brighton, MI 48116

The Food and Heat Producing Solar Greenhouse
Bill Yanda and Rick Fisher
1976, 1980/208 pp./$8
John Muir Publications
Box 613
Santa Fe, NM 87501

All of the basics, in detail, about building, buying, and using a solar greenhouse. Four elements are involved in this design: the most efficient collection of solar energy; the storage of solar energy; the reduction of heat loss during and following collection periods; and zone layout for the particular light and temperature requirements of various plants. The benefits of this design are: surplus thermal energy for use to heat an adjoining structure immediately or stored for later use; independence from mechanical heating and cooling devices powered by fossil fuel; and fresh vegetables through the winter season. Included are illustrated directions for building your own solar greenhouse, as well as information about manufacturers of greenhouse units.

The Solar Greenhouse Book
James C. McCullagh, Editor
1978/328 pp./$14.95
Rodale Press, Inc.
Organic Park
Emmaus, PA 18049

Growing food and collecting heat for the home with a solar greenhouse gets a thorough presentation in this book, the work of several contributors. Of particular value are the opening chapters, which not only explain how the green-

house works, but also give a very understandable introduction to solar energy in general. The whole range of greenhouse varieties is covered, with construction details and directions combined with drawings and photos. In addition, there are over one hundred pages on growing crops in the units, as well as a listing of materials, equipment, and manufacturers.

How to Buy Solar Heating without Getting Burnt!
Malcolm Wells and Irwin Spetgang
1978/262 pp./$6.95
Rodale Press, Inc.
Organic Park
Emmaus, PA 18049

This book's subtitle is its best description: *A Consumer's Guide to Choosing, Financing and Installing Solar House-Heating Equipment.* Everything is explained: how it works, what is involved, how it is installed, and how much it costs. There is careful coverage of such aspects as the legal considerations of access to sunlight, as well as contracting with architects, installers, and suppliers. The authors present both advantages and disadvantages and report the results of their survey of homeowners using solar heating. Manufacturers are listed, and there are numerous drawings and photos.

Harrowsmith Magazine
$13.50/8 issues per year
Camden East, Ont.
Canada KOK 1J0

Here is a magazine that would be well worth

American appropriate technologists will begin to regain the ability to use tools and shape their working and living environments. This is an ability that most people in the rural areas of developing countries have not lost, and in that sense we, not they, are underdeveloped.

Ken Darrow and Rick Pam, *Appropriate Technology Sourcebook,* Vol. 1 (Stanford, Calif.: Volunteers in Asia, 1981).

the trip across the border to Canada—by mail—for a regular update on developments in self-sufficiency. The publication covers all aspects of the subject—from alternate-energy resources to growing your own food, do-it-yourself tools, and skills. The articles are written with expertise and style, and the photographs—many in color—are a pleasure for the eye. The magazine regularly devotes its issues to special coverage of specific topics: a recent issue, for instance, carried several articles by the builders of owner-built homes.

The Harrowsmith Sourcebook

James Lawrence, Editor
1979/319 pp./$7.95
Camden House Publishing, Ltd.
Camden East, Ont.
Canada KOK 1J0

This catalog of things and information for self-sufficiency is thick with hundreds of listings of manufacturers, suppliers, book publishers, government information sources. Most of the entries are for Canadian sources, many are for sources in the United States, but all of them are useful to all because our common border is open both ways. You will find everything here from wood stoves to solar-heating equipment, gardening and farming tools, supplies, and know-how.

The Do's & Don't's of Methane

Al Rutan
1975, 1979/160 pp./$9.95
Rutan Publishing
Box 3585
Minneapolis, MN 55403

Methane gas (or biogas) produced from waste material—for lighting, heating, cooking—has a tested technology. Its use, however, has been very limited—except in China, where it has even been tried in the internal-combustion engine. The

TAX CREDITS FOR ENERGY-CONSERVATION, SOLAR AND WIND-POWER INSTALLATIONS

Federal tax-credit incentives can reduce the costs of energy-conservation measures and solar and wind-power installations in your residence. These credits are subtracted from the total amount of income tax you owe—they are not merely deductions that reduce your total taxable income.

Qualifying energy-conservation measures include: insulation; storm or thermal windows or doors; caulking or weather stripping; fuel-efficient furnace burner; device for modifying flue openings to make heating system more efficient; furnace ignition system that replaces a gas pilot light; thermostat with automatic setback; meter that shows cost of energy used.

Conservation measures are eligible only in dwellings built before April 20, 1977. Measures paid for after April 19, 1977, and before January 1, 1986, receive a tax credit of 15 percent of costs up to $2,000. If you spend $1,000 you get $150, if you spend $2,000 you get $300.

Solar and wind-power installations are eligible regardless of the age of the dwelling. Installations paid for after December 31, 1979, and before January 1, 1986, receive a tax credit of 40 percent of costs up to $10,000. If you spend $1,000 you get $400, if you spend as much as $10,000 you get the maximum of $4,000.

Qualifying installations include both active and passive solar systems, and wind-power systems that produce either electricity or mechanical energy.

Federal tax credits cover the costs of equipment and materials as well as installation, but the dollar value of your own labor may not be claimed. For detailed information about the credits, contact your local office of the U.S. Internal Revenue Service.

Many of the states are now also offering similar income-tax credits. For information, contact your state's energy department or tax agency.

author tells how the process works, and how to make and operate a digester safely. There are explanations of the chemistry of the process, as well as drawings and plans. If you live where there is a source of the right waste material, here is a way to cut your gas bill.

Harnessing the Wind for Home Energy
Dermot McGuigan
1978/144 pp./$4.95
Garden Way Publishing
1538 Ferry Rd.
Charlotte, VT 05445

This report on wind power covers power potential, siting, costs, and selection of equipment, with descriptions of various wind systems and products. The author details specific working installations, with illustrations. There is an index of equipment manufacturers and their products. (If ordering from publisher, add $1 for postage and handling.)

Home Wind Power
U.S. Dept. of Energy
1981/208 pp./$10.95
Garden Way Publishing
1538 Ferry Rd.
Charlotte, VT 05445

By generating your own electricity, it is possible not only to reduce your utility bill, but also to earn money by selling excess power when production exceeds your need. Originally prepared by the federal government, this book covers the subject from evaluation of your site to selection, installation, monitoring, and maintenance of a home wind-energy system. (If ordering from publisher, add $1 for postage and handling.)

WIND-POWER
EQUIPMENT

Pan Tech markets several lines of wind turbines for generating electrical power: Winco Wincharger, Sencenbaugh, Dunlite, Enertech. The various units range from a 24-watt battery charger to a 20-kilowatt induction generator. The Enertech line, for example, begins with the model 1800 ($4,250), which has a capacity of 1.8 kilowatts and is designed to produce up to 60 percent of

the electricity used by a typical household when favorably sited for wind. Rotor and generator components are combined and mounted on towers forty feet high and higher. The Enertech model 4000 ($7,400) has a 4-kilowatt capacity. The firm also sells the Sparco wind-powered water pumps ($375), in a piston model which draws water from a well directly below with a lift of thirty-three feet, or in a diaphragm model which will lift water thirteen feet over a horizontal distance of thirty feet. Write for brochures and prices:

Pan Tech Energy Systems
175 W. Main St.
Babylon, NY 11702

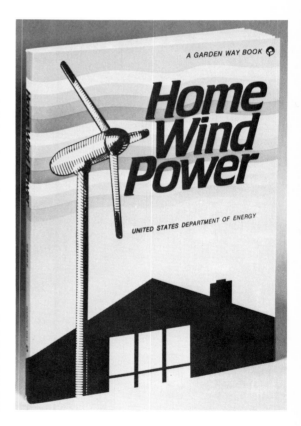

Enertech model 1800 wind turbine, from Pan Tech Energy Systems.

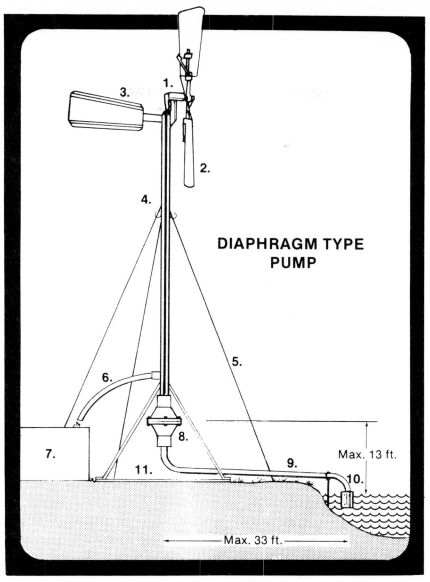

DIAPHRAGM TYPE PUMP

1.

2.

3.

4.

5.

6.

7.

8.

9.

10.

11.

Max. 13 ft.

Max. 33 ft.

Sparco wind-powered diaphragm-type water pump, from Pan Tech Energy Systems.

Wind Power for Farms, Homes and Small Industry

Jack Park and Dick Schwind
1978/232 pp./$18.50
National Technical Information Service
U.S. Department of Commerce
5285 Port Royal Rd.
Springfield, VA 22161

When you have gotten past the initial researching and decided to put the wind to work for you, this is the kind of book you will want to study. It covers the subject thoroughly, with advice on how to evaluate wind-power equipment.

Wind Energy Resource Atlas

Pacific Northwest Laboratory
Volumes 1 through 12
Superintendent of Documents
U.S. Government Printing Office
Washington, DC 20402

Each of the volumes of this atlas covers a specific region of the United States, giving wind and geographic data. There are maps showing topography and power density, as well as data on wind-speed frequency and seasonal variations. Prices for the individual volumes vary between $4.50 and $6.50. Write for a listing of the volumes to determine the one for your area.

Alternate Sources of Energy

$15/6 issues per year
Alternate Sources of Energy, Inc.
107 S. Central Ave.
Milaca, MN 56353

Published by a nonprofit organization, this magazine reports on research and innovation in the use of alternate and renewable energy sources. It deals with solar, wind, and biogas (methane) topics, as well as energy-related inventions and books.

Appropriate Technology Sourcebook, Vol. 1

Ken Darrow and Rick Pam
1976, 1981/320 pp. $5.50

Appropriate Technology Sourcebook, Vol. 2

Ken Darrow, Kent Keller, and Rick Pam
1981/496 pp./$6.50

Appropriate Technology Project
Volunteers in Asia
Box 4543
Stanford, CA 94305

These two volumes present reviews of various books and plans on energy sources, farm implements, workshop tools, agriculture, housing, health care, water supply: vol. 1 covers 385, and vol. 2 offers 500. Published by an organization devoted to technical assistance in Asian countries, the two volumes emphasize the use of basic skills and improvised materials for making tools and equipment. Sample drawings from the reviewed publications illustrate the volumes, and vol. 2 goes beyond the categories of vol. 1 to cover such subjects as fish farming, forestry, and transportation. (When ordering from publisher, add $1 for postage and handling for vol. 1 and $1.50 for vol. 2.)

SELF-SUFFICIENCY INFORMATION

The Farallones Institute is a nonprofit educational organization devoted to research on self-sufficiency and appropriate technology—for both urban and rural settings. It maintains study centers that deal with solar energy, organic agricul-

In primitive societies bartering is often the only game in town, with bartered items used, worn, or eaten; traded for other things; or kept to exchange for future needs. In different civilizations and geographical areas, the objects bartered can be material things such as shells, mats, baskets, cloth, tea, gold dust, skins, or dog teeth; or immaterial things such as songs, dances, planting, or even sorcery techniques.

Constance Stapleton and Phyllis C. Richman, *Barter* (New York: Scribner's, 1978).

ture, waste management, land-use planning, structural design. Write for literature:

Farallones Institute
15290 Coleman Valley Rd.
Occidental, CA 95465

Village Technology Handbook
Volunteers in Technical Assistance
1970/390 pp./$9.95

VITA
3706 Rhode Island Ave.
Mt. Rainier, MD 20822

This manual of small-scale technology is designed for Third-World development, but it is a treasury of how-to information whatever world you live in. Construction plans range from well digging to food storage, sanitation, and hand-powered appliances. There are photos, charts, graphs, and line drawings.

14
HEALTH

How to Be Your Own Doctor—Sometimes
Keith W. Sehnert, M.D., with Howard Eisenberg
1975/353 pp./$5.95
Grosset & Dunlap
51 Madison Ave.
New York, NY 10010

This book will not teach you how to perform surgery, but it will instruct you in dealing with common illnesses and handling medical emergencies. It is written in an informal style and with careful detail that is intended to save you unnecessary visits to the doctor. Within the book is a special 127-page section titled "The Self-Help Medical Guide," which is illustrated with drawings. Especially useful is a chapter devoted to medications, with a list of basic items for your medicine cabinet. Also valuable is a section on pamphlets and booklets available for free or a nominal fee from health and medical associations, governmental agencies, and such sources as pharmaceutical companies.

The Well Body Book
Mike Samuels, M.D., and Hal Bennett
1973/350 pp./$7.50
Random House, Inc.
201 E. 50th St.
New York, NY 10022

A guide to home medical care, this book ex-

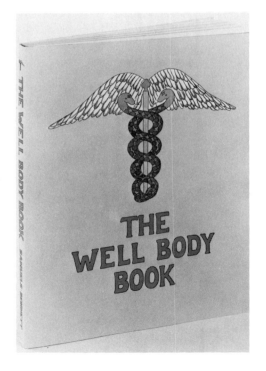

plains the elements of good health, as well as the diagnosis and treatment of common illnesses. The authors discuss how the body heals itself and emphasize the daily practices of preventive self-care. The book is extensively illustrated with drawings.

Medical Self-Care
Tom Ferguson, M.D., Editor
1980/320 pp./$8.95
Simon and Schuster
1230 Avenue of the Americas
New York, NY 10020

This collection of book excerpts and magazine articles—chiefly from *Medical Self-Care* magazine—is a valuable resource for learning about and being self-sufficient about your health. The selections range from such topics as the idea of self-care itself to nutrition, childbirth, drugs, exercise, sexuality, and medical consumerism. Also included are reviews of further information sources.

Take Care of Yourself
Donald M. Vickery, M.D., and James F. Fries, M.D.
1981/370 pp./$9.95
Addison-Wesley Publishing Co.
Jacob Way
Reading, MA 01867

A guide to self-sufficient health and medical care, with detailed directions for home treatment that are combined with a system of evaluation that tells you when you must see a physician. The book begins with a thorough introduction to such aspects of self-care as living habits, preventive measures, dealing with physicians and hospitals, and medications for home care and their costs. The larger part of the book then covers specific conditions, injuries, and illnesses, with detailed explanation of symptoms and treatment.

Taking Care of Your Child
Robert H. Pantell, M.D., James F. Fries, M.D., and Donald M. Vickery, M.D.
1977/409 pp./$7.95
Addison-Wesley Publishing Co.
Jacob Way
Reading, MA 01867

A useful companion volume to *Take Care of Yourself,* this book employs the same system of detailed directions for home treatment combined with a charted evaluation that specifies when a physician must be consulted. The authors provide health and medical directions in introductory chapters that begin with pregnancy and proceed through the child's early years. More than half of the book is devoted to detailed coverage of common illnesses and injuries, their symptoms and treatment.

The Well Baby Book
Mike Samuels, M.D., and Nancy Samuels
1979/402 pp./$9.95
Simon and Schuster
1230 Avenue of the Americas
New York, NY 10020

This large-format book provides an education for parents and a guide for caring for the newborn. The authors are concerned with the whole experience of parents and child. They begin with such background as a short history of how babies faced life in the past and an introduction to the resources of modern medicine. In a way, the book is about babies as survivors. Chapters cover the time of pregnancy, birth, early months, early years. The second half of the book is devoted to treatment of injury and illness, with detailed and illustrated directions for self-help and care by a physician.

Another reason for the book's fascination is that it is natural for us to thrill to any good story in which man overcomes natural obstacles. Have you considered how great Crusoe's victory was? He found a desert island and left it a civilization. He domesticated animals, he established a settlement, and, with the coming of Friday, he started a colonial government. In his small way he is a symbol of man himself, in his ascent from the cave to his present condition.

Clifton Fadiman, afterword to, Daniel DeFoe,
Robinson Crusoe (New York: Macmillan, 1962).

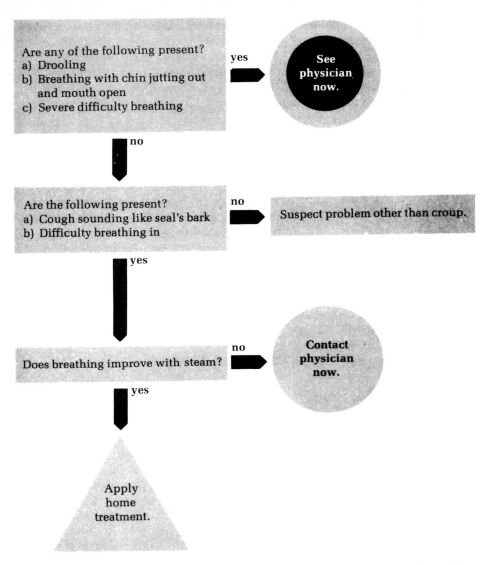

Chart gives directions for evaluating croup symptoms in a child (from *Taking Care of Your Child*).

Within the chart:

Are any of the following present?
a) Drooling
b) Breathing with chin jutting out and mouth open
c) Severe difficulty breathing

— yes → **See physician now.**

— no ↓

Are the following present?
a) Cough sounding like seal's bark
b) Difficulty breathing in

— no → **Suspect problem other than croup.**

— yes ↓

Does breathing improve with steam?

— no → **Contact physician now.**

— yes ↓

Apply home treatment.

Baby and Child Care
Benjamin Spock, M.D.
1945, 1976/666 pp./$8.95
Simon and Schuster
1230 Avenue of the Americas
New York, NY 10020
    Dr. Spock has coached millions of parents through the infancy and early childhood of their offspring. His book covers every aspect of the physical, medical, and emotional needs of the child, answering the hundreds of questions that arise and saving many a phone call or trip to a doctor's office.

MEDICAL KIT: THE FAMILY BLACK BAG

This kit contains stethoscope, blood-pressure cuff, otoscope for examining ears, high-intensity penlight, oral and rectal thermometers, tongue depressors, and a dental mirror. The kit comes with a black vinyl bag, a self-help guide by Keith Sehnert, M.D., and instructions for using the instruments, as well as health-record forms. Sold by a nonprofit health organization, the kit provides the basics for medical care on a continuing basis or in an emergency situation. Price is $83. For information write:

Health Activation Network
Box 923
Vienna, VA 22180

Textbook for Midwives
Margaret F. Myles
1953, 1981/890 pp./$29.75
Churchill Livingstone, Inc.
19 W. 44th St.
New York, NY 10036

This large book comes from Britain, where it is a standard textbook and where midwives are a basic element in the medical-care system. There the midwife provides prenatal care, delivers the baby, and attends to mother and child during the postnatal period: the physician is called in only if there are complications. Thus the book is a complete course and a prime survival resource. The book is illustrated extensively with photos and drawings.

The Family Black Bag: kit includes stethoscope, otoscope, and blood-pressure cuff, sells for $83.

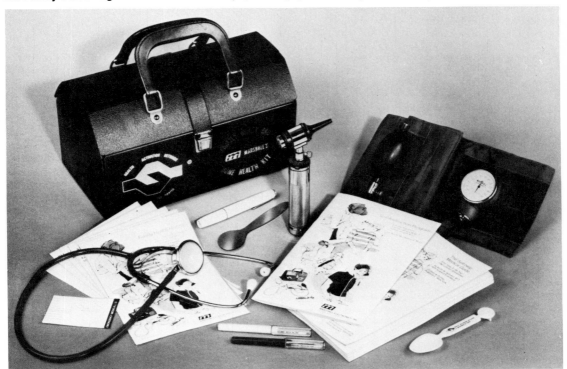

15

TRANSPORTATION

YAMAHA MOTORCYCLES—AND 100-MPG MOTORBIKES

Yamaha sells a full line of motorcycles and trail-bike models—machines that can give you low-cost transportation on the road as well as off. The firm also manufactures three motorbike models designed for high fuel-efficiency travel: Yama-hopper ($479) and Towny ($569), with EPA ratings of over 100 mpg, and Chappy ($659), with a rating of over 85 mpg. Write for literature and dealer/price information:

Yamaha Motor Corp., U.S.A.
Box 6555
Cypress, CA 90630

SUZUKI: MANY MODELS FROM JAPAN

Suzuki offers motorcycles, trail bikes, and motor-bikes in a variety of models. The fuel-tank capacities of three typical bikes suggest a story of gasoline economy: the GS450E motorcycle holds 3.8 gallons, the SP500 trail bike carries 2.4 gallons, and the FA50 motorbike—called the Economy Commuter—has a capacity of only 0.7 gallon. Write for catalog and dealer/price information:

U.S. Suzuki Motor Corp.
3251 E. Imperial Hwy.
Brea, CA 92621

What it is, if I raise something and you make something can't we make a trade? We could send 'em all the politicians they need. For instance, Russia some Senators for some vodka. Little Nicaragua some Congressmen for some bananas. I tell you, the whole fool scheme is worth trying, just for the sake of this last part. If you can furnish the world with our politicians we can compete with 'em.

Will Rogers (Quoted by Constance Stapleton and Phyllis C. Richman, Barter **[New York: Scribner's, 1978].)**

From Yamaha: from top, model IT175J trail bike, $1,599; and Tri-Moto bike, $1,299, shown with accessory carrying racks.

Suzuki FA50 Economy Commuter motorbike, $479.

SELECTING AND ADJUSTING YOUR BICYCLE SEAT FOR COMFORT AND SAFETY

The bicycle saddle is an important part of your bike and your attitude toward commuting. The selection of the proper saddle is a personal choice and is best handled slowly and with care. Try different saddles at a bicycle shop. Your saddle should be positioned so as to allow your leg to be almost straight when your foot is on the pedal. Saddle height is the distance from the pedal axle, in its lowest position (when aligned with the seat tube), to the top of the saddle. One method of determining the correct saddle height for you has been recommended by several experienced bicyclists. They believe that by multiplying the inseam measurement (crotch to floor without wearing shoes) by 1.09, the correct saddle height is found. In adjusting your saddle height, be sure to leave at least 2½ inches of seat post down inside the seat tube. This prevents a loose seat which is unsafe for riding.

From: *The Bicycle: A Commuting Alternative*, by Frederick L. Wolfe (Edmonds, Wash.: Signpost Books, 1979).

HARLEY-DAVIDSON MOTORCYCLES

If the costs of running a car make you think of the motorcycle alternative, one company you will have in mind is Harley-Davidson. In the United States the name has always meant motorcycle. However, while there is the gas savings, some of the firm's eleven models can cost as much as, and more than, some cars. Write for catalog:

Harley-Davidson Motor Co., Inc.
Box 653
Milwaukee, WI 53201

The Bicycle: A Commuting Alternative
Frederick L. Wolfe
1979/154 pp./$7.95
Signpost Books
8912 192nd St. S.W.
Edmonds, WA 98020

The costs of car and public transportation—as well as the value of exercise for physical fitness—have made the bicycle a new kind of tool. It is no longer a plaything. This book tells all about how to use a bike to get to and from your work, whether it is an office or a factory. The author explains the bicycle's advantages and covers ways to handle its disadvantages. A separate chapter deals with biking safely and comfortably in city traffic, and another discusses the bicycle itself—its types, accessories, and maintenance. The book is illustrated with photos and drawings.

BICYCLING: *YOU* MAKE IT GO—AND YOUR GAS COSTS ARE ZERO

If the bicycle is to be your means of transportation—and physical conditioning—for survival, you will want to use a ten-speed bike and be able to maintain and repair it. This firm's mail-order catalog—*The Handbook of Cyclology*—offers almost two hundred pages of parts, accessories, and tools. The section on tools, in particular, makes this a useful source. Write for catalog ($4):

Cycle Goods Corp.
2735 Hennepin Ave.
Minneapolis, MN 55408

16
SOURCES OF INDEPENDENT INCOME

Handbook of Trade and Technical Careers and Training
National Association of Trade and Technical Schools (NATTS)
1980/48 pp./free

Getting Skilled
Tom Hebert and John Coyne
1976, 1980/145 pp./reference

NATTS
2021 K St. N.W.
Washington, DC 20006

This association of trade and technical schools offers its handbook as a directory of accredited schools. The booklet catalogs and describes a variety of work specializations and lists the schools that provide training for them: a free copy is available on request. Its reference book—*Getting Skilled*—is not offered for sale: the association makes the book available to public libraries and to high-school and other career-counseling agencies. The book is a useful source of advice about making your choice of training and selecting a school for it.

How to Find a Job: Start a Business
Donald R. Brann
1981/210 pp./$6.95
Easi-Bild Directions Simplified, Inc.
Box 215
Briarcliff Manor, NY 10510

This is a book of ideas for earning a living in such one-man jobs as carpentry, plumbing, and bricklaying. Its chapters cover such possibilities as house remodeling, chimney repair, and burglarproofing. The idea is to develop your skills for a small-scale service business. This book refers the reader to the author's previously published series of how-to books for detailed introductions to the various skills involved. Write for catalog.

Handbook for Prospectors
Richard M. Pearl
1943, 1973/472 pp./$27.50
McGraw-Hill Book Co.
1221 Avenue of the Americas
New York, NY 10020

Revised and rewritten many times since its origin early in the century as the work of M.W. von Bernewitz, and now in its fifth edition, this book covers all of the basics of prospecting. The text is illustrated with both drawings and photos to show the reader the way to minerals, metals, chemicals, and gemstones. There are chapters on elementary geology and mineralogy, as well as the specific targets of prospectors—from gold and silver and uranium to fertilizers, abrasives, ceramic, and metallurgical materials. If you have thought about going all the way back to the land to earn your bread by extracting what lies beneath it, this is the kind of handbook you will need to start on your way.

Earning Money without a Job
Jay Conrad Levinson
1979/204 pp./$4.95
Holt, Rinehart & Winston
521 5th Ave.
New York, NY 10175

This is a book of ideas for ways to self-employed earnings. The author spells out hundreds of possibilities and tips. One main piece of advice is to combine several small-scale incomes. His suggestions range from sales opportunities—including mail-order selling from your home—to diving for golf balls on the local course. Many of his ideas involve no capital, some a minimum amount. If you have a vehicle—car, van, truck, jeep—he has suggestions for turning it into a money-maker. Throughout, the emphasis is on work that requires little skill, or skills that can be learned quickly.

The Incredible Secret Money Machine
Don Lancaster
1978/159 pp./$5.95
Howard W. Sams & Co., Inc.
4300 W. 62nd St.
Indianapolis, IN 46268

If you have a skill or skills, and you are working for somebody else—or between "workings-for-somebody-else"—the heart of your economic-survival problem may be that you should be working for yourself. The author talks about such skills as computer programmer, potter, writer—and, by extension, plumber, sign painter, auto mechanic, bookkeeper, portrait painter. His premise is that you can earn a happier and more secure living with your work if you do it as a one-person business. He concentrates on the nuts and bolts of this kind of adjustment, and with enough humor to make all things seem possible.

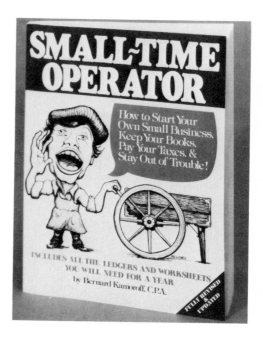

Small-Time Operator

Bernard Kamoroff
1976, 1981/190 pp./$7.95
Bell Springs Publishing
Box 640
Laytonville, CA 95454

This book, written by a certified public accountant, is one to start with if you are thinking about going into business for yourself. He begins with advice and ideas about starting a small business, and then shows you how to run it. He covers location and financing, federal and state regulations, insurance, bookkeeping, credit sales, expansion, partnership, incorporation, taxes. The end section of the book provides the various ledgers and forms needed for a year of bookkeeping. (If ordering from publisher, add $1 for postage and handling.)

Working for Yourself

Geof Hewitt
1977/320 pp./$7.95
Rodale Press, Inc.
Organic Park
Emmaus, PA 18049

If self-sufficiency through self-employment is on your mind, here is a book that could show you the way. The author bases this book on the experiences of people who earn their living with their own business, trade, or profession—many of them in farming.

Barter

Constance Stapleton and Phyllis C. Richman
1978/195 pp./$6.95
Charles Scribner's Sons
579 5th Ave.
New York, NY 10017

Barter is the "purchasing" of goods or services with your own goods or services, instead of money. You don't have to wait until you run out of money—or it ceases to exist—to practice barter. For instance, if caring for your young child prevents you from taking a job, and you are an accomplished piano player, you might trade piano lessons for someone's baby-sitting services. Or, if you have a surplus crop in your backyard garden, you trade carrots and tomatoes with a mechanic for a tune-up of your car. The possibilities are almost endless, and this book tells you how to make the most of them.

Let's Try Barter

Charles Morrow Wilson
1960, 1976/184 pp./$4.95
Devin-Adair Co.
143 Sound Beach Ave.
Old Greenwich, CT 06870

Bartering goods and services goes way back to the beginnings of human affairs; money exchange is a relatively new thing. This book traces the history of barter and brings it up to date with accounts of current practices. The trading post, for instance, is still very much alive, particularly in the form of swap shops, and bartering in organizations is as widespread as bartering arranged by agencies for a fee. Individuals more and more are practicing bartering, and the author tells all about why and how it is done, giving many specific examples in detail. An example on a larger scale than, say, trading potatoes for hardware: you own a piece of real estate that has appreciated greatly in value with inflation; you want to buy property in another state—perhaps a farm, or retreat land—so you trade your real estate for the desired property and thus legally avoid a capital-gains tax.

Raising Earthworms for Profit

Earl B. Shields
1959/127 pp./$3.50
Shields Publications
Box 669
Eagle River, WI 54521

Earthworms have a market as bait for fishermen, as breeding stock for those who want to grow them, and for gardeners and farmers who use them for soil improvement. Here is a book that shows you how to get into this business, with all the details you need for growing and marketing your crop. On the other hand, you might simply want to grow earthworms for your own use, on a fishhook or in your garden. (If ordering from publisher, add $.95 for postage and handling.)

Mail Order Moonlighting

Cecil C. Hoge
1976/399 pp./$7.95
Ten Speed Press
Box 7123
Berkeley, CA 94707

Here is a thorough presentation of how you can earn your way with a mail-order business in your own home. The book covers such aspects as how to select the products you will sell, how much to pay for them, and how to price them for sale.

WHEN THE SPRING MEETS THE FALL ON THE FOURTH OF JULY

The climate of the northern states was transformed. In a band from Washington and Oregon across the country to New England, average annual temperatures fell four degrees over twenty years.

Mercifully, the transformation was gradual. Temperature averages went down in small increments, and there were some years when they went back up slightly. But by the mid-1990s, the overall climate was three degrees colder, and the mercury continued to fall.

The climate change was worldwide, of course, though not uniform. There were complex transformations in different parts of the globe, some of them unexpected. Scientists could not agree on the reasons for the deterioration, and at the end of the century the only common view was that the trend was likely to continue indefinitely. The arctic regions were expanding toward the equator, and this was intensifying the effects of the climate change.

The most noticeable effects were in altered local weather patterns and shorter growing seasons. In the far northern states of the United States, winters became increasingly more severe and snow accumulations set records on top of records for a decade. Then, toward the end of the century, the region began experiencing almost snowless winters while cities like New Orleans had frequent snowfalls.

The shortened growing seasons affected the northern states first, and by 1995 agriculture had ceased in the Dakotas, Minnesota, Wisconsin, and Michigan, as well as in New York and most of New England.

Northern populations began migrating southward long before that time. Chicago and Detroit became Siberian cities and their industries vanished. Ice blocked shipping on the Great Lakes and St. Lawrence Seaway for two-thirds of the year. New York and Boston lingered on as major population centers for many years, but Seattle had become a ghost town by the end of the century.

Alaska became a primitive arctic outpost, peopled only by Indians, Eskimos, and pipeline workers. Canada's dwindling population emigrated, many coming to the United States, until strict quotas were set.

There were no glaciers in sight yet, but by the beginning of the twenty-first century the population of the United States had become concentrated in the southern states. The climate change brought great social and economic changes with it. The Americans who managed the adjustment best were those who had migrated early and established themselves and their skills in the middle states of the country, where agricultural lands could support expanded populations. In the states of the Gulf region and the east and west coasts, crowding made survival grim for even the most adept . . .

The #1 Home Business Book
George and Sandra Delany
1981/168 pp./$4.95
Liberty Publishing Co.
Box 298
Cockeysville, MD 21030

The heart of this book is its 100 pages of itemized ideas—400 of them—for starting your own business. The ideas range from dog-obedience training and auto tune-ups to packing box lunches for local business offices and neighborhood housecleaning. Each suggestion is presented with the basics involved, enough to get your mind working to test your interest and aptitude for the business. All of the ideas are one-person operations and all can be pursued at or from your household. The opening chapters of this valuable book are an introduction to the practical aspects of turning a dream into income-producing reality, working for yourself instead of at a job: the starting-up process, advertising and marketing, keeping your books.

School at Home
Darcy Williamson
1979/91 pp./$9.95
Maverick Publications
Drawer 5007
Bend, OR 97701

What if you don't want to send your child to a public or private school? What if there are no longer any schools available? You can teach your child yourself, at home, and here is a guide for doing it. The author discusses home instruction thoroughly, covering both the advantages and disadvantages. Included is a chapter on some of the home-study correspondence programs available, as well as a chapter with a state-by-state listing of laws regulating compulsory school attendance.

Consumer Reports
$12/11 monthly issues plus December-issue *Buyer's Guide*

Consumer Reports Buyer's Guide
$3.50/annual

Consumers Union News Digest
$36/24 issues per year

Consumers Union
256 Washington St.
Mt. Vernon, NY 10550

Consumers Union has a long-standing reputation for objective reporting about the retail marketplace. Its publications are a sound investment of time and/or money for self-sufficiency. The monthly *Consumer Reports,* in magazine format, devote each issue to special coverage on some single topic (saving energy costs in the home, for instance), along with rating reports on various products. The *Buyer's Guide* is an annual report, with ratings of products by category. The *News Digest* presents extracts from newspapers and magazines to keep you current in a variety of categories important to the individual consumer (automotive safety, banking and personal finance, taxes, product safety, and a broad spectrum of other topics). All of these publications are available in most local libraries.

We must dare to think "unthinkable" thoughts. We must learn to explore all the options and possibilities that confront us in a complex and rapidly changing world. We must learn to welcome and not to fear the voices of dissent. We must dare to think about "unthinkable things" because when things become unthinkable, thinking stops and action becomes mindless.

James W. Fulbright, speech in U.S. Senate (1964)

PART

3

FACING AND SURVIVING THE WORST

Life After Doomsday: A Survivalist Guide to Nuclear War and Other Major Disasters

Bruce D. Clayton
1980/185 pp./$8.95
Dial Press
c/o Doubleday & Co.
Mail Order Dept.
500 Franklin Ave.
Garden City, NY 11530

Civil-defense preparedness in the United States has declined almost to nonexistence after a period of heightened awareness following World War II. At the same time, our chief adversary in the nuclear confrontation, the Soviet Union, has developed elaborate and costly preparations. The Chinese appear to have based their programs largely on self-sufficiency measures, while the completely neutral Swiss have perhaps the most extensive civil-defense system of all. In this country the survivalism movement has been developing a kind of do-it-yourself approach, which in some ways takes the form of the posse or vigilante solutions to the weakness or absence of governmental authority and law and order in the

Drawing below illustrates radiation shielding provided by the interior of a wood-frame house (*PF* stands for "protection factor"). The greatest shielding is at the lowest level of the basement corner, represented by the figure of a person lying down. Inset diagram at left shows overall *PF* values within the structure. (from *Life After Doomsday: A Survivalist Guide to Nuclear War and Other Major Disasters*)

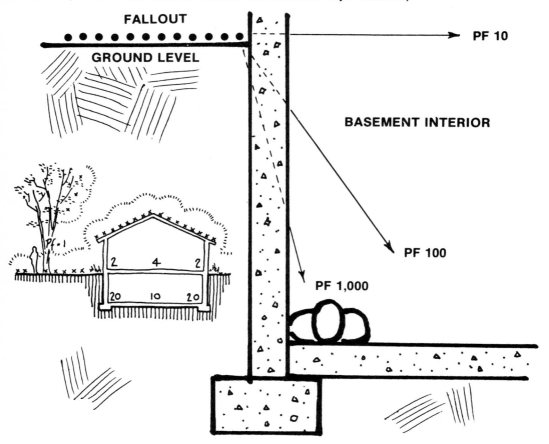

Old West of the 1800s. As the author of this book points out, survivalism has become a multi-million-dollar market for suppliers of storage foods, medical supplies, survival literature, and equipment—with the emphasis on radiation-detection devices, and personal weapons of all kinds, particularly firearms that have military applications. This manual provides a thorough introduction to survivalism and preparedness for both natural and man-made disasters. Nuclear war is the focus here, and a large part of the text and illustrations is devoted to a detailed explanation of all aspects of the subject. The author's premise is that—contrary to widespread popular belief—most of the population would live through a nuclear attack. The long-term survivors will be those who are prepared for the aftermath. Shelters, food and medical supplies, equipment of all kinds, self-defense weapons and methods are covered.

SURVIVAL PUBLICATIONS AND CONSULTATION SERVICES

This publisher specializes in books, bibliographies, and article collections on the subject of "retreating." The term generally refers to a home or other structure prepared as a refuge for a time of crisis. But the topics covered range from retreat siting (including the use of earth-sheltered building design) to food and water supply, nuclear safety, tools and equipment, guns and accessories. The firm also offers consultation services on survival questions and retreat design. Write for brochure:

Stephens Press
Drawer 1441
Spokane, WA 99210

Below, map indicates military target areas in the United States. Solid black represents primary targets; the open circles show secondary targets. (from *Life After Doomsday: A Survivalist Guide to Nuclear War and Other Major Disasters*)

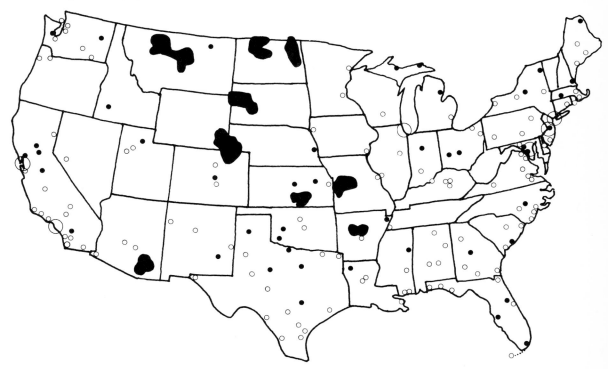

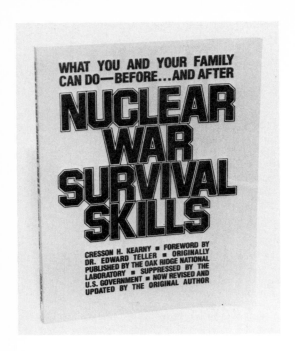

Nuclear War Survival Skills
Cresson H. Kearny
NWS Research Bureau
1980/232 pp./$9.95
Caroline House Publishers, Inc.
920 W. Industrial Drive
Aurora, IL 60506

Originally researched and written while the author was on the staff of the Oak Ridge National Laboratory, this manual is a valuable how-to guide for do-it-yourself civil defense. Included is a clear presentation of the hazards of nuclear weapons. The author gives directions and plans for building fallout shelters and making ventilation and sanitation equipment for them. There are chapters on providing food, water, light, and medical care, as well as improvised clothing and protective items. The how-to plans include a hand-made fallout meter, as well as expedient blast shelters. Photos and drawings illustrate the book throughout.

FEMA: WASHINGTON'S NEWEST NAME FOR CIVIL DEFENSE

The Federal Emergency Management Agency is the current name for our national civil defense program. Dating back to WWII when it was called

Drawing illustrates directions for making a siphon-operated water-supply system for a belowground fallout shelter (from _Nuclear War Survival Skills_).

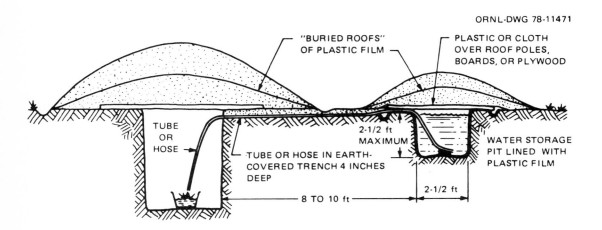

ORNL-DWG 78-11471

the Office of Civil Defense, the program later was reorganized and redesignated as the Defense Civil Preparedness Agency, a branch of the U.S. Department of Defense. The current agency offers the public a selection of informational material. *Protection in the Nuclear Age,* a 68-page booklet published in 1977 by the Defense Civil Preparedness Agency, covers the basics of the subject. Also available from FEMA are six pamphlets that present directions and plans for building home fallout and blast shelters:

Drawing illustrates a lean-to fallout shelter for basement location (from *Home Fallout Shelter/H-12-F*).

- **Home Fallout Shelter** (H−12−C/4 pp./1980): use of common lumber and concrete blocks for a permanent structure in a basement corner

- **Home Fallout Shelter** (H−12−E/4 pp./1980): for basement location, a wooden unit hinged to a wall is tilted up to rest on a stacked brick or concrete-block wall and unit is filled with blocks for overhead protection

- **Home Fallout Shelter** (H−12−F/4 pp./1980): a lean-to design for basement location, prebuilt wooden components are filled with bricks or concrete blocks for radiation shielding

- **Home Shelter** (H−12−1/8 pp./1980): an outside underground concrete shelter for homes without basements, designed for fallout, blast and thermal protection

- **Aboveground Home Shelter** (H−12−2/8 pp./1980): constructed of concrete blocks and designed for fallout and limited blast protection, this unit can also be used as a tool shed or workshop

- **Home Blast Shelter** (H−12−3/8 pp./1981): an outside underground concrete shelter designed for protection from fallout, blast and thermal effects

Federal Emergency Management Agency
Office of Public Affairs
Washington, DC 20472

In an age characterized by leisure, most people depend too much on push buttons, time clocks, and other indoor conveniences for their daily survival. Consequently, they do not develop the abilities or skills which could enable them to survive stresses encountered in the wilds. History is full of war-ruined civilizations that have fallen from indoor luxury to outdoor desperation in only a few hours.

Editor's Note, Larry Dean Olsen, *Outdoor Survival Skills* (Provo, Utah: Brigham Young University Press, 1980).

Drawing illustrates outside underground concrete blast shelter (from *Home Blast Shelter/H-12-3*).

THE BEST DEFENSE?

It all began with an incident on the East German border. Communist artillery training on a gunnery range sent several live rounds just over the boundary line. A village was hit, and several West German civilians were killed. A week later the supposed error was duplicated from the western side, though it has never been learned exactly where those rounds originated.

Three days after that, a dozen American soldiers were reported killed by machine-gun fire while on patrol along the border at night. Before morning, a salvo of artillery flew over the line, supposedly aimed at the East German unit responsible for the killings.

A week of relative calm ensued while diplomats talked. That truce was tested by a series of sniping incidents, and finally broken when a Russian tank unit crossed the border claiming pursuit of a West German patrol for violating Communist territory. The Russian tanks, cut off by American armor, refused to surrender, and an overnight standoff developed.

At dawn, three columns of Russian tanks crossed the border, joined the surrounded unit, and set up positions on West German soil. The NATO allies delivered an ultimatum: the intrusion would be considered an act of war unless the Russians withdrew within four hours. The Russians stayed, and exactly one minute into the fifth hour a tactical nuclear weapon was fired into the massed tanks.

That night Russian missiles struck Detroit and St. Louis with nuclear warheads, leveling both cities. The United States retaliated with nuclear strikes against Stalingrad and Kiev.

The deadly exchange of weaponry and its aftermath was entirely out of proportion to the border incident that precipitated it. Years of competition and confrontation between East and West had set the scene, of course. But there was no real warning for any of the victims—neither the soldiers in the tanks nor the civilians in the four cities—because no one ever truly expected it to happen.

The populations of Kiev and Stalingrad at least had the limited benefit of an elaborate civil-defense program.

In the United States at that time there was no such program, on any meaningful scale. Thousands died immediately from the blasts in Detroit and St. Louis, with thousands dying in the following days because medical care was not delivered to them.

Populations near the blasts and in the path of the resulting fallout suffered high casualty rates in deaths and radiation sickness because public fallout shelters were not available and few were educated in the use of improvised shelters.

Even with the whole of the nation mobilized for the relief of the affected states, there were many deaths due to starvation and epidemic disease. Existing relief programs simply were not organized on a scale large enough and practical enough to deal effectively with the massive numbers of victims.

Americans who had made private preparations for catastrophe were noteworthy among the survivors. They knew how to shelter from fallout and they had food and medical supplies to fall back on. Rigid martial law—rather than civil disorder—was an immediate consequence of the nuclear attacks. Those who had prepared armed retreats found that their strongholds isolated them from relief and recovery programs . . .

I do not believe that civilization will be wiped out in a war fought with the atomic bomb. Perhaps two thirds of the people of the earth might be killed, but enough men capable of thinking, and enough books, would be left to start again, and civilization would be restored.

Albert Einstein, in *Atlantic Monthly* (1945)

The Effects of Nuclear War

Office of Technology Assessment,
Congress of the United States
1979/151 pp./$5.50
(S/N 052-003-00668-5)
Superintendent of Documents
U.S. Government Printing Office
Washington, DC 20402

If you are going to take steps to be prepared for survival, this is one of those books you must read. Written for our representatives in the Congress, the book summarizes what actually can be expected to happen to us if there is nuclear war. Projections of attacks by the Soviets are presented with detailing that ranges from numbers of short-term and long-term dead and injured to prospects for local and national recovery. Such cities as Detroit and Philadelphia are involved in the scenarios. Civil-defense methods and strategies are covered, as are such practical measures as fallout-shelter design. The book is illustrated with photos, drawings, and maps.

These native American people were corn farmers who moved across the plains to the base of the Rocky Mountains and established small towns about 900 A.D. They settled in an area with tall grass on the hills where they hunted deer, and woods in the valleys where they raised corn. Then a remarkably long drought began, and within about twenty years the tall grass gave way to shorter varieties and the forests dried up except for some willow and cottonwood trees along the streams. The deer that had comprised about 97 percent of the Mill Creek people's diet disappeared, and bison, a grazing animal, became the meat staple. Food was less plentiful, and farming settlements were forced out of existence to the west. "That drought lasted 200 years," says Reid Bryson. "Clearly two hundred years of drought in the 'breadbasket' of North America is possible."

Stephen H. Schneider with Lynne E. Mesirow, *The Genesis Strategy: Climate and Global Survival* (New York: Plenum Press, 1976).

Drawing and its caption explains how to adapt the basement of a stone house as a fallout shelter (from *The Effects of Nuclear War*).

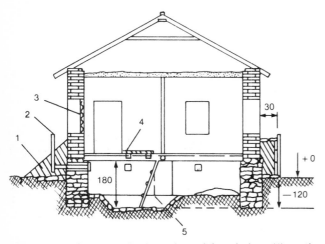

Basement of a stone house adapted for shelter: (1) earth embankment; (2) exhaust duct; (3) curtains on windows; (4) airtight hatch; (5) recessed pit. Material requirements: lumber, 0.5 m³; nails, 1 kg; earth, 3 to 5 m³; labor, 15 to 29 hours (man-hours).

Some structures, particularly those designed for the purpose, offer substantial protection against direct nuclear effects (blast, thermal radiation, ionizing radiation, and related effects such as induced fires). Since blast is usually the most difficult effect to protect against, such shelters are generally evaluated on blast resistance, and protection against other direct effects is assumed. Since most urban targets can be destroyed by an overpressure of 5 to 10 psi, a shelter providing protection against an overpressure of about 10 psi is called a blast shelter, although many blast shelters offer greater protection. Other shelters provide good protection against fallout, but little resistance to blast—such "fallout shelters" are discussed in the next section. Blast shelters generally protect against fallout, but best meet this purpose when they contain adequate life-support systems. (For example, a subway station without special provisions for water and ventilation would make a good blast shelter but a poor fallout shelter.)

Nuclear explosions produce "rings" of various overpressures. If the overpressure at a given spot is very low, a blast shelter is unnecessary; if the overpressure is very high (e.g., a direct hit with a surface burst), even the best blast shelters will fail. The "harder" the blast shelter (that is, the greater the overpressure it can resist), the greater the area in which it could save its occupants' lives. Moreover, if the weapon height of burst (HOB) is chosen to maximize the area receiving 5 to 10 psi, only a very small area (or no area at all) receives more than 40 to 50 psi. Hence, to attack blast shelters of 40 to 50 psi (which is a reasonably attainable hardness), weapons must be detonated at a lower altitude, reducing the area over which buildings, factories, etc., are destroyed.

The costs of blast shelters depend on the degree of protection afforded and on whether the shelter is detached or is in a building constructed for other purposes. However, a large variation in costs occurs between shelters added to existing buildings and those built as part of new construction. The installation of shelters in new construction, or "slanting," is preferable, but it could take as long as 20 years for a national policy of slanting to provide adequate protection in cities.

An inexpensive way to protect population from blast is to use existing underground facilities such as subways, where people can be located for short periods for protection. If people must remain in shelters to escape fallout, then life-support measures requiring special preparation are needed.

Other lethal nuclear effects cannot be overlooked. Although, as noted above, blast shelters usually protect against prompt radiation, the shelters must be designed to ensure that this is the case.

Another problem is protection against fallout. If a sheltered population is to survive fallout, two things must be done. First, fallout must be prevented from infiltrating shelters through doors, ventilation, and other conduits. Other measures to prevent fallout from being tracked or carried into a shelter must also be taken. More important, the shelter must enable its occupants to stay inside as long as outside radiation remains dangerous; radiation doses are cumulative and a few brief exposures to outside fallout may be far more hazardous than constant exposure to a low level of radiation that might penetrate into a shelter.

Since radiation may remain dangerous for periods from a few days to several weeks, each (blast) shelter must be equipped to support its occupants for at least this time. Requirements include adequate stocks of food, water, and necessary medical supplies, sanitary facilities, and other appliances. Equipment for controlling temperature, humidity, and "air quality" standards is also critical. With many people enclosed in an airtight shelter, temperatures, humidity, and carbon dioxide content increase, oxygen availability decreases, and fetid materials accumulate. Surface fires, naturally hot or humid weather, or crowded conditions may make things worse. If unregulated, slight increases in heat and humidity quickly lead to discomfort; substantial rises in temperature, humidity, and carbon dioxide over time could even cause death. Fires are also a threat to shelterees because of extreme temperatures (possibly exceeding 2,000 degrees F) and carbon monoxide and other noxious gases. A large fire might draw oxygen out of a shelter, suffocating shelterees. World War II experience indicates that rubble heated by a firestorm may remain intolerably hot for several days after the fire is put out.

Fallout protection is relatively easy to achieve (in contrast to blast protection). Any shielding material reduces the radiation intensity. Different materials reduce the intensity by differing amounts. For example, the thickness (in inches) of various substances needed to reduce gamma radiation by a factor of 10 is: steel, 3.7; concrete, 12; earth, 18; water, 26; wood, 50. Consider an average home basement that provides a protection factor (PF) of 10 (reduces the inside level of radiation to one-tenth of that outside). Without additional protection, a family sheltered here could still be exposed to dangerous levels of radiation over time. For example, after 7 days an accumulated dose of almost 400 rems inside the basement would occur if the radiation outside totaled 4,000 roentgens. This could be attenuated to a relatively safe accumulation of 40 rems, if about 18 inches of dirt could be piled against windows and exposed walls before the fallout begins. Thirty-six inches of dirt would reduce the dose to a negligible level of 4 rems.

Over the years, home fallout shelters have received considerable attention, with the government distributing plans that could be used to make home basements better shelters. Such plans typically involve piling dirt against windows and (if possible) on floors above the shelter area, stocking provisions, obtaining radios and batteries, building makeshift toilets, and so forth. Such simple actions can substantially increase protection against radiation and may slightly improve protection against blast. However, few homes in the South and West have basements.

With adequate time, instructions, and materials, an "expedient" shelter offering reasonable radiation protection can be constructed. This is a buried or semiburied structure, shielded from radiation by dirt and other common materials. Expedient shelter construction figures prominently in Soviet civil defense planning.

From: *The Effects of Nuclear War*, by the U.S. Congress, Office of Technology Assessment (Washington, D.C.: U.S. Government Printing Office, 1979).

But, then, what other form of energy is so unsafe that it is uninsurable and requires a law (the Price-Anderson Act) that limits liability and prevents the injured, sick, and damaged from recovering compensation to the full limit of the assets of the utility or reactor manufacturers? What other form of energy produces wastes that are lethal for some 250,000 years and for which there is no safe, proven storage technology? What other form of energy can produce a disaster rendering hundreds of square miles, or more, of this country uninhabitable?

Ralph Nader, introduction to, Environmental Action Foundation, *Accidents Will Happen: The Case against Nuclear Power* (New York: Harper & Row, 1979).

Expedient Shelter Handbook
George A. Cristy and Cresson H. Kearny
1974/250 pp./$10.60
National Technical Information Service
U.S. Dept. of Commerce
5285 Port Royal Rd.
Springfield, VA 22161

Prepared at the Oak Ridge National Laboratory, this manual presents building plans for fifteen expedient shelters. Such shelters are designed primarily for protection from fallout and are structures that can be built within forty-eight hours by unskilled labor using available materials and equipment. The shelters are improvised with such materials as earth, doors, and plastic sheeting. Plastic garbage bags and cloth pillowcases are used for sandbags. Line drawings detail the building directions.

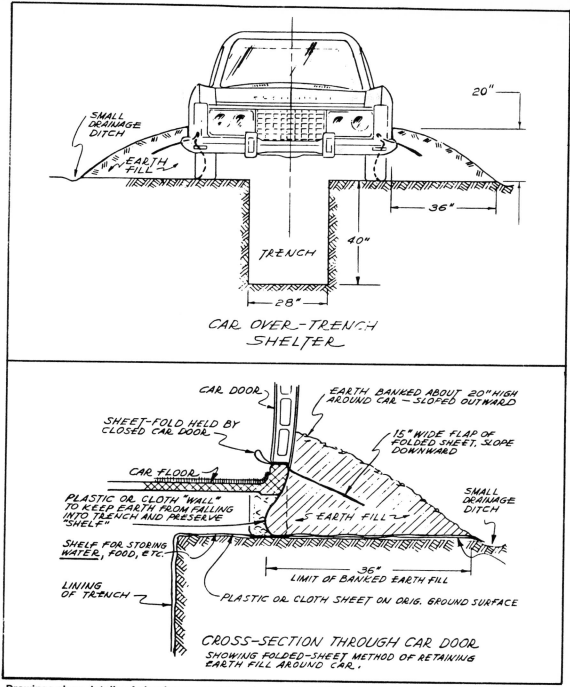

20"

SMALL DRAINAGE DITCH

EARTH FILL

36"

TRENCH

40"

28"

CAR OVER-TRENCH SHELTER

CAR DOOR

EARTH BANKED ABOUT 20" HIGH AROUND CAR — SLOPED OUTWARD

SHEET-FOLD HELD BY CLOSED CAR DOOR

15" WIDE FLAP OF FOLDED SHEET, SLOPE DOWNWARD

CAR FLOOR

SMALL DRAINAGE DITCH

PLASTIC OR CLOTH "WALL" TO KEEP EARTH FROM FALLING INTO TRENCH AND PRESERVE "SHELF"

EARTH FILL

SHELF FOR STORING WATER, FOOD, ETC.

36"
LIMIT OF BANKED EARTH FILL

LINING OF TRENCH

PLASTIC OR CLOTH SHEET ON ORIG. GROUND SURFACE

CROSS-SECTION THROUGH CAR DOOR
SHOWING FOLDED-SHEET METHOD OF RETAINING EARTH FILL AROUND CAR.

Drawings show details of plan for car-over-trench expedient fallout shelter (from *Expedient Shelter Handbook*).

Civil Defense: A Soviet View

P. T. Yegorov, I. A. Shlyakov, and N. I. Alabin
1970, 1976/374 pp./$4
(S/N 008-070-00382-1)
Superintendent of Documents
U.S. Government Printing Office
Washington, DC 20402

This translation of a Soviet manual provides a detailed view of the Russian emphasis on civil defense, with practical information for anyone studying the subject. The book covers the effects of nuclear, chemical, and biological weapons in warfare, and includes blast and fallout shelters as well as such individual measures as gas masks and protective clothing. Shelter designs are presented with building plans, and the book is illustrated throughout with how-to drawings.

NBC Warfare Defense Ashore

U.S. Dept. of the Navy
1978/521 pp./$6.50
(S/N 008-050-00165-8)
Superintendent of Documents
U.S. Government Printing Office
Washington, DC 20402

Defense measures in nuclear, biological, and chemical warfare situations are covered in extensive detail in this publication. It is a technical manual and deals exclusively with military equipment and procedures, but it would be a practical resource for anyone researching the subject. The book is illustrated with photos, drawings, and charts.

Your Chance to Live

Tamara C. Lowery, Editor
1973/111 pp./$3.25
(S/N 008-040-00072-9)
Superintendent of Documents
U.S. Government Printing Office
Washington, DC 20402

A publication of the Defense Civil Preparedness Agency prepared by the Far West Laboratory for Educational Research and Development, this is a book for children. It introduces youngsters to survival methods in situations ranging from forest fires to storms, earthquakes, nuclear accident, or warfare. Illustrated with drawings, the book has an easy style—and offers lessons for adults as well as children.

The Survivalists

Patrick Rivers
1975/224 pp./$4.95
Universe Books, Inc.
381 Park Ave. S.
New York, NY 10016

The author writes about the unarmed "survivalists" who believe that today's society has entered a trend of marked decline. But unlike the armed survivalists, they do not see the immediate threat in the sudden violence of war, economic collapse, or natural catastrophe. Instead, they are alarmed by what is seen as a self-destructing element in our technological society, in the form of environmental damage and the waste of human and natural resources. The solution pursued by these survivalists is a society based on alternate-energy sources, appropriate and alternative technology, rural self-sufficiency. The author bases his book on research among such survivalists both in Britain and the United States.

Cannibals and Kings

Marvin Harris
1977/351 pp./$2.95
Vintage Books
201 E. 50th St.
New York, NY 10022

When a people "uses up" its environment securing the means of its livelihood through its existing technology, it goes into a decline that can only be reversed through development of new—"appropriate"—technology. The decline requires a reversal of population expansion as well as improvisation in securing the necessities of life. Warning that it is a fatal mistake to assume that a way of life will continually improve, this anthropologist tests his hypothesis with studies of societies in history. The Aztecs, for instance, conducted extensive warfare, collected prisoners by the thousands, and used them in human-sacrifice rituals that were combined with institutionalized cannibalism. Going back to the beginnings of recorded history, infanticide—in various forms—has been an institution for population control. Early civilizations used labor-intensive irrigation systems to rescue their depleted environments in order to provide minimum food supplies. Ever newer and newer technology has, at times, forestalled the complete decline of a people, but ultimately an environment can only

Upper drawing shows building plan for an underground fallout shelter in sandy soil, lower drawing illustrates evacuation of a shelter (from *Civil Defense: A Soviet View*).

sustain a limited level of use. This book is sobering—sometimes grisly—reading, but it is an education in looking into the future by means of the past.

The Genesis Strategy: Climate and Global Survival

Stephen H. Schneider with Lynne E. Mesirow
1976/419 pp./$17.50
Plenum Publishing Corp.
233 Spring St.
New York, NY 10013

This is a book of science for the layman about global climate and weather, and how they affect the present and future survival of mankind. The term of the book's title is biblical, referring to the story of Joseph, who advised the pharaoh to lay away seven years of plentiful harvests against the years of famine to come. The present low level of world grain reserves is related to two of the major elements in this book: the question of whether human activities are disturbing the balance of the earth's climate system, and the possibility that current climate is a moderate or mild interlude in a general trend toward severe glacial temperatures. The author, who has been deputy head of the climate project at the National Center for Atmospheric Research, examines the history of world climate, covering such aspects as the "little ice age" of 1550–1850. He also reports on how modern science confronts politics in preparing for the future. Drawings, diagrams, maps, and photos illustrate the text.

The Dorset Disaster

Alexander Sidar III
1980/276 pp./out of print
The Stonesong Press, Inc.
Grosset & Dunlap, Inc.

The author supposes that a nuclear-reactor power plant in Connecticut has a runaway accident. He presents an hour-by-hour account of how the disaster becomes a catastrophe, telling the story as it is experienced by all of the people involved. The book is based on scientific projections and is illustrated with photos, drawings, and maps. As an education in what the future may hold for us, this out-of-print book is well worth a search in public libraries or secondhand bookstores.

Passport to Survival

Esther Dickey
1969, 1981/180 pp./$6.50
Bookcraft, Inc.
1848 W. 2300 St. S.
Salt Lake City, UT 84119

The author supposes that the potential for civil upheaval, famine, and war is real enough so that everyone should have a basic survival-food capacity. She builds this capacity on four basic food elements—wheat, powdered milk, honey, and salt—and explains methods of food preparation, preservation, and storage that can yield a sustaining diet from them. There are over one hundred recipes using the four basics. The author includes a chapter on cooking and handling foods outdoors, as well as one on self-help health care.

SURVIVAL, INC.: STORAGE FOOD, APPLIANCES, SURVIVAL GEAR

This firm is one of the largest in its field, specializing in an extensive variety of storage foods, both freeze-dried and dehydrated, as well as such bulk materials as grains and beans, all packed in cans. Prices range widely, depending on quantity and type of food: a Maxi Unit supply for one person for one year costs $1,630, plus shipping. The firm also sells a variety of food-processing appliances such as grain mills and food dryers, as well as a large collection of survival gear that includes radiation detectors, knives, personal-defense weapons, tools, heaters, stoves, survival kits, vaults, and storage containers. Write for catalog ($2):

Survival, Inc.
Box 5509
Carson, CA 90749

VACUUM-PACKED SEEDS FOR PLANTING OR BARTER

Survival Inc. sells a variety of vegetable seeds vacuum-packed in cans. One selection, in a no. 10 can weighing 3½ pounds, sells for $29.95. The Survival Garden selection, 1½ pounds in a

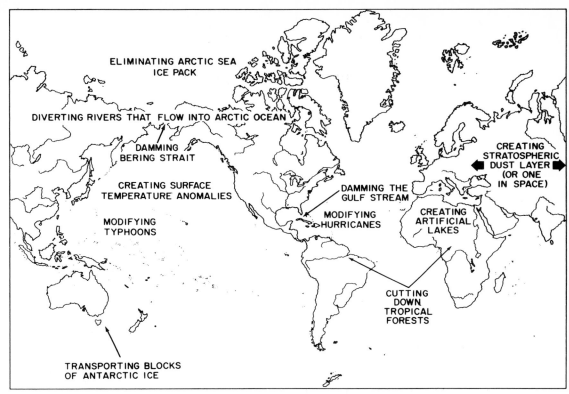

ELIMINATING ARCTIC SEA ICE PACK

DIVERTING RIVERS THAT FLOW INTO ARCTIC OCEAN

DAMMING BERING STRAIT

CREATING SURFACE TEMPERATURE ANOMALIES

MODIFYING TYPHOONS

CREATING STRATOSPHERIC DUST LAYER (OR ONE IN SPACE)

DAMMING THE GULF STREAM

MODIFYING HURRICANES

CREATING ARTIFICIAL LAKES

CUTTING DOWN TROPICAL FORESTS

TRANSPORTING BLOCKS OF ANTARCTIC ICE

Schematic map shows a number of deliberate climate-modification projects that have been proposed or are likely to be projected in the future (from *The Genesis Strategy: Climate and Global Survival*).

FRUIT GROUP
1 Apple Granules
2 Apple Slices
1 Apricot Slices
1 Pineapple (FD)
1 Prunes, Pitted
1 Raisins
1 Fruit Blend
1 Pear Slices

FATS AND OILS GROUP
2 Margarine Powder
2 Shortening Powder
2 Salad Oil

GRAIN GROUP
2 Corn Meal
2 Quick Oats
2 White Rice
30 Whole Kernel Wheat
2 Spaghetti, Elbo
6 Flour, White
4 Wheat, Cracked

ADJUNCTS GROUP
1 Orange Drink
1 Cocoa
2 Salt, Iodized
1 Peppers, Green Bell
1 Baco Dices
1 Gelatin, Orange
18 Honey

VEGETABLE GROUP
1 Cabbage Dices
2 Carrot Dices
2 Corn, Sweet
2 Peas, Garden
4 Potato Granules
3 Potato Dices
2 Tomato
2 Beans, Green Cut
1 Celery, Stalk
2 Potato Slices
1 Spinach Flakes
2 Stew Blend

PROTEIN GROUP
1 Cheese Omelette
3 Egg Solids, Mix
12 Milk Solids, Nonfat Regular
1 Cheese, Powdered
1 Beans, Red
1 Beans, White GN
1 Peas, Green Split

FREEZE DRIED MEAT GROUP
1 Hamburger Patties
1 Diced Beef
1 Beef Steak
1 Beef Stew
1 Sausage
1 Potatoes & Beef

TOTAL NUMBER OF CANS . . . 138 Packed in 23 Easy to stack same-size cartons.
Stores in an area 36" wide, 18½" deep, 54" high.

A MAXI UNIT WILL SUPPLY APPROXIMATELY THE FOLLOWING:
2400 Calories and 85 Grams of protein per day for ONE PERSON for ONE YEAR.
2400 Calories and 85 Grams of protein per day for TWO PEOPLE for SIX MONTHS.
1960 Calories and 65 Grams of protein per day for FIVE PEOPLE for THREE MONTHS.
1800 Calories and 60 Grams of protein per day for TWO PEOPLE for EIGHT MONTHS.

From the Survival, Inc., catalog: chart shows contents of Maxi Unit, designed to provide basic nutritional needs for one person for one year, priced at $1,630, plus shipping costs.

no. 3 can, is $10.50 and includes green beans, beets, cabbage, carrot, corn, onion, peas, spinach, squash, tomato. The seeds are selected for several years of storage and planting in any climate. In a variation of packaging, another selection of twenty-five different seeds is packed in individual six-ounce cans and priced at $35 a case.

Survival, Inc.
Box 5509
Carson, CA 90749

WINNEBAGO: SURVIVING WITH A HOUSE ON WHEELS

A motor home requires a substantial investment, but these self-contained dwellings can transport you and your household far out of harm's way. Winnebago is widely known for its line of motor homes, varying in price from upwards of $18,000 to as high as $28,395 for a Chieftain model. The units, powered by V-8 engines, are completely furnished and include kitchen facilities as well as toilet and bath. Write for product and dealer information:

Winnebago Industries, Inc.
Box 152
Forest City, IA 50436

Sailing the Farm
Ken Neumeyer
1981/192 pp./$7.95
Ten Speed Press
Box 7123
Berkeley, CA 94707

On a boat under sail you could not only live out of reach of a troubled society, but you could also make the sea your retreat from natural and man-made catastrophe. The author calls his book a survival guide to homesteading on the ocean. While many people have made their homes on boats moored at docksides, he has spent several years of traveling and living at sea aboard his thirty-foot boat. Even in these times, there are remote stretches of coast and deserted islands that civilization barely touches. The practical details of such a life—outfitting a boat, providing for food and water, dealing with difficulties—are presented. The book is illustrated with over one hundred diagrams and sketches.

Living Aboard
Jan and Bill Moeller
1977/305 pp./$17.50
International Marine Publishing Co.
21 Elm St.
Camden, ME 04843

The idea is not new—making a cruising sailboat your permanent home—but it does have a new application in these times. It can be an economical way of life—traveling with the wind and living on the seafood you catch. And being at sea when nuclear war explodes could ensure your survival. Living on a sailboat can have disadvantages as well, however, and the authors tell both sides of the story in this book. They cover selection of boat, living costs, and the many aspects of a comfortable life on board. The book is illustrated with photos and drawings.

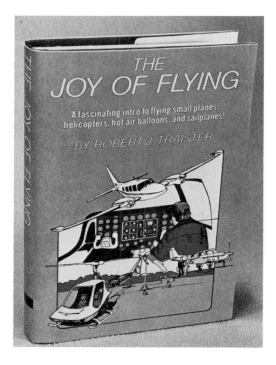

The Joy of Flying
Robert J. Traister
1981/272 pp./$9.95
TAB Books, Inc.
Blue Ridge Summit, PA 17214

Another way to retreat for survival is to fly away

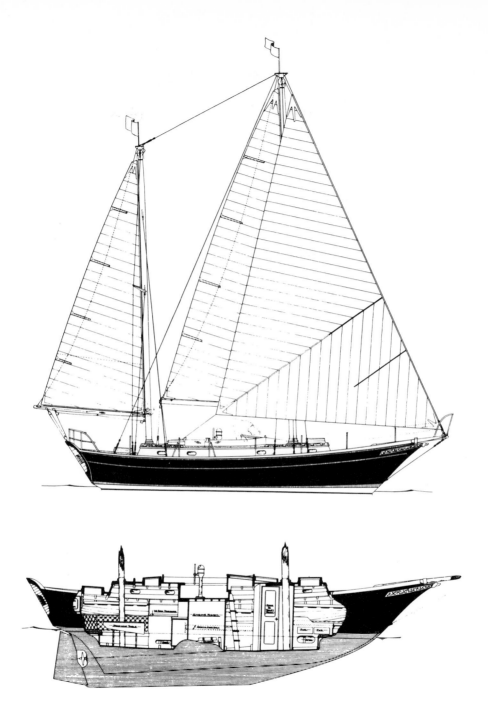

Drawing shows a Mason 37 stern cabin ketch, with view of living space in cabin area (from *Living Aboard*).

from threat. This book is a useful introduction to flying, mainly covering small aircraft, but also dealing with helicopters, gliders, sailplanes, and hot-air balloons. For the beginner, the book gives a short course in the workings of a small plane, as well as a detailed discussion of the steps involved in getting a pilot's license. Along with covering the costs involved in flying a plane, the author reviews the single-engine aircraft on the market with details on such popular models as the Piper Super Cub, Cessna 152, and Beechcraft Skipper. Photographs illustrate the how-to material and product reviews.

Nothing could have been more obvious to the people of the early twentieth century than the rapidity with which war was becoming impossible. And as certainly they did not see it. They did not see it until the atomic bombs burst in their fumbling hands.

H. G. Wells, *The World Set Free* (1914)

FROM BAD TO WORSE

The economic depression should not have become the social catastrophe that it did. It had been coming for years, and the federal and state governments should have been much better prepared.

In fact, it was the years of decline preceding the depression that had set the scene for the havoc that developed. State and local governments had already cut services to below absolute minimums, and the few demoralized public employees who were left refused to work for an inflated currency that became worthless overnight.

Police departments were not functioning, and when the crash came they were abandoned altogether in many places. National Guard and federal military units were ineffective and unreliable; most troops had not been paid in months, and whole companies began deserting.

All banks were closed on the day after the Monday collapse of the stock markets. Across the country, rioting broke out when crowds tried to break into banks for money that had little purchasing power. In Cleveland, National Guard units were called out, but the troops looted stores instead of maintaining order. Federal troops were brought in, only to join the Guard units in looting—an occurrence repeated in city after city.

Within a week there were bands of armed soldiers foraging everywhere. Civilian groups were formed to oppose the troops, but in many cases they too became foragers. In the beginning there were ample food supplies, but they quickly disappeared from the marketing system, either stolen or destroyed by looters or bought up by hoarders in a black market that used precious metals and gems for exchange.

Washington declared martial law on a national basis. Using elite troops, Congress restored a semblance of order by the end of the year, but the Constitution remained suspended until the elections two years later. The country's vulnerability to foreign attack passed as the monetary collapse spread around the world, and the nations that posed a threat were themselves paralyzed by internal disorder.

Few Americans were prepared for the upheaval, and most of those who had armed themselves and stocked retreats in isolated areas discovered that martial law reached everywhere. Their careful preparations did give them an advantage during that first winter, however. Most of the population went hungry until the following spring, when the military government commandeered all private food stocks, instituted rigid rationing, and confiscated all firearms . . .

INITIAL EMERGENCY MEDICAL CARE FOR PERFORATING CHEST INJURIES

The victim almost always has an obvious penetrating injury of the chest wall, producing a so-called "sucking wound" since air is sucked in through the wound during inspiration. Due to the impairment in respiration the patient begins fighting for air almost immediately and soon becomes cyanotic, loses consciousness, and goes into shock if untreated.

The hole in the chest must be tightly closed at the earliest possible moment in order to restore respiratory function. The best method of closing such a wound is with sterile, fine-mesh, Vaseline-impregnated gauze and an outer, thick, sterile dressing. However, the cleanest available substitute must be utilized immediately: a clean handkerchief, or even a parka can be stuffed over the opening. *The hole must be closed immediately or without exception the patient will die.* A more ideal dressing may be applied later, but air must not be permitted to enter the chest while the coverings are being switched.

From: *Medicine for Mountaineering*, by James A. Wilkerson, M.D., Editor (Seattle, Wash: The Mountaineers, 1976).

If peace and survival are to be achieved, the search must almost certainly go beyond the effort to find a balance in thermonuclear terror.

John Kenneth Galbraith, *The Affluent Society* (1958)

The 25 Most Practical Homebuilt Aircraft
Peter M. Bowers
1978/174 pp./$5.95
TAB Books, Inc.
Blue Ridge Summit, PA 17214

If the prospect of flying your own small plane in retreat from danger attracts you, you might want to consider building the plane yourself. The author presents twenty-five such plane designs, all of them models for which plans can be purchased. They are small planes, many of them single-seaters, but any one of them could be your do-it-yourself starting point. The book is illustrated with photos of the aircraft.

Where There Is No Doctor
David Werner
1977/409 pp./$7.50
Hesperian Foundation
Box 1692
Palo Alto, CA 94302

Originally written in Spanish, this book has already been translated into several languages, largely for use in underdeveloped countries. Its intended audience is the remote village community, but its usefulness as a health-care resource makes it a prime book for anyone's survival kit. With a team of medical specialists to advise him, the author has covered all aspects of health care. The presentation is easy to read and simple to follow, with drawings throughout. Symptoms are described and illustrated, action is prescribed. Where a physician or health-care worker is required, the book says so. A special forty-page section covers medicines and drugs. The book is complete and could save your life one day. (If ordering from publisher, add $.50 for postage and handling.)

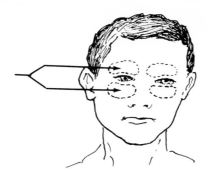

If a person has continuous severe gut pain with vomiting,
but does not have diarrhea, suspect an acute abdomen.

Acute abdomen:

**Take to a hospital—
surgery may be needed**

- continuous severe pain that keeps getting worse
- constipation and vomiting
- belly swollen, hard, person protects it
- severely ill

Less serious illness:

**Probably can be treated
in the home or health center**

- pain that comes and goes (cramps)
- moderate or severe diarrhea
- sometimes signs of an infection, perhaps a cold or sore throat
- he has had pains like this before
- only moderately ill

If a person shows signs of acute abdomen,
get him to a hospital as fast as you can.

**Above, drawing shows locations of sinuses, below,
chart gives directions for stomach pain and
associated symptoms (from *Where There Is No
Doctor*).**

The Essential Guide to Prescription Drugs

James W. Long, M.D.
1977, 1980/864 pp./$25
Harper & Row
10 E. 53rd St.
New York, NY 10022

This reference book profiles 212 prescription and over-the-counter drugs, presented by generic name and with listings of 1,466 brand names. The profile format explains how the drug works, conditions under which it should not be taken or when a physician should be consulted, possible side or adverse effects, as well as other specific cautions.

Medicine for Mountaineering

James A. Wilkerson, M.D., Editor
1967, 1975/367 pp./$7.95
The Mountaineers
719 Pike St.
Seattle, WA 98101

This is a book of first aid—"plus second aid"—written by a team of doctors for people who climb mountains and get hurt or sick in remote places where, literally, no doctor can get to. It is one of those survival books you want to have in hand for the day when *you* have to be the doctor. Written for the layperson, but presupposing a minimum of specialized training to make its in-

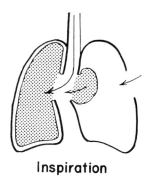 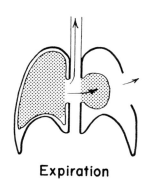

Inspiration   Expiration

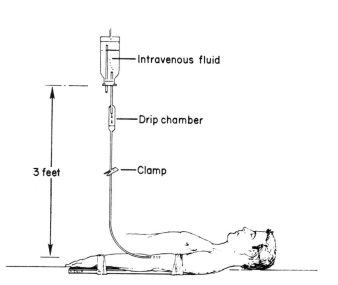

Intravenous fluid

Drip chamber

3 feet

Clamp

Upper drawings show lung function with a punctured chest wall, lower drawing illustrates administration of intravenous fluids (from *Medicine for Mountaineering*).

struction useful and safe, the book is a complete textbook in emergency medical care, including sections on both oral and injectable medications.

is illustrated with both photos and drawings. (When ordering from publisher, add $.75 for postage and handling.)

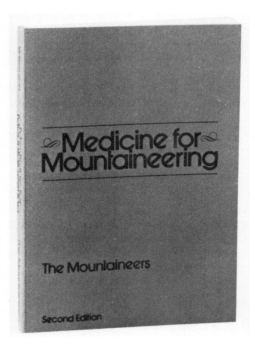

Wilderness Medicine
William W. Forgey, M.D.
1979/124 pp./$5.95
Indiana Camp Supply, Inc.
Box 344
Pittsboro, IN 46167

Written specifically for backpackers, mountaineers, and other wilderness travelers, this book covers the prevention, diagnosis, and therapy of over two hundred medical conditions. A clinical index provides quick reference. Both medical and surgical techniques are covered with directions for injecting painkillers, suturing wounds, and dealing with such emergencies as appendicitis (though not the major-surgical procedure of appendectomy). Both nonprescription and pre-scription-drug medical kits are outlined, including a 29½-ounce prescription kit designed for care of up to ten people for up to three months. The book

Army Medical Handbook of Basic Nursing/TM 8-230
U.S. Dept. of the Army
1970/634 pp./$7.55
(S/N 008-020-00336-1)
Superintendent of Documents
U.S. Government Printing Office
Washington, DC 20402

This large-format book is the army's manual for training medics for the battlefield as well as dressing-station and hospital service. It is the book that could be your lifesaver in an extreme survival situation—particularly if combined with advanced-first-aid or paramedical training. The manual covers all of the basic phases of medical care, including drugs and drug administration, as well as obstetrical, pediatric, and geriatric nursing care. Extensively illustrated with detailed drawings.

FORMING A SQUARE KNOT USING A NEEDLE HOLDER

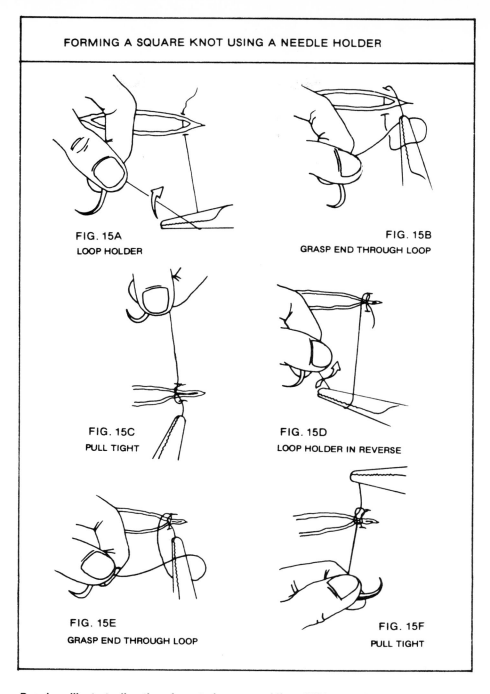

FIG. 15A
LOOP HOLDER

FIG. 15B
GRASP END THROUGH LOOP

FIG. 15C
PULL TIGHT

FIG. 15D
LOOP HOLDER IN REVERSE

FIG. 15E
GRASP END THROUGH LOOP

FIG. 15F
PULL TIGHT

Drawings illustrate directions for suturing a wound (from *Wilderness Medicine*).

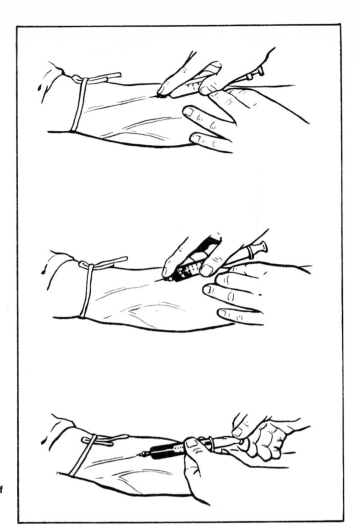

Three drawings from a sequence of eight, showing step-by-step procedure for use of syringe in a vein (from *Army Medical Handbook of Basic Nursing***).**

The Merck Manual
1899, 1977/2,188 pp./$9.75
Merck & Co., Inc.
Box 2000
Rahway, NJ 07065

A professional reference manual for physicians and nurses. It is not a first-aid handbook by any means. But in an extreme survival situation, with complete isolation from professional care, it could become *your* reference—especially if you have gained advanced first-aid and paramedical training and experience.

SURPLUS: IMPROVISING FOR SURVIVAL

Like other firms in this field, Airborne Sales offers both new and used government surplus as well as new consumer items. You could buy a forty-eight-gallon gas tank for $99.50, to be used in a jeep, truck, or motor home, or for fuel storage. You could also buy a Sperry gunsight made for the 40mm antiaircraft cannon and use it as a spotting scope or cannibalize it for optics, gears, and controls: it cost the government $3,510, you pay $89.50. The firm offers all kinds of pumps, gearboxes, electrical controls. There are survival items such as inflatable rafts and navy distress signals, as well as camping gear, compasses, binoculars. Write for catalog ($1):

Airborne Sales Co., Inc.
Box 2727, Dept. C-81B
Culver City, CA 90230

ELECTRONICS EQUIPMENT AND COMPONENTS: MILITARY AND INDUSTRIAL SURPLUS

This mail-order company specializes in electronics equipment, components, and parts. This is new and used material, military and industrial surplus and "seconds," that can be used as is, repaired, modified, or employed to build things. There are computer components, cathode-ray tubes, keyboards, switches, transistors, electric motors, relays. A recent catalog offered miniature solar cells ($5 and up) and solar panels ($40 to $400) for charging batteries (photovoltaic). The U.S. Army walkie-talkie PRC-6 sells for $25, plus $5 for antenna, a forty-channel Panasonic CB radio sells for $15. Write for catalog:

Meshna, Inc.
Box 62
East Lynn, MA 01904

How to Buy Surplus Personal Property from the Department of Defense
23 pp./$1.50
(S/N 008-007-02939-8)
Superintendent of Documents
U.S. Government Printing Office
Washington, DC 20402
There are two main ways of buying federal-government surplus. The simple way is to go to your local "army-navy store" or its equivalent (a retailer or wholesaler who buys from the government). Or, you can deal directly with federal agencies (which, as you can imagine, can become complex). The surplus available from the government ranges from battered helmets and rifles to tanks and missile silos, from mess-hall cooking equipment to sailing vessels and land. But you have to deal with various agencies, offices, bids, auctions, catalogs, inspections, and regulations. This booklet, however, will explain the basics of the process for you. It concentrates on the Department of Defense, but it also covers the other agencies that are involved.

MILITARY FIELD EQUIPMENT

P&S Sales is a mail-order firm specializing in new, unused military field equipment: packs, ammo pouches, utility bags, canteens, boots, field jackets, sleeping bags. For instance, it offers the Army LC-1 (Medium) ALICE combat pack for $59.95 (*ALICE* stands for All-Purpose Lightweight Individual Carrying Equipment), with the ALICE pack frame for $49.50. Write for catalog:

P&S Sales
Box 45095
Tulsa, OK 74145

CRIME-PROTECTION DEVICES

One of the oldest ways of safeguarding your cash is the money belt: here is one of cowhide with removable buckle for $12.95. This mail-order house also sells a battery-powered device ($24.95) which you hang on the inside doorknob: when someone tries the knob from the outside, an alarm goes off. Write for catalog:

Brookstone
127 Vose Farm Rd.
Peterborough, NH 03458

The Complete Security Handbook
C. A. Roper
1981/511 pp./$13.95
TAB Books, Inc.
Blue Ridge Summit, PA 17214
A comprehensive manual of home-security devices and systems covering locks and alarms of all kinds (including smoke and heat detectors and other fire-safety precautions) as well as the use of automatic electronic systems combined with perimeter exterior and interior lighting. Closed-circuit television systems as well as safe units for securing valuables are discussed. The book lists the manufacturers in this field, and the author details do-it-yourself security systems and product installation. Illustrated throughout with photos and drawings.

PERSONAL PROTECTION: POCKET-SIZE TEAR-GAS UNIT

The "Equalizer II" fits in pocket or purse, delivers a nonlethal aerosol stream of tear gas, has a safety lock to prevent accidental firing, and costs $5.95. Carried in a high-crime area, it could save your life. Write for literature and dealer information:

Penguin Industries, Inc.
Airport Industrial Mall
Coatesville, PA 19320

"Equalizer II" delivers a nonlethal aerosol stream of tear gas.

How to Crimeproof Your Home
1979/18 pp./$2
Consumer Information Center
Department DD
Pueblo, CO 81001
   This booklet tells how to use landscaping, lighting, doors, windows, locks, and alarms to protect your home. There are also tips for apartment dwellers. The Consumer Information Center is a federal agency, and its catalog of books and booklets is available free.

Survival Guns
Mel Tappan
1976, 1980/458 pp./$9.95
Janus Press
Box 578
Rogue River, OR 97537
   If you are pondering whether to arm yourself for survival—with handgun, shotgun, rifle, or otherwise—here is a guide to know-how about firearms as weapons. The author reviews guns of all kinds, both sporting arms and military

Aside from regulatory and utility officials, everyone said the evacuation plan would not work. And it didn't. When the reactor on the Hudson River north of New York City failed, it went into a meltdown and released huge amounts of radiation.

There were only five hours of evacuation warning. Perhaps if there had been more time, the plan would have had a better chance of working effectively.

It was September, the weather was mild, and the evacuation began calmly. Within two hours, however, all of the highways in the metropolitan region were clogged. An untangling began, and the civil authorities were making headway when the reactor gave out its poison. There was panic, and it was thirty-six hours before the roadways were cleared.

Those who ignored the evacuation order generally fared better than most. They took shelter in their homes, apartments, and public buildings. Those in the path of the fallout suffered lower rates of radiation contamination in their shelters than the hundreds of thousands caught out in the open in their cars and public transportation. People fled for cover, but the movement was disorganized and largely ineffective.

Wind directions that day produced the maximum of contamination in the region. When the meltdown occurred shortly after noon, there had been a light summer breeze blowing from north to south. The one nuclear unit affected the two reactors adjoining it, and the whole mass of radioactive debris was blown out into a plume whose finer particles rose several thousand feet. Brisker air movement at higher elevations quickly began pushing the radioactive cloud southward. Then, toward evening, as it reached New York City, the cloud fanned out like an umbrella, met countering air currents from the Atlantic, and began moving northeast along the heavily populated coast.

All along its course, the toxic cloud was spreading its load of radioactive particles on the land below. The largest concentration of matter fell on New York City and the New Jersey communities just to the west.

There were no official public fallout shelters anywhere and the authorities used radio and television to broadcast hasty instructions for improvised shelter. But to a large extent this was counterproductive. Many people lingered too long listening to the broadcasts when they should have been making hurried preparations. Generally speaking, the public did not respond effectively to the instructions they received for escaping the invisible poison. Many of those who did take cover in the basements of public buildings—or under stacks of furniture in private dwellings—failed to supply themselves with enough food and water. They came out of hiding too soon and ended up as radiation casualties after all.

Hundreds of thousands did come through the catastrophe unscathed, though.

First of all, there were the ones who were upwind or completely clear of the path of the cloud—or who succeeded in fleeing to safety in time. And there were those who had supplied themselves with food and water and know-how in their prepared or improvised fallout shelters in basements, sewers, and subway tunnels. In all cases, they stayed under cover for the many days it took for the danger to pass.

New York City itself was so thoroughly contaminated that its surviving population was relocated to other parts of the country. Many never returned. The skyscrapers remained empty for months, and the effects of the disruption on the national economy lasted for decades . . .

weapons, citing their availability, capabilities, and costs. Also covered are such nonfirearm survival weapons as airguns, crossbows, blowguns, boomerangs, and slingshots. (When ordering from publisher, add $1 for postage and handling.)

SURPLUS RADIATION DETECTORS

This firm sells two Radiac units, both self-contained and battery-powered. The army model is about the size of a schoolchild's lunchbox, weighs eight pounds, and is priced at $54.50. It is rated to detect gamma radiations up to 50,000 milliroentgens per hour. The navy model is a little larger than a car battery, weighs twenty-five pounds and is priced at $89.50. It indicates beta and gamma rays by means of a meter or by headphones. Catalog ($1) gives detailed information:

Airborne Sales Co., Inc.
Box 2727, Dept. C-81B
Culver City, CA 90230

TWO RADIATION DETECTORS

Here are two detectors that combine the features of a geiger counter and a radiation alarm. The larger, the Nukebuster, weighs fourteen ounces, costs $279.95, and monitors alpha, beta, gamma, and X rays. Flashing red lights and audible tones signal any rise in radiation level, and meter and alarm can be set to signal at various ranges. The unit can be plugged into the lighter socket of a car, a 110-volt socket with adapter, or a battery pack for portable use. The smaller detector, the Radiation Alert—Mini, weighs six ounces without its nine-volt battery, fits in the palm of the hand, costs $199, is sensitive to the same radiation, and also uses lights and audible tones to signal as selectable exposure rates are reached.

Solar Electronics
156 Drakes Lane
Summertown, TN 38483

Nuclear war is not a comfortable subject. Throughout all the variations, possibilities, and uncertainties that this study describes, one theme is constant—a nuclear war would be a catastrophe. A militarily plausible nuclear attack, even "limited," could be expected to kill people and to inflict economic damage on a scale unprecedented in American experience; a large-scale nuclear exchange would be a calamity unprecedented in human history. The mind recoils from the effort to foresee the details of such a calamity, and from the careful explanation of the unavoidable uncertainties as to whether people would die from blast damage, from fallout radiation, or from starvation during the following winter.

U.S. Congress, Office of Technology Assessment, *The Effects of Nuclear War* (Washington, D.C.: U.S. Government Printing Office, 1979).

Nukebuster radiation detector and alarm.

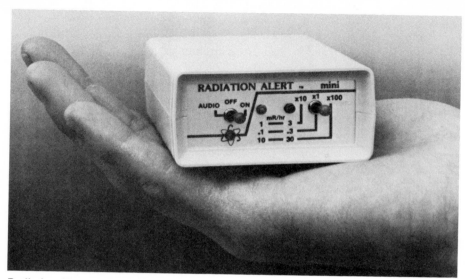

Radiation Alert—Mini detector and alarm.

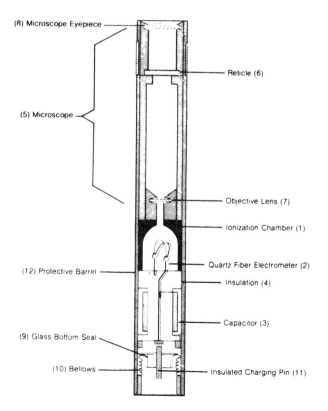

(8) Microscope Eyepiece

Reticle (6)

(5) Microscope

Objective Lens (7)

Ionization Chamber (1)

(12) Protective Barrel

Quartz Fiber Electrometer (2)

Insulation (4)

Capacitor (3)

(9) Glass Bottom Seal

(10) Bellows

Insulated Charging Pin (11)

QUARTZ-FIBER DOSIMETER: drawing shows components of this direct-reading dosimeter, with entire system—sealed in protective barrel—weighing less than a pound, and reading taken visually through microscope eyepiece, at top. Price $92.50 (Survival, Inc., Box 5509, Carson, CA 90749).

SELECTING A RADIATION DETECTOR

A basement fallout shelter would be incomplete without a device for detecting radiation. Emergency radio broadcasts would tell you about general levels of radiation in your area, but a personal detector will measure radiation immediately inside and outside your home.

The most practical kind of detector for the home is the civil-defense type, which measures radiation into the high levels that threaten life. Government-surplus units made for the civil-defense program can sometimes be purchased for about $100. Bought new, similar models are available for about $200 and up. Surplus equipment from the army and navy, providing comparable detection, can be found for under $100.

A second type of detector is the dosimeter.

These units are tube shaped and typically small enough to be carried continuously by a person—clipped on a belt, for instance. Radiation dosage is read from an internal scale seen through an eyepiece. These units can be purchased for about $100, but they require a separate recharging unit costing about the same amount.

Also on the market are highly sensitive meters for measuring very low levels of radiation in such applications as health physics. This type of detector does not provide the broad measurement essential for fallout protection, though it would be useful for decontamination. Such a detector is not a basic item of equipment for a household shelter, and prices range up to several hundred dollars.

---

1. On paper, civil defense looks effective . . .
2. However, no one at all thinks that the United States has an effective civil defense . . .
3. U.S. civil defense capability is weakened because some elements are in place while others are not or have not been maintained . . .
4. Faced with drastic technological change, moral and philosophical questions about the desirability of civil defense, and budgetary constraints, Federal plans have been marked by vacillations, shifts in direction, and endless reorganization.

U.S. Congress, Office of Technology Assessment, *The Effects of Nuclear War* (Washington, D.C.: U.S. Government Printing Office, 1979).

Survival, Evasion and Escape/FM 21–76
U.S. Dept. of the Army
1957, 1969/431 pp./$6.05
(S/N 008–020–00157–1)
Superintendent of Documents

U.S. Government Printing Office
Washington, DC 20402

The second half of this handbook and training manual is devoted to instructions for military personnel cut off or captured by enemy forces. As a resource for civilians facing enemy forces in wartime, it offers a guide to methods, skills, and tactics that could mean your survival. The emphasis is on how to elude the threatening enemy, on one hand, and surviving imprisonment psychologically and practically, on the other.

We are here to make a choice between the quick and the dead. That is our business. Behind the black portent of the new atomic age lies a hope which, seized upon with faith, can work our salvation. If we fail, then we have damned every man to be the slave of fear. Let us not deceive ourselves: we must elect world peace or world destruction.

Bernard Baruch, address to the U.N. Atomic Energy Commission (1946)

EVADING ENEMY TROOPS IN WARTIME: SOME EXPERT ADVICE FROM THE ARMY

A difficult task in any situation is the attempt to cross the forward edge of the battle area. If unable to determine the general direction to friendly lines, remain in position and observe the movement of enemy military forces or supplies, noise and flashes of the battle area, or the orientation of enemy artillery. After arriving in the combat zone, select a concealed position from which as much of the battle area as possible may be observed. Select a route and critical terrain features on which you can guide when exfiltrating back to friendly positions under the cover of darkness. Several alternate routes should be selected with care to avoid "easy" approaches to friendly lines which are more likely to be covered by friendly fires and enemy patrols. If in uniform, select exposure time during daylight hours and be close enough to be easily recognized by friendly troops.

Watch for friendly patrols. Once a patrol is spotted, remain in position and allow the patrol to approach. When the patrol is close enough to recognize you, display a white cloth and call out a greeting that is clearly and unmistakably of American origin. It is imperative that, at the time of contact, there is sufficient light for the patrol to identify you. In the event you elect not to establish contact, you should, if possible, observe their route and approach friendly lines at approximately the same location. This will enable you to avoid mine fields and booby traps.

If unable to contact a friendly patrol, the only alternative may be to make a direct approach of front line positions. This will require crawling through the enemy's forward positions to a position near forward friendly elements. This action should be accomplished during the hours of darkness. Once near friendly lines, however, do not attempt to make contact until there is sufficient light for you to be recognized. As in establishing contact with a friendly patrol, call out something typically American and wave a white cloth.

From: *Survival, Evasion and Escape*/FM 21–76, by the U.S. Dept. of the Army (Washington, D.C.: U.S. Government Printing Office, 1969).

INDEX

251

252

256